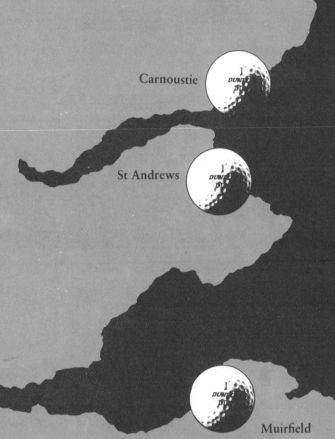

Carnoustie

St Andrews

Gleneagles

Muirfield

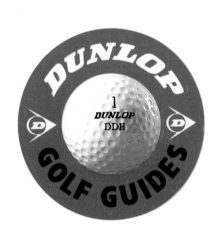

# The Championship Courses of SCOTLAND

Sandy Lyle
with Bob Ferrier

World's Work Ltd

First published 1982 by
World's Work Ltd
The Windmill Press
Kingswood, Tadworth, Surrey

Paintings by Ken Turner
Photography by David Pocknell

Copyright © Lennard Books Ltd 1982

SBN 437 09060 4

Made by Lennard Books
The Old School
Wheathampstead, Herts AL4 8AN

Editor Michael Leitch
Designed by David Pocknell's Company Ltd
Production Reynolds Clark Associates Ltd
Printed and bound in Belgium by
Henri Proost & Cie, Turnhout

Back cover photograph by
Lawrence Levy

# CONTENTS

The game of golf is very old. The first set of rules was formulated in the middle of the 18th century, and still forms the basis of the existing code, even though golf in various forms was played for centuries before then. In its beginnings in Scotland, the game was played among sand dunes by the seashore – indeed the word 'links' refers specifically to the stretch of broken ground behind a beach. At St Andrews and Carnoustie, the same terrain has been in use for golf for centuries, and of our other Scottish championship courses, the Ailsa Course at Turnberry, Royal Troon and Muirfield use precisely the same type of links ground. The King's Course at Gleneagles Hotel is the one exception in our six; but, as we shall see, it has its own particular and compelling claim to be examined here.

These great courses, and the men who tended them and played over them, have made a critical contribution to the development of golf as a world game. In the great international explosion towards the end of the 19th century, Scots spread the game to all the countries of the British Empire, to Europe and to North America. Scottish professionals and designers influenced all subsequent golf architecture throughout the world, and this influence was based on what they had known, and left behind, in the Old Country.

This is why anyone who has ever played golf, to whatever standard, should make a pilgrimage to play one if not all of these courses, accepting their particular demands and challenges. The experience will certainly be memorable, and some preparation is essential. These courses require respect – respect for their history and traditions, and for their design and architecture. The rewards they can provide will more than repay the effort, as numerous great champions will testify.

It is important to accept that, on links courses above all others, golf is a point-to-point game, and not a distance-for-its-own-sake game. Brute strength has no place here. You will be required to hit the ball precisely to position A, to position B, to position C; if you do that, you will find that these courses will reward you most handsomely. What you must *not* do is pack fear, or self-pity, in your golf bag. As you stand on the first tee of the Old Course at St Andrews, in front of those tall clubhouse windows, or advance towards them up the 18th, with such names as Morris, Strath, Forgan, Auchterlonie in your mind, not to mention Jones and Hagen, Snead and Cotton, Palmer and Nicklaus, Thomson and Locke, it may be difficult not to shiver. Or as you try to hit and hold wickedly trapped, mounded and hump-backed greens such as the 13th at Muirfield or the 16th at Carnoustie, and attempt carries over 150 yards of heather on a blind line, you may find the depth of the pot bunkers, the adhesiveness of the heather, the wicked lies and uneven stances make you mumble about the unfairness of it all. But remember Bernard Darwin's words: 'It's not supposed to be fair.' Fairness has nothing to do with it, and that is an intrinsic part of links golf.

You must give some thought to strategy and tactics. Strategy has been described as 'what you want to do' and tactics as 'how you decide to do it'. Do you want to break 90? 80? What score will content you? Decide that, then decide on the tactics which will give you that score – where you must make par, where you hope to make birdies, where you are prepared to surrender a stroke or strokes, which positions you plainly cannot reach and where else you should therefore go.

The best way to make these preparations in advance is to obtain the Dunlop Golf Guide for the course (they are individually available as paperbacks) or one of the other little brochures which also give a detailed plan of each hole, showing clearly all the hazards and all the distances, from the tees to the greens, and the depths of the greens. One hour of studying this will pay much in the way of dividend – especially if you carry it with you on the round, and *refer* to it. A first-class caddie on the day will be invaluable, but make sure he is not merely a bag-carrier, which is entirely different. And, if you can, play each course more than once. The more often you play them, the more you will learn of their subtleties.

Wind and weather, and the speed of the course, will compromise all this. For example, Billy Joe Patton, famous American amateur and Walker Cup player of the Fifties and Sixties, tells how on the same day, playing the short 8th at St Andrews – flat, nondescript and, many would say, the weakest and easiest hole on the course – he hit a 2-iron 'with every bone in ma body', then 'nudged' an 8-iron a few hours later, such was the effect of a complete wind change. The hole is 178 yards.

Above all, warm up in advance, and bring a swing with you. As the professionals say, 'If you haven't brought it with you, you won't find it here.' Be in good form. Spend some time on the practice ground before you tee off. By the time you get to the first tee, have faith in your swing. And always play your shots positively and calmly. Most of the time you will do just as well hitting with three-quarter power.

Donald Ross, a Dornoch man who became famous as a golf architect in the US (Seminole, Pinehurst No 2 and numerous others), has said: 'The championship course . . . should call for long and accurate tee shots, accurate iron play, precise handling of the short game, and finally consistent putting. These abilities should be called for in a proportion that will not permit excellence in any one department of the game to offset too largely deficiencies in another.' And A. W. Tillinghurst, another distinguished golf architect in America (Baltusrol, San Francisco GC), has said: 'A controlled shot to a closely guarded green is the surest test of a man's golf.'

You will be tested by these great courses. But be assured that this book is not written for expert professionals. When we talk here of the average player, we mean with a handicap of, say, seven and upward. When we talk of the good player, we mean with a handicap below seven.

Putting I have not mentioned. It represents, as we all know to our cost, some 50 per cent of the game, and therefore is of critical importance. But it is terribly subjective, with an endless number of systems, methods and theories applied to it. What I would say is that before you tackle any of these courses, practice your putting! Practice until you have a comfortable and consistent stroke, and until the putter feels like a friend. You will be faced with huge greens, such as the Old Course 'twins' where you might well have putts of 30 or 40 yards. You will be faced with greens which have double tiers, such as the 5th at Carnoustie, the 9th at Gleneagles, the 8th at Turnberry. You will be faced with greens which are fast, are set in hollows, plateaued, sunken. In dealing with them, concentrate more on distance than on line. Do not be afraid of these greens. Do not be afraid of these courses. Take to them respect, preparation, accuracy, control, rational thinking and sound judgment. If you do, you will be richly rewarded.

One thing more. Save a little time for the flora and fauna, the landscape and skyscape. Depending on the season, you may see deer and fox and pheasant at Gleneagles, seals basking in the Eden estuary, the diving gannets off Turnberry Point, skylarks, redshanks, even a kestrel at Troon, heather and broom and bracken everywhere, and the blinding sunsets of the West of Scotland. Above all else, enjoy your time there – the round, the day, the memory.

### Good golf is a state of mind

'Golf is deceptively simple, and endlessly complicated. A child can play it well, and a grown man can never master it. Any single round of it is full of unexpected triumphs and seemingly perfect shots that end in disaster.

It is almost a science, yet it is a puzzle without an answer. It is gratifying and tantalising, precise and unpredictable. It requires complete concentration and total relaxation. It satisfies the soul and frustrates the intellect.

It is at the same time rewarding and maddening – and it is without doubt the greatest game mankind has ever invented.'

# ST ANDREWS

## St Andrews

Golf has been played at St Andrews, on the ground of the present Old Course, for more than 500 years. And the Royal and Ancient Golf Club of St Andrews, governing body of the game throughout the entire world with the exception of the USA, has been in existence in St Andrews for more than two centuries. Thus the history and significance of both course and club will be well established in the mind of anyone who goes to St Andrews and claims to be a golfer.

The course may be considered an ancient monument. As such, if for no other reason, it must be preserved. It is certainly an enigma, its tests and its problems varying almost from hour to hour with the fickle changes of Scottish wind and weather. It is rather less a product of nature's evolution than the purists would have you believe. The hand of man has certainly touched it over the decades. It has been condemned as an anachronism, as defying all the philosophies of modern design – and certainly the massive talents of the modern champion professional golfer have overwhelmed it when the course is soft and the weather still.

It is unique. A links course, it is nevertheless different from all other links courses. So for the golfer coming to it for the first time, as perhaps for the man coming to it for the 100th time, some advance preparation is necessary. It is as well to give some thought initially to the nature of the beast. The course runs more or less straight out in a line to the north-west for seven holes, squiggles round a fish-hook loop at the end and runs back to the south-east, with holes 1 to 7 on the way out sharing fairways with holes 12 to 18 on the way in. Most share common or double greens, and the fairways are separated by a central and intermittent line of bunkers, or a slight fall in the ground.

The outward line of the course is protected on the right side by banks of gorse bushes, containing many hidden bunkers, which separate it from the New and Jubilee Courses. The inward line on the right side is mainly defined by gorse, stone walls and disused railway lines, all of which serve to mark out-of-bounds borders and separate the Old Course from the Eden Course. The Old Course is essentially flat. The highest point of the

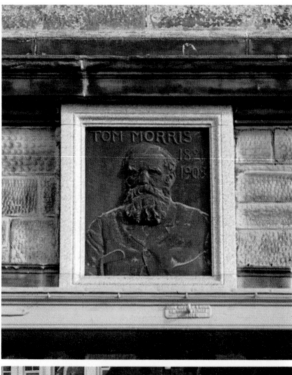

Tom Morris, R & A professional and four times Open

property can scarcely be 40 feet above sea level.

Yet despite the general flatness there is no more

Champion. His shop still stands beside the 18th green

restless golfing ground anywhere in the world. With the exception of the 1st and 18th, and perhaps

the 9th and 10th fairways, the ground is an endless ocean of ripples, ridges, mounds, dips, swales, gulleys and plateaux, often carried into the greens and fiendishly splashed with heather and gorse. A man can drive the ball into what he thinks is absolutely the required place and find it some 12 inches above his stance, on a downslope, with a minor mountain in front of him, while only a few yards away is a stretch of perfectly flat fairway offering an open shot from a proper stance.

Thus the course is not fair – but then no great golf course is intended to be fair, no great game is ever fair; so dismiss that from your mind. If you study the place closely and for long enough, you will always find a way. Here are three guiding principles for the average player:

1 For safety, play to the left.
2 If you get into a bunker, *get out*.
3 Never despair.

The right side of every hole on the course is defended by major hazards. The shot to the left is almost always sensible, if conservative, and offers a position from which to advance cleanly.

Bunkers on the Old Course are seemingly everywhere. They are very powerful, deep, with high fronts and faces. You must get out first time at all costs, even if you have to play backwards. The course, just as it can consume you in an instant (if you ignore the bunker advice, for example), can also reward you in a remarkably benign fashion for one simple but correct golf shot. So never quit on the Old Course.

The greens also are special. Almost all of them are built up from

Laurie Auchterlonie, the legendary club-maker, and a crowded corner in his famous workshop

the immediate fairway into plateaux, if only two or three feet higher. Many of them fall away from front to back. Many of them have a hollow or a ridge or a mound directly in front of them,

and almost all of them have a bunker, large or small, at the front left-centre – to protect them from the golfer who is approaching from the left. So the Old Course confirms the age-old maxim that golf is not a power game but a point-to-point game; it also sustains the notion that the game and the golf hole should be played 'from the flagstick outwards'.

The player should know where the flagstick is on the green; where he wants to land his ball on the green; the point on the fairway from which to play to the green, and where to drive the ball to get to that point. So, first time out at St Andrews, the best advice I can give is that you should take a caddie. Make sure he is an experienced, local caddie, and not just a bag-carrier.

Robert Trent Jones, the American golf architect, has written: 'The first few rounds a golfer plays on the Old Course are not likely to alter his first estimate that it is vastly over-rated. He will be puzzled to understand the rhapsodies that have been composed about the perfect strategic positioning of its trapping, the subtle undulations of its huge double greens, the endless tumbling of its fairways, which seldom give him a chance to play a shot from a level stance. Then as he plays on, it begins to soak in through his pores that whenever he plays a fine shot he is rewarded; whenever he doesn't play the right shot he is penalized in proportion, and whenever he thinks out his round hole by hole, he scores well. This is the essence of strategic architecture; to encourage initiative, reward a well-played, daring stroke more than a cautious one, and yet to insist that there must be planning and honest self-

The caddie master's office

appraisal behind the daring.'

If you absorb all that and do, at least in part, what Trent Jones recommends, you will walk up that 18th fairway with deep pride and satisfaction no matter how you may have scored.

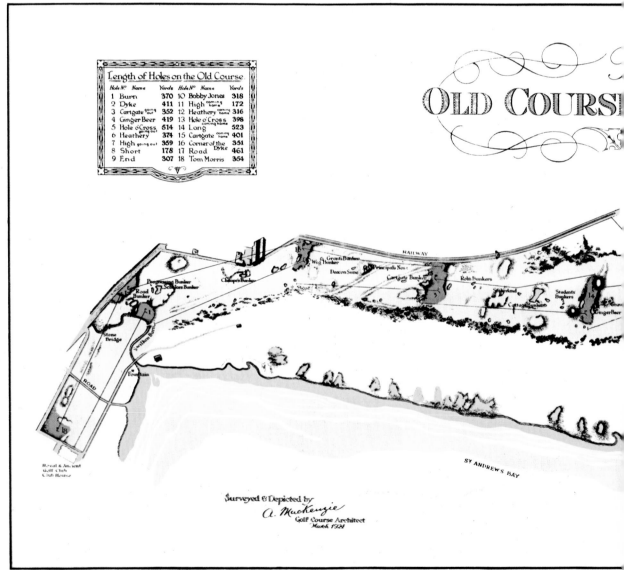

| Length of Holes on the Old Course | | | | |
|---|---|---|---|---|
| Hole Nº | Name | Yards | Hole Nº | Name | Yards |
| 1 | Burn | 370 | 10 | Bobby Jones | 318 |
| 2 | Dyke | 411 | 11 | High coming home | 172 |
| 3 | Cartgate going out | 352 | 12 | Heathery coming home | 316 |
| 4 | Ginger Beer | 419 | 13 | Hole o'Cross coming home | 398 |
| 5 | Hole o'Cross going out | 514 | 14 | Long | 523 |
| 6 | Heathery | 374 | 15 | Cartgate coming home | 401 |
| 7 | High going out | 359 | 16 | Corner of the Dyke | 351 |
| 8 | Short | 178 | 17 | Road | 461 |
| 9 | End | 307 | 18 | Tom Morris | 364 |

OLD COURSE

Surveyed & Depicted by
*A. Mackenzie*
Golf Course Architect
March 1924

## LOCAL RULES

### 1 OUT OF BOUNDS (Def 21 Rule 29-1)

(a) Beyond any wall or fence bounding the Course.

(b) Beyond the Swilcan Burn on the right of the 1st hole and in or beyond the trench marked by stakes on the right of the 2nd hole.

(c) Beyond the fence behind the 18th green and 1st tee and on or over the white line between sections of this fence.

*Note: The trench on the right of the 12th and 13th holes is not out of bounds.*

### 2 WATER HAZARDS (Def 14 Rule 33)

(a) Those parts of the Swilcan Burn which are unmarked or are marked with yellow stakes are ordinary water hazards (Rule 33-2).

(b) Those parts of the Swilcan Burn to be treated as lateral water hazards are marked with red stakes (Rule 33-3).

### 3 GROUND UNDER REPAIR (Def 13 Rule 32)

Play is prohibited within a GUR demarcated area; Rule 32-2 applies.

### 4 ROADS AND PATHS

All roads and paths are integral parts of the Course (Def 20c). The ball must be played as it lies or declared unplayable.

### 5 OBSTRUCTIONS (Def 20 Rule 31)

March stones are immovable obstructions (Rule 31-2).

### 6 POP-UP SPRINKLER HEADS

All pop-up sprinkler heads are immovable obstructions (Def 20) and relief from interference by them may be obtained under Rule 31-2.

In addition, if such an obstruction on, or within two club-lengths of, the putting green of the hole being played intervenes between the ball and the hole, the competitor may obtain relief, without penalty, in the following circumstances: —

(a) If the ball lie on the putting green, it may be lifted and placed, not nearer the hole, at the nearest point at which intervention by the obstruction is avoided.

(b) If the ball lie off the putting green (but not in a hazard) and is within two club-lengths of the intervening obstruction it may be lifted, cleaned and dropped as in clause (a) above.

### ETIQUETTE

Don't play until the match in front is out of range, but don't delay your own game.

If you are overtaken by other players while you are looking for a lost ball, or because of your own slow play, call the other players on, then wait until they are out of range before you continue your own game.

When you've finished putting, don't loiter on the green; there are other people waiting to play.

### EMPLOYMENT OF CADDIES

Caddies are not employed by the Management Committee but, for the convenience of players, caddies are permitted on the courses provided they are in possession of a current licence. Caddies must be engaged through the Caddie Master. Do not employ an un-licensed caddie without permission of a course officer or official.

4 BALL STROKE PLAY IS NOT PERMITTED.

PLEASE REPLACE DIVOTS AND REPAIR PLUG MARKS ON THE GREEN.

LINKS MANAGEMENT COMMITTEE OF ST ANDREWS
GOLF PLACE, ST ANDREWS, FIFE KY16 9JA

*Printed in Scotland by Woods of Perth (Printers) Ltd., 3/5 Mill Street, Perth PH1 5JB*

**MEN SSS 72**   **LGU SS 75**

**HOMEWARD PLAYERS HAVE THE RIGHT OF WAY**

| HOLE | MEN YARDS | MEN METRES | PAR | LADIES YARDS | LADIES METRES | PAR | STR. ALLCE. | SELF | PARTNER | OPP. | OPP. | + − | HOLE |
|------|-----------|------------|-----|--------------|---------------|-----|-------------|------|---------|------|------|-----|------|
| 1 | 370 | 338 | 4 | 339 | 310 | 4 | 15 | | | | | | |
| 2 | 411 | 377 | 4 | 375 | 343 | 5 | 3 | | | | | | 1 |
| 3 | 352 | 322 | 4 | 321 | 293 | 5 | 13 | | | | | | 2 |
| 4 | 419 | 383 | 4 | 401 | 366 | 5 | 9 | | | | | | 3 |
| 5 | 514 | 470 | 5 | 454 | 415 | 5 | 1 | | | | | | 4 |
| 6 | 374 | 342 | 4 | 325 | 297 | 4 | 11 | | | | | | 5 |
| 7 | 359 | 328 | 4 | 335 | 307 | 4 | 7 | | | | | | 6 |
| 8 | 178 | 163 | 3 | 145 | 132 | 3 | 18 | | | | | | 7 |
| 9 | 307 | 281 | 4 | 261 | 238 | 4 | 5 | | | | | | 8 |
| OUT | 3284 | 3004 | 36 | 2956 | 2701 | 38 | | | | | | | 9 |
| 10 | 318 | 291 | 4 | 296 | 271 | 4 | 10 | | | | | | OUT |
| 11 | 172 | 157 | 3 | 150 | 137 | 3 | 17 | | | | | | 10 |
| 12 | 316 | 289 | 4 | 304 | 278 | 4 | 6 | | | | | | 11 |
| 13 | 398 | 364 | 4 | 377 | 345 | 5 | 12 | | | | | | 12 |
| 14 | 523 | 478 | 5 | 487 | 445 | 5 | 2 | | | | | | 13 |
| 15 | 401 | 366 | 4 | 369 | 337 | 4 | 8 | | | | | | 14 |
| 16 | 351 | 321 | 4 | 325 | 297 | 4 | 14 | | | | | | 15 |
| 17 | 461 | 421 | 4 | 426 | 389 | 5 | 4 | | | | | | 16 |
| 18 | 354 | 324 | 4 | 342 | 312 | 4 | 16 | | | | | | 17 |
| IN | 3294 | 3011 | 36 | 3076 | 2811 | 38 | | | | | | | 18 |
| OUT | 3284 | 3004 | 36 | 2956 | 2701 | 38 | | | | | | | IN |
| TOTAL | 6578 | 6015 | 72 | 6032 | 5512 | 76 | | | | | | | OUT |

| | | | | HANDICAP | | | | TOTAL |

PLAYER ...............................

| | | | | NETT SCORE | |

MARKER ...............................

COMPETITION ...............................

DATE ...............................

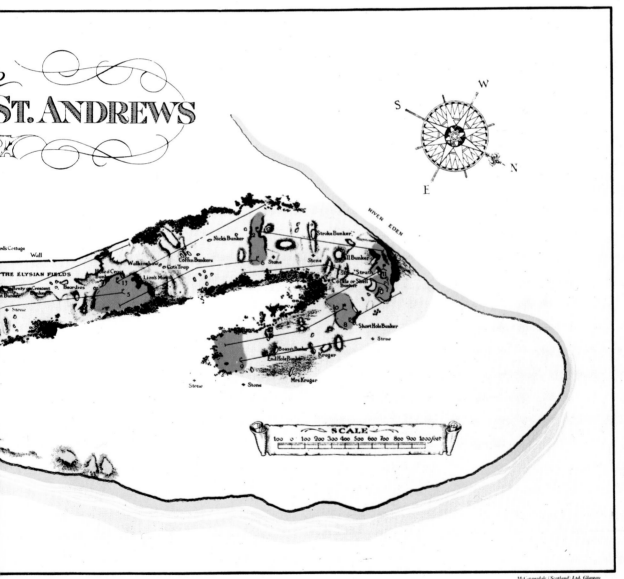

ST. ANDREWS

W

S

E

N

RIVER EDEN

Nick's Bunker

Stroke Bunker

Coffin Bunkers

Hell Bunker

Stone

Stone

Strath

rds Cottage

Wall

Walkinshaw

Cat's Trap

THE ELYSIAN FIELDS

Hole o'Cross

Lion's Mouth

Cockle or Shell Bunker

13

nity or Crescent

Beardies

5

Stone

Short Hole Bunker

Stone

Boase's Bunker

End Hole Bunker

Kruger

Stone

Stone

Mrs Kruger

SCALE
100  0  100 200 300 400 500 600 700 800 900 1000/feet

M. Corquodale (Scotland) Ltd. Glasgow

OLD COURSE
HOLE NO. 1
BURN
370 YDS.
PAR 4 STR. 15

Here you are at last, at the Mecca for golfers. As you stand on the huge teeing ground, behind you is the old, grey clubhouse with its tall, ground-floor windows; the long sweep of St Andrews Bay reaches off to the right; the golf shops and houses and Rusack's Hotel form file down the left. Before you is a vast expanse of fairway, embracing the 1st and 18th holes, a double fairway surely 150 yards across without a single bunker in sight. Your first problem will be to stay sufficiently relaxed and in control of yourself for the shot in hand. You will be well aware of where you are, and the whole ambience can be overpowering, no matter how often you stand on this first tee. You will be well aware that the clubhouse behind you is more than 100 years old, that the Royal and Ancient Golf Club which inhabits it is more than 200 years old, and that golf has been played here or hereabouts for the best part of five centuries. In fact you would be a poor golfer indeed if all of this did not give you a twinge or two.

I have some consolation for you. The first hole of the Old Course is just about the easiest opening hole of any championship course anywhere. You have a flat, abundant fairway to aim at. Granny Clark's Wynd, a narrow metal roadway, crosses the fairway about 130 yards out – no problem. The main characteristic, in fact the only characteristic, of this hole is the Swilcan Burn, which crosses the front of the green hard by the putting surface, then turns and comes back part of the way up the right side of the fairway. The presence rather than the perils of this burn preoccupy the golfer, and it has produced some adventures for the best of them.

In the 1970 Open Championship, Tom Shaw of America putted his third shot, from the back of the green, all the way into the burn. He then dropped a ball under penalty on the far side of the burn, and promptly chipped back over it onto the green and directly into the hole – score 5! In the same championship Doug Sanders pitched into the burn with the second shot of his first round, and scored six on the hole. Yet he almost won the championship, missing a three-foot putt on the 72nd hole which brought him a losing play-off, decided again on the very last green, with Jack Nicklaus.

The only danger on the drive, once you have your nerves and concentration under control, is the right side, where an out-of-bounds fence runs all the way along. If you hit the ball

The 1st tee and the Royal and Ancient clubhouse

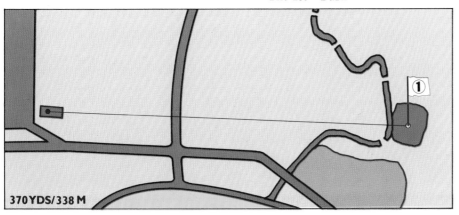

**370YDS/338M**

too far (!), the side sector of the burn might just be in play. So drive to the left, on the left corner of the green. You can aim even further left, on the bridge over the burn, if you prefer.

With the pin in the centre of the green, in fact anywhere but at the front, you have a perfectly straightforward, orthodox shot to it. In still air, if you have driven the ball out a bit

more than 200 yards, you will have a mid-iron to play. If the pin is at the front, which could mean only five or six yards from the edge of the burn, ignore it. Go for the centre or back of the green, where there is no trouble.

The essential point is to start your Old Course round sensibly. Knock the drive down that wide fairway. Pop the second to the middle of the

green. It is quite big enough for anyone to hit. Take your two putts and settle for a comfortable par, and compose yourself for the adventures ahead.

### What's in the name?

The burn or stream is the Swilcan Burn which loops round to guard the green.

Go for the centre or back of the green to avoid possible trouble

*The 1st Green and the Swilcan Burn*

OLD COURSE
HOLE NO. 2
DYKE
411 YDS.
PAR 4 STR. 3

The Old Course and Carnoustie, above all other links courses, can be disquieting in particular respects. They have so many flat tees, so much broken or dead ground that it is often difficult to know how far or where to go, quite apart from how to get there. This is not so much a question of blind shots as of blind lines, and in knowing on what precise line the ball should be hit, particularly from the tees. The second at St Andrews is a vintage Old Course hole, and your first real introduction to the variety of hazards and variations of routes that have to be considered on this extraordinary golf course.

The second tee is hard by the first green and is quite flat. For the first time we meet a long bank of gorse which guards much of the right side of the fairway and marches out in a line all the way to the 7th hole and the end of the course, separating it from the parallel New Course. Like all these outward holes, the 2nd is something of a driving hazard.

All the same, I would not be too fidgety about your drive. There is a

Above:
The ridge hiding the green

Bunker divides the 2nd and 16th greens

Ridge protects the right side of the green

2nd shot at the 2nd

16

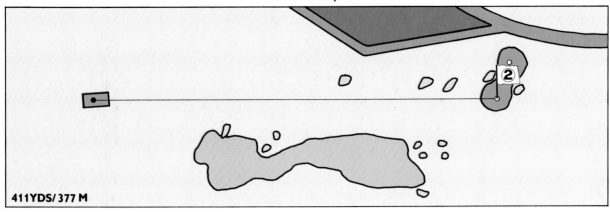

**411YDS/377 M**

reasonably wide fairway to find, with the line to the left of the whins (gorse). There is a bunker on the right side, about 130 yards out, with two little pots beyond it, at around 180 yards. On the left, between the 2nd and 17th fairways, is the bigger Cheape's bunker, 250 yards away, and if your driving line bisected that right bunker and Cheape's, you would be in an excellent position. The line of the teeing ground itself should keep you right.

The second shot is the main challenge on this hole, and is perhaps one of the most difficult on the course. The nature of the green makes it so. It is long from left to right, the first of St Andrews's famous double greens, and is coupled with the 16th. It is probably as much as 55 yards across, with its twin. A bunker at the front, eating into the putting surface, 'divides' the second from the 16th, and the right half, which we are concerned with, has a ridge dead in front of it. The green behind that ridge slopes away, and in fact a slight rise towards the back of the green, stiffened by the Wig bunker, gives the green a hollow effect.

The ridge is more pronounced on the left, and if the flagstick is to the left, you will not see all of it. You would then have to pitch the ball short, and hope it runs up and over the ridge onto the green. With the pin to the right, everything is much more open, and this underlines one of the basic tenets for playing the Old Course, which is that the tightest driving lines are down the right. These also happen to be the more dangerous driving lines. If you can drive down a tight line along these whins on the opening holes, and avoid the bunkers, which are scattered, almost all of them hidden, amongst and beyond the whins, you are likely to be in a good position. On almost every hole on the Old Course, the right side of the fairway, with access to the easier right side of the greens, is the more rewarding place to be.

Provided you find the right side of the fairway, your second or approach shot will be a good deal less risky. If you have any doubts about making the distance on your second, aim for the right-front corner of the green. If anywhere, that is the area in which to be short. Despite a good deal of undulation in the ground there, you have a chance to chip the ball close with your third.

There are two big bunkers, not always easy to see, on the left some 70 yards and 40 yards short of the green. Most of the ground in front of the green is undulating, and your best bet, as ever, is to fly the ball if you can all the way to the putting surface. If you cannot, hope for a bit of luck in getting a decent lie and stance for the third! And don't be embarrassed, ever, at St Andrews, by luck: everyone who plays this course will need some, and everyone who plays the course can expect some – both good and bad.

## What's in the name?

The dyke marked the boundary of the railway property, now owned by the Old Course Hotel.

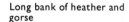

Long bank of heather and gorse

## St Andrews

OLD COURSE
HOLE NO. 3
CARTGATE
352 YDS.
PAR 4 STR. 13

The 3rd hole follows the pattern of the 2nd, but although substantially shorter, it is perhaps progressively more difficult, certainly on the tee shot. It too illustrates a basic tenet, this time of golf architecture: the more the player takes advantage of the safe or easy way on shot A, the more complicated should be the subsequent challenges on shot B.

Again, there is not a lot to see, no clearly defined target, as you line up your drive. You could safely follow the line of the teeing ground and aim for a point 20 yards inside, or to the left of, that persisting border of whins. Alternatively you could go well to the left, out towards the Principal's Nose bunkers on the adjoining 16th fairway, which are about 190 yards from your tee, but the more left you go, the tighter your second shot will be.

The adventurous driving line is again down the right, just inside the line of gorse, but hidden along that right side is a minefield of bunkers from 170 yards to 240 yards, any of which can be penal. The

On this hole there is no clearly defined target from the tee

Never expect a true bounce in these bumps and hollows

Approach shot must pitch on the green and hold

The 3rd Green

18

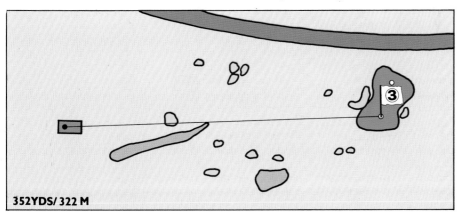

**352YDS/ 322 M**

optimum line might be just on the right of a central fairway bunker, 120 yards out.

A series of ridges runs in diagonally across this fairway, from 10 o'clock to 4 o'clock, advancing from the left and the 16th fairway. These make for, at best, uneven stances on your approach shot, which poses stiff problems, as at the 2nd hole. Here, the green is rather deeper, from front to back, but with an entrance very much nipped in by the huge Cartgate bunker hard by the putting surface on the left. This green also has a pronounced slope from left to right. There is a mass of uneven ground in front of it, and in there you will be entirely at the mercy of the

bouncing ball.

The further right you have driven, the more open the second shot will be, but that will mean you have flirted with pot bunkers and banks of gorse. The further left you have driven, the more into play will come that big Cartgate bunker, closing out pretty effectively the left half of the green. And if the hole is cut behind Cartgate, as it would be at least once in every championship, for example, then the shot required will be quite fearsome.

If the pin is at the right back, you will probably not see the bottom of it, even when you are only 20 yards short of the green, so strong are the slopes and contours. There is a

small bunker at the back of the green, just to complicate your complications. But such a mass of difficulties often produces simple decisions. You must drive carefully here, on line, and hit a decent shot. You should then be playing a pitching club with which, at all costs, you *must* hit the green.

The real difficulty here, as everywhere on the Old Course, is in not quite knowing where to go, and not being able to see. Even second or third or fourth time round, you will not know exactly where the humps and hollows are, and where you can land the ball safely and where not. You must never really expect to get a straight and true bounce here.

And you must not allow yourself to become impatient with this golf course. Don't rush it. Let it all come to you; it will, in time.

## What's in the name?
This refers to the gate in a cart track which led out towards the Eden estuary, and was used by fishermen.

## St Andrews

The first thing the average player should do here is take a careful look at the yardage. This hole can be a puzzle, and much depends on the conditions. For instance, I can imagine a first-class amateur playing it, in still air, with a drive and an 8-iron. On the other hand, in air that is less than still, it can be two woods, particularly in cold weather or with the wind against. So the average player should realistically deem it a par 5 and play it accordingly.

It is a long hole, but at least we can see the green, or at any rate the flagstick, far ahead down the line of the teeing ground. This line is hard along the right side with its now customary perils, but again it is the more adventurous line, and will give a better view of, and better access to, the green on the second shot.

In a sense the Ginger Beer can be likened to a valley, running between the higher ground to the left along which the 15th hole runs, and the 'wall' of gorse to the right. But it is not exactly a quiet, pastoral valley. Several

The direct line appears to run through a valley

Mounded fairway ridge defending the green

Approach to the 4th

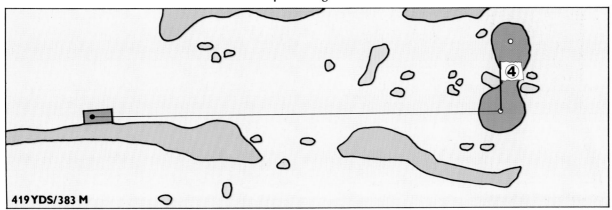

**419 YDS/383 M**

Wall of gorse on the right

ridges enter from the left, from the 15th, and out on the left side of the fairway is what I can only describe as a hump. Many people tend or elect to drive over there, and if you were planning to hit a massive hook anywhere on the Old Course, this might be the place to do it. Nowhere are you guaranteed a level lie for the second shot on this fairway, but if you can get beyond the ridges and beyond a big bunker on the right, the back of which is 220 yards from the tee, you might be lucky since the fairway opens out there into a reasonable area, and gives you some comforting space to work with.

From there, as you contemplate your second shot, you are faced with a mounded fairway ridge defending the green, a good distance short of it but five or six feet high. Past this ridge, the ground is nothing but humps and hollows all the way to the putting surface.

The green is quite big. Although present, no bunkers are to be seen, the reason being that none is effectively in play. There is the usual big one, front left, bisecting the double green, and just short of this a trio of 'Student's' bunkers, none of these really in line. What there is to perplex you is the mound or ridge short of the green. If you can carry that, you should never be too far from the centre of the

green. If you feel you cannot carry it, play just short of it, favouring the right – your ball will probably break to the right in any case. From that little corner you can attack the flagstick fairly well. But note that the green is long, a good 40 yards, with firm folds in it. If you do hit the green with your second, you may still be facing a long putt which will need a good deal of work, so the clubbing on the second shot is very important, and the accuracy of the chip shot, if you need one, no less so.

**What's in the name?**

In the last century one Daw (David) Anderson had a ginger-beer stall; it must have been a memorable brew.

OLD COURSE
HOLE NO. 5
HOLE O' CROSS
514 YDS.
PAR 5 STR. 1

**H**ole o' Cross (Out) is the first of only two par-5 holes on the Old Course. It runs beside and contra to the other, the 14th or Long Hole on the inward half of the course.

The drive here continues to pose problems we have faced on the earlier holes, with the

The view from the tee emphasizes the need to play to the left

line of gorse running down the right side, past the Pulpit bunker which is about 150 yards out, and concealing beyond it no fewer than six bunkers of varying size but equal ferocity – deep and very straight-faced. These range from 200 yards to 255 yards, so you *must* keep the ball to the left of that line. There is plenty of room to go left, and the man who draws the ball will have an advantage here. But for first-timers it poses again the question of exactly where to go. The perfect line in still air would be just to the left of that Pulpit bunker. There is a stone marker down there, which is exactly the place to hit.

The left side is interesting. Here we are probably at the narrowest point on the course, not

much more than 100 yards across the joint 5th and 14th fairways, yet there seems plenty of room to the left of that driving line – further evidence that nothing is simple at St Andrews. The 14th fairway is higher than the 5th, and an escarpment of three or four feet in height lines the left side of this hole. Inside it, the ground is very uneven, falling, tumbling, making a level stance unlikely. However, if you could possibly get your drive out 250 yards or more, along that left line, you might well run into a level area of fairway. If the course is dry, if you are downwind, if you hit your best shot, it would certainly not be impossible.

Almost every shot on this course calls for decision-making, and the

second shot at the 5th is no exception. You will be faced with a high ridge crossing the entire front of the green, with only the white flag itself showing above it. Two bunkers are set into this ridge, rather like The Spectacles on the 14th at Carnoustie, but set wider apart. The ridge is approximately 410 yards from the medal tee. Immediately in front of it is a piece of honest, level fairway which should give you a good stance and lie. If you carry this ridge with a good, positive shot, you might well be on the front of the putting surface; the ground beyond the ridge is reasonable, and will certainly move the ball forward *unless* the big gulley behind the ridge smothers the ball.

If I say you can

High ridge containing two bunkers crosses the front of the green

2nd shot at the 5th

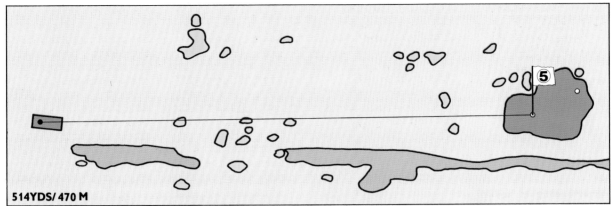

**514YDS/ 470 M**

consider this a birdie hole, choke back your surprise. You must think positively and optimistically on this course. If you are downwind, which means with a south or south-east wind, it need not be beyond your talents.

So now we come to the point of decision. Can you carry that ridge comfortably? That depends on your drive, your lie and stance, the wind and the weather and your shot-making. If you think you can do it – go ahead, do it. Don't think defensively. The line would be right between the bunkers or marginally left of that. If you have any doubts about making the carry, don't think defensively, think tactically, and play short of the ridge. That will almost certainly give you a good stance and lie and leave you a third shot, a pitch of 120–130 yards to what may appear the biggest green on any golf course that you have seen. If you are into a headwind, of course, your decision will probably be made for you – you will have to play short. But if you are short of the ridge in two, for whatever reason, walk forward to the top of it, and have a look beyond. That might be just as important as anything you do on this hole.

**What's in the name?**

Probably a reference to a cross that once stood here rather than any crossing of the course.

**For safety on the 2nd shot aim for a patch of level fairway short of the ridge**

OLD COURSE
HOLE NO. 6
HEATHERY
374 YDS.
PAR 4 STR. 11

**A**t first glance, this looks no more than a hit-and-hope job. Immediately in front of the tee there is nothing but a mass of gullies, gorse and heather, with a path snaking somewhere through it. It all underlines the value, first time round, of investing in an experienced caddie.

The line of the teeing ground here seems to me to be slightly too far to the right of the ideal line, and I think your direction should be on the hangars of the RAF station at Leuchars in the distance, across the estuary of the River Eden.

Still the bank of heather and gorse runs along the right, rising now, with a more powerful appearance. Again there is the cluster of bunkers, four this time in the range 210 yards to 230 yards on the right

side, which you will not see. On the left are the two very big Coffins bunkers, perhaps 200 yards away. Between the Coffins and the right-hand bunkers is (by St Andrews standards) good fairway space. So if you had your drive out 220 yards or more on my line, you would be 150 yards or less from the middle of the green and in a good position for the approach shot. Downwind, in dry conditions, your best shot could take you really quite close to this green.

As always on the Old Course, the green demands the closest attention and concentration. The problem here may well be holding

the green with your approach, or at least getting decently close to the flagstick. There are not too many greens on this course which rise nicely to the back to hold your shot, with completely clear, uncluttered entrances. This time there is no screening ridge compromising the front; instead, a dip or gulley runs across. This then rises quite quickly to the putting surface, which in turn slopes away from you.

The green is long from left to right, quite deep from front to back, and most of it, certainly the right half, can be clearly seen. Given a

good drive, you might like to consider running the ball on, hitting a low shot with, say, a 6- or 7-iron, pitching the ball perhaps 30 yards short of the putting surface and taking a chance with the bounce. In any event, you do have some options with the second shot. It is the drive, and getting the right driving line, which provides the major challenge on the hole.

### What's in the name?

In former times the heather grew abundantly here, though there is less of it now.

**374 YDS/342 M**

The fairway ridge hides bunkers to left and right

Green slopes away at the back

Cluster of bunkers at 210–250 yards

2nd shot at the 6th

OLD COURSE
HOLE NO. 7
HIGH
359 YDS.
PAR 4 STR. 7

HOMEWARD
PLAYERS
HAVE RIGHT
OF WAY

A view from the tee of the adventurous direct route

**W**orking out your driving line is your first problem. In front of the tee, and quite close to it, is a large heather-covered bank which makes the drive blind. Pressing in on the right, thankfully for the last time, is our now-familiar line of gorse bushes, but this time instead of ignoring it and in general playing away from it, we can make it an ally. Beyond this frontal high ground, we play into the only zone that passes for a valley at St Andrews, at least until we get to the 18th. It is a wide expanse of fairly true ground where the 7th hole and the short 11th cross. From somewhere in that area, we then have to play to possibly the most complicated green on the course.

If you take the shortest, most direct and most adventurous – and also the best – route to this hole you have to drive along the line of the gorse on the right, almost clipping the bushes. On that line you will have to carry 220 yards to be safely in the valley, but a solid hit on that line can put you in the perfect position for your second shot. A more conservative line would be to hit directly over the bunker on the bank or hill in front of the tee. That bunker is 170–180 yards from the medal tee, and there is some 20

The Strath bunker

The 7th green from the right-hand rough

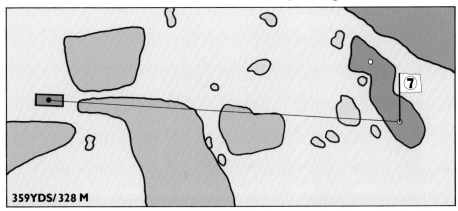

**359YDS/328 M**

yards of bad ground behind it.

When you come over the hill, the prospect is unique. The 11th and 7th greens form yet another of the Old Course's famous double greens, the 11th occupying the left part, and the 7th with its white flag – your target – to the right. This double green is probably the longest from left to right, if not the largest in area, on the course and lies 'across' the approach shot on the 7th, running from 8 o'clock to 2 o'clock. If you have driven to the left, your approach shot will be longer but will be played more down the length of the green. The huge Cockle bunker, some 20 yards short of the putting surface, is on a direct line tee-to-green and covers the front (it is driveable by supermen provided the conditions are right).

The bunker to the left of the Cockle digs right into the putting surface and is usually taken as marking the extreme left of the 7th, and the extreme right of the 11th, in target terms. So if your drive has been 'straight', on the more dashing line along the whins, you will be closer to Cockle and the green, but will require a different approach shot – shorter, but probably higher, a softer, holding pitch into a green running across the shot.

When you come to look at this green more closely, you can hardly imagine it existing anywhere but St Andrews. It slopes quite severely downwards from its left, or if you prefer back, and falls away at the back, or to the right, towards the 8th tee. There are ridges and rises at the very front of the green which you must carry. In fact at the front of the green, actually on the putting surface, there is first a slight dip, then a quick rise up to the plateau green proper. In addition, there is a spine running through the green, so that the factor of luck, as the ball pitches and runs along it, is great. If the ball should come to rest in the wrong place, a good deal of hard work will have to go into the putting. The second shot must therefore be very positive, from whatever angle, and aimed to pitch on the putting surface.

### What's in the name?

The most mountainous sector of the baffling undulations that give the Old Course so much of its character.

The huge Cockle bunker

Green falls away at the back and on the right

The most direct, though adventurous, line is tight on the right

The Old Course has but two par 5s and two par 3s. This is the first of the short holes and in yardage it is not too forbidding, although it can play very long into wind (south-east). Billy Joe Patton, the famous American amateur and Walker Cup player, has told how he played this hole in successive rounds, when the wind changed course, with a 2-iron ('Ah hit that bawl with every bone in ma body') and then an 8-iron ('Ah jes' tried to bleed it a little').

The green doubles

Above:
The Short Hole bunker

The Short Hole bunker is well
short of the green

The short 8th

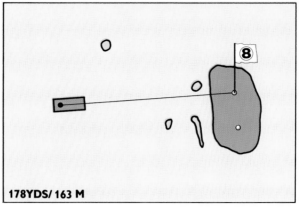

**178YDS/ 163 M**

with the 10th. It is very big and quite long from left to right, and frankly it is hard to miss. The hole has but one real routine defence, the Short Hole bunker, slightly off the centre line to the left and a long way short of the green. There are modest grass banks which disguise the front of the green to some extent, and club selection is obviously important here.

The 8th is probably the first really unsubtle hole on the course, and you really must make par or better here. We are now into The Loop, which does exactly what it says. From the 7th hole to the 11th, the course loops round in a fishhook so that, come the 12th tee, we are now pointed back towards the town on a run of holes which parallel directly the first half-dozen outward holes.

Holes 8, 9 and 10 are perhaps the easiest on the course for various reasons. They are all flat and open, without blind shots, set out plainly before you with every-thing to be seen; all are on the short side, and there is very little undulation in the ground. One advantage is that they give the player a period of rest and recuperation, without forbidding challenges, before the major problems ahead on the final third of the course. Even more important, they can be used to hold the score together. Holes 7 to 12 have been played in successive threes by more than one golfer, and even the average player must score relatively well, certainly from 8 to 11, to protect his card.

The 8th could never be called a severe hole, but it has to be tackled with some care. The main danger is under-clubbing.

**What's in the name?**

Here at the top of the 'loop' is the first of the two short holes on the course.

OLD COURSE
HOLE NO. 9
END
307 YDS.
PAR 4 STR. 5

**T**his hole is entirely flat, straight-forward and straight-away, with everything visible from the tee. The fairway is very wide, and is shared with the 10th hole, rather like the 1st and 18th. Here a few bunkers and occasional light rough separate the two and give them at least some definition.

The 9th gives you plenty of options, or

Boase's bunker and the End Hole bunker narrow the approach to the green

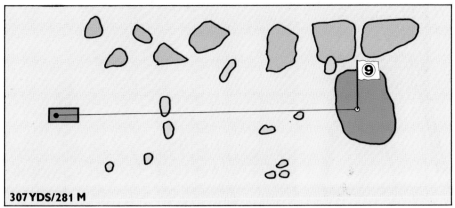

**307 YDS/281 M**

more accurately plenty of margins, on the drive. A pair of cross-bunkers called Kruger, not much more than 100 yards away, lies directly across the fairway. The driving line from tee to centre of green would take you over the gap between these two bunkers. You should aim slightly to the left of that point. If you took the dead-centre line you might well finish in the End Hole bunker, which is 240 yards from the tee and 70 yards from the centre of the green on the direct line. Short of, and wider than, the End Hole bunker is Boase's bunker, which can catch a sliced shot.

There are two large bunkers in the left rough, one about 170 yards from the tee (Mrs Kruger), the other just wide of the left front of the green; but neither should be in play and the End Hole bunker should only be a problem on the drive.

The second shot, yet again, is testing, but not for a typically St Andrews reason. The single green is very big, very flat, and is simply an extension of the fairway. This makes the second shot rather difficult to judge. Depending on your position, you may have to pitch the ball all the way to the hole, or pitch and run it there, or give it the old 'Musselburgh scuffle' – all the way along the ground. Indeed, if you have driven the ball well in good conditions, you may even think of putting from off the green.

Tony Jacklin, in his freakish round in the 1970 Open Championship, holed out in two here for an outward half of 29, with a shot that might well have gone over the green, but instead whacked the flagstick and fell into the hole!

## What's in the name?

The 9th green marks the end or turning-point, and the beginning of the long walk home.

Large flat green and flat approach

End Hole bunker at 240 yards

*From the 9th Tee*

OLD COURSE
HOLE NO. 10
BOBBY JONES
318 YDS.
PAR 4 STR. 10

**T**his is the return hole, very like the 9th, and in common with it increases in interest and character the closer you get to the green. There is a trio of bunkers only just in the left rough 100 yards out. The straight line from tee to green will be directly over them. You will see the End Hole and Boase's bunker on the right, and the Kruger bunkers in the distance. None of these should concern you, but just beyond Kruger and to the left is a 10th-hole bunker some 240 yards from the medal tee. That bunker, provided you do not drive into it, is a good driving line, or preferably a little to the left of it. You would then be driving at the midpoint between that bunker and the trio on the left. This is your best driving line, and it also gives you a good deal of margin.

**What's in the name?**

A tribute to the great American amateur, whom some rate as the greatest player in the history of golf.

The 10th Green

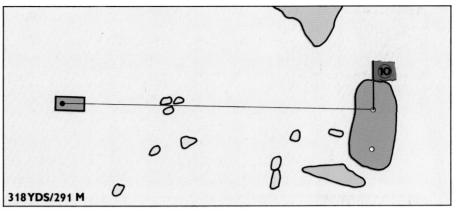

318 YDS/291 M

Unlike the 9th hole, in the general driving area here, say over the final 100 yards to the green, the ground is undulating. The green is raised slightly at the front, and then slopes away from you and to the left. This is the green which is twinned with the short 8th. All kinds of approach shots are 'on', though all pose slightly stronger problems than at the 9th. If you go for the full-blooded pitch, it might be difficult to stop where you want to on the green. If you decide to run the ball, then stance, lie and the contours of the ground between you and the green will make the shot intriguing. So once again this old course remains in character. Even on its easiest holes, which so far you might judge to be 1, 8, 9 and 10, there is always a puzzle, however minor, for the player.

The green, too, undulates a good deal more than the part which serves the 8th hole, and there are some definite borrows to be coped with. But since this is a very short par 4, anything more than par on the hole can be counted a failure.

Left:
Undulating ground in front of the green

Green is raised slightly at the front and slopes away and to the left

The 10th Hole bunker

33

OLD COURSE
HOLE NO. 11
HIGH
172 YDS.
PAR 3 STR. 17

This is one of the world's greatest, most celebrated and most demanding short holes, regardless of conditions. It is the most clearly defined target on the course, yet also the most clearly and powerfully defended.

The green is very narrow from front to back. It slopes upwards severely, then falls over into a rough-strewn bank, down to the estuary of the River Eden, and you can consider that a disaster area. At the front, it is resolutely defended by the very large, very deep Hill bunker on the left, and by the smaller but equally vicious Strath bunker on the right. These are possibly the two most fearsome bunkers on the course. The entire contouring of the area short of the green, and the very front portions of the putting surfaces, will gather shots towards these bunkers. And since we are at the end of the course, on the brink of the Eden estuary, there is almost always some wind, and since the green is totally exposed on that sharp slope, it is always inclined to be fast. That is more than

Above:
The Strath bunker and the steep sloping green

The Hill bunker

The Strath bunker

*from the 11th Tee*

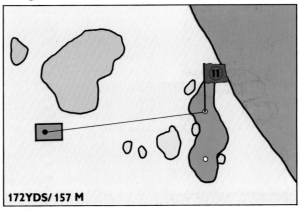

**172YDS/ 157 M**

enough to make the 11th tee a terror tee, a real danger point on the Old Course. Anything pitching 20 yards short is likely to break towards the Strath bunker. Go over the back of the green, and you will be pitching out of strong, tangly rough onto a slippery downslope.

There are nevertheless some tactically sound points to be made. Regardless of pin position, you should try to be at the front of the green, so that you have an uphill putt to the flag. And if possible make sure that, if you are going to need a second putt, it too is directly uphill. Side-hill putts on this green take an unbelievable amount of borrow. If the hole is cut directly behind either of the frontal bunkers, aim instead for the front centre of the green. On the whole it is better to be short than over the back. If you do get into one of these deep traps, *get out*, first time, even if it means playing backwards to the fairway.

This is a very demanding par 3. If you score more than that, do not let it upset your composure. Gene Sarazen, one of the few men to have completed golf's Grand Slam, and who was both Open Champion and US Open Champion in the same year, once made six at this hole – including three shots in Hill bunker.

### What's in the name?

The short 11th shares its relative heights with the 7th, which it crosses.

OLD COURSE
HOLE NO. 12
HEATHERY
316 YDS.
PAR 4 STR. 6

The Heathery is a tricky, fidgety hole, getting its name no doubt from the heather banks on the left which spread away in front of the 7th tee. It is a short par 4, and for this and other reasons it presents many problems, for the long hitter in particular. From the high tee by the 11th green, above the estuary, there is a positive stew of bunkers on the straight line to the green.

The key factor dominating the drive is the big Stroke bunker, dead ahead in the centre of the fairway 175 yards out. Another smaller bunker is set just past it and slightly wide of it. A pair of bunkers, unseen from the tee, backs it up at 215 yards. Thus the strategy requires you to go wide of Stroke on either side.

The green is very narrow, only some 15 yards from front to back, and it rises abruptly into a shelf. There is a single bunker 40 yards short on the direct tee-to-green line, and the ground immediately in front of the green is very uneven. The optimum shot to

Uneven ground in front of the green

Approach to the 12th

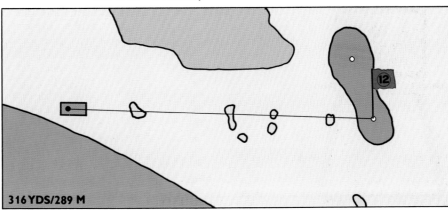

**316 YDS/289 M**

such a narrow green, then, would be a high, soft pitch which you would hope to see settle down and stop quickly.

But from which side to attack this green, since a drive directly on line is not recommended? The long hitters who could get the ball out 240–250 yards might pass all the obvious hazards. The general consensus is that you should go left of Stroke, but not too far left, where the banked heather comes into play. The smart shot might well be to get the ball out 190–200 yards, just to the left of that big bunker, then go for a pitch from

that side. This would give you rather more of the length of the green to work with.

Mercifully, there is no trouble over the back of the green, so the pitch shot can be over- rather than under-clubbed. If you go well wide to the right of Stroke, where there are no hazards as such, you are into very uneven ground, and pitching to the narrowest of greens. Even on this short par 4, there are enough complexities to illustrate what a unique golf course it is. Whether you care for it or not, you have to agree that it is uncommon!

And by the way, from the tee, just about the most distant point on the course, there is the most wonderful panorama of the Eden estuary, the rolling hills above the Leuchars road, and the well-loved prospect of the distant, 'auld grey toon'. Take a moment to savour it, before you set out on the long, hard road home.

### What's in the name?

Heathery (In) gets its name from the heather which runs along the left-hand side of the fairway.

The approach from the left directly over the bunker

Narrow green but no trouble behind

**OLD COURSE
HOLE NO. 13
HOLE O' CROSS
398 YDS.
PAR 4 STR. 12**

This is the first of a run of five holes, from 13 to 17, which collectively form the main single challenge of the Old Course. In general, they run in a south-easterly direction and so are most likely to be running across the prevailing wind, a right to left wind. With the possible exception of 15, all are very severely restricted by subtle or substantial hazards, natural or otherwise, and all of them demand resolution on the part of the player – clear thinking, correct decision-making, positive shot-making, too, but above all resolution in facing up to the demands these holes make.

The structure of Hole o' Cross (In) is quite marvellous. There is a wide dense bank of heather and gorse running down the right side for most of the hole. About 220 yards from the tee, it branches left into what I can only call a range of foothills, which cross the fairway and continue in front of the 6th tee, the parallel hole, and create the blind tee shot which we experienced there. Down the centre line between the two fairways, and establishing more or less the left side of the 13th, is a parade of bunkers of various sizes. Thus our first thought on the 13th tee is of driving into a rectangle confined by the gorse on the right, the bunkers on the left, and the 'foothills' at the end.

Probably the first governing factor here will be the playing conditions. Into a head-wind, this hole will play very long, and in some circumstances even a professional player will need two woods. The first bunker, Nick's, is only 120 yards out. Behind it on the left are the Coffins, two very big traps covering the range 150–190 yards. Beyond them, at the left end of the cross ridge, is another pair, Cat's Trap and Walkinshaw's, about 260 yards out.

There are three options on the drive:
1 You can drive straight ahead into the rectangle. You should not go more than 200 yards. Beyond that you may dribble into the foothills.
2 You can go directly over Coffins. You should not then go more than 240 yards or you will be flirting with Cat's Trap.
3 You can go positively left of Coffins. You should not then go more than 240 yards, or you will be tangling with more foothills.

The second shot brings no relief from decisions, decisions. The three drive placements have one thing in common. They demand a second shot which is all carry. The ground to the green is so badly broken that the approach shot cannot possibly be landed short with any hope that it will run truly on. The direct route, from drive 1, is effectively closed out by the Hole o' Cross bunker, dead in front of the right half of the green and hard into the putting

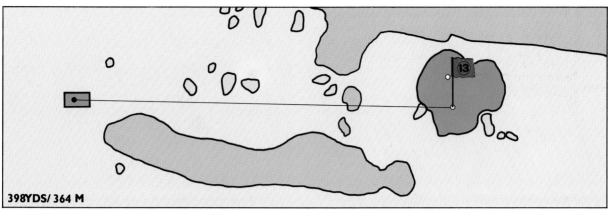

**398YDS/ 364 M**

surface. The best bet here, even if it does seem a touch cowardly, is to aim for the left half of the double green, on the white flag marking the 5th hole. Otherwise you might well be saddled with a shot of 180 yards which would have to carry well into a huge green.

If you have gone left, or followed either drive 2 or 3, you have diminished the threat of Hole o' Cross bunker, and will have a slightly shorter shot, but it will be essentially the same shot in that it must carry, and you should still favour the white flag on the 5th green.

There is just one possible escape route if you have taken the drive 1 route, and if you are not sure you can make the distance on the second shot. To the right of that Hole o' Cross bunker, to the right of the green and towards the 14th tee, is a piece of perfectly fair ground. You might think of popping your second over there, then chipping to the flagstick. However you make par here, it is a par well made, and if you are one over, fret not. As you see, it is a hole of unrelenting perplexity.

### What's in the name?

Hole o' Cross (In) shares its name with the 5th hole and the cross is thought to have stood by the shared green.

Broken ground right through to the green

Foothills cross the fairway at 220 yards

Approach to the 13th

Far left:
The view of the foothills from the tee

OLD COURSE
HOLE NO. 14
LONG
523 YDS.
PAR 5 STR. 2

**T**his is potentially the most destructive hole on the course. In Open Championship play, Gene Sarazen and Bobby Locke have scored 8, and Peter Thomson 7. Gary Player was once in one of the Beardies bunkers and declared that it had not been raked 'since it was made', which we can suppose was rather a long time ago.

The 14th is a long, sapping hole, demanding three fine hits from a professional player (you will be asked for three shots averaging 175 yards from the medal tee). So the thing to do is stand still for a moment, get your breathing right, give some thought to what you are about, and take a long hard look at the thing. Having said that, I must tell you that you will not see very much!

A stone wall squeezes into the fairway from the right, before turning back outwards again. It marks an out-of-bounds line. The first hazard on the left side is the Beardies, a set of bunkers making, with the angle of the wall, a rather narrow gap. The Beardies comprise one large and three small traps extending from 160 yards to 200 yards from the medal tee. In a left to right wind, the narrow gap between them and the wall makes this a terrifying drive to get

right. The line should be on the spire at the right-hand end of the distant town. Needless to say, you cannot see the green from the tee, but when you do, you will find that it is very big, and can be attacked from a variety of angles.

Although you cannot see them very clearly, it is essential that you pass the Beardies to the right, staying between them and the wall. If you have driven up level with them, or slightly past them, you will have entered the Elysian Fields, perhaps the only piece of honest, ordinary, recognizable fairway to be found beyond the 1st and 18th. The Elysian Fields extend perhaps a couple of hundred yards towards the green. At the end of them, the ground closes in from both sides in yet another tangle of broken, unreliable ground with heather and foothills and so on, which persists for a

further 100 yards almost to the green. There are two small bunkers along the left side, Benty and Kitchen, but dominating the scene, and the tactics from now on, is a huge and famous bunker, apparently as big as a tennis court – the very properly named Hell.

For a long hitter who has got one of his very best shots out well past the Beardies, the choice may be simple. He can go for an enormous smash past Hell, but again it will have to be his very best shot. For the

average chap, who perhaps has hit a good drive of say 225 yards, and is in a good position, the choice is not so easy. He will then be 180 yards from the centre of Hell bunker and 300 yards from the centre of the green! One thing at least he can be sure of: if he is playing into wind, he has absolutely no chance of carrying Hell bunker.

The conservative player will knock the ball forward, 100 yards or so, towards the end of the Elysian Fields, and go for a third shot of about 170

It can be sensible to use the full width of the double green

Hollows in front of the green

*The Approach to the 14th and Hell Bunker*

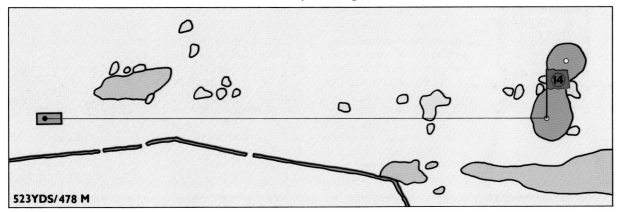

**523YDS/478 M**

yards to the green. Another obvious possibility for the same man is to blast the ball straight over Hell, if he thinks he can make the carry. He should be warned, however, that some 80 yards beyond Hell – and out of sight, of course – are other traps, principally Grave and Ginger Beer, protecting that line and the left half of the green.

Happily there is a well-established third course, used often by the best of players. It is to play the second shot to the left, aiming a good 50 yards to the left of Hell bunker, into the lower 5th fairway, and taking a line on the white flag on the 4th green. There is good ground there, more or less level with the leading edge of Hell bunker, and you have a fair chance of a decent stance and lie for what might be a mid-iron or long pitch shot to the green. A sensible line to keep your par within reach, even on the third shot, would be on the white flag, and reckon on getting down with two solid putts from there.

Although the double green is broad from left to right, the 14th green has hollows in front from which it rises steeply up a frontal bank, then falls away to the back quite sharply, so that many approaches will go all the way to the back, or even off the green. People also have trouble putting up and over that rise to the flag, if the approach has been left short. You must forget here, as at so many other Old Course greens, the business of running or bumbling the ball on.

The 14th is a critical hole. You must play it deliberately, using sensible tactics for the conditions, and above all, you must keep the ball in play. All those bunkers – Beardies, Benty, Kitchen, Hell, Grave, Ginger Beer – are penal. Get in any of them, and you have certainly lost one shot.

## What's in the name?

Long *is* long, and is made longer by its most evil traps – Beardies, Benty, Kitchen, Hell and Grave.

OLD COURSE
HOLE NO. 15
CARTGATE
401 YDS.
PAR 4 STR. 8

Into wind, this can turn into quite a longish hole, demanding two good hits. However, on a still day, it is a drive and moderate iron to a big green and altogether a much more simple hole than the others on this inward half. If you can relax anywhere in this stretch, it may well be here.

Along the right side of the hole is the usual file of gorse, although towards the green the old railway line comes into view on the right, but is not, I think, in play. As the railway appears, the gorse fades out, and you will be relieved to know that, from that point on, you are once and for all finished with gorse. On the left side, the big Cottage bunker starts about 140 yards out and leads off to the left. Beyond it, and hidden, at 200 yards' range, is the sneaky little Sutherland pot bunker. The driving line is to the right of Cottage where there is fair space, aiming on that same church spire in St Andrews town (see 14th). This should bring you to a flat area of fairway, and if your drive gets nicely along into a slight gully between mounds, you will be in a perfect position for a confident thrust at the green.

About halfway to the green on the second shot, more or less on line, is the trio of Rob's bunkers, but they should not concern you. As usual at St Andrews, the left half of this green is guarded by a pot bunker, but again the green is huge, and will take three or four clubs' difference from front to back. This and a good deal of dead ground in front of the green make club selection on the second shot very important. I would be inclined always to take one club more than it looks.

Finally, it should be said that the fringe of the green, at the immediate front and right side, is altogether more friendly than you have come to expect on the Old Course. The ground is reasonable. You will have a fair chance to chip or putt from off the green close to the flag, and although there is not one single hole on this course which you dare not respect, I would guess that there is more pleasure from less hard work to be won from the 15th than most.

The huge double green with its solitary pot bunker

Cartgate (In) shares its name and its green with the 3rd hole.

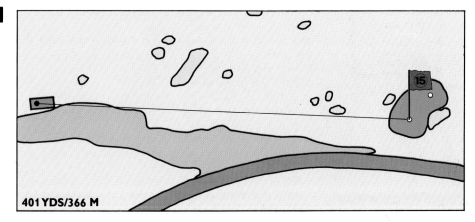

**401 YDS/366 M**

Left side of the green is guarded by a pot bunker

Green is huge and it is easy to under-club the 2nd shot

2nd shot at the 15th

OLD COURSE
HOLE NO. 16
'CORNER O' DYKE'
351 YDS.
PAR 4 STR. 14

**T**his is one of the most dangerous holes on the course. The disused railway line runs hard by the tee, all the way along as far as the green; it

closes off the entire right side of the hole, since it marks out-of-bounds. A group of three bunkers, Principal's Nose, is slightly left of the direct line to the flag, covering 170–190 yards from the medal tee, and leaving the narrowest of gaps – it looks little more than 15 yards across – to the railway line. And past Principal's Nose, 40 yards on, is Deacon Sime bunker, placed to trap anyone who flies directly over that trio of hazards.

The ambitious driver can have a go directly for the green, between these traps and the railway. This makes for a shorter, easier second shot into the green. It also requires

an act of cold courage, or, if you prefer, an act of madness. It is difficult to imagine anyone tackling it in a hard left-to-right wind.

The alternative way is to go left of Principal's Nose, or on a line directly over the left bunker of the three, which should keep you wide of Deacon Sime. About 230–240 yards out on that line is a friendly fairway, but from there the line of the second shot is compromised by Grant's bunker, 20 yards short of the putting surface, and Wig bunker which eats into the left front of it.

The green itself, as usual, is raised on a

plateau, with devious little gullies in front and at the back, and the ground just short of it tends to throw everything to the right, towards the railway fence. The ground between the right side of the green and the railway fence is fair, but there is not a lot of it – only a few feet.

In the 1978 Open Championship, Simon Owen and Jack Nicklaus came to this hole together in the last round, Owen leading the championship by one stroke from Nicklaus. He nailed a long drive down the right side, on the more dangerous line, and at a time like that, at the very climax of the champion-

ship, it took a lot of guts to do it. Nicklaus drove to the left. Then Owen, over-excited no doubt, hit his approach over the green, chipped back, and missed the putt. Nicklaus pitched on – and holed his putt. So the Open was lost and won, with a swing of two strokes on this 16th hole. It is that kind of golf hole, a short par 4, but with its variety of challenges and options a very subtle hole indeed.

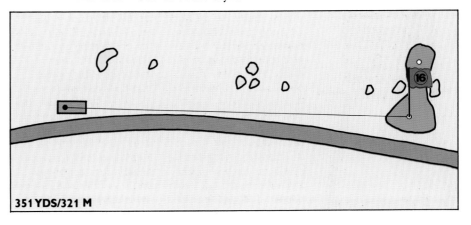

**351 YDS/321 M**

### What's in the name?

The green is tucked into the corner of the dyke which also gives its name to the 2nd hole.

Devious gullies in front of the raised green

Old railway line runs beside the green

The 16th Green

Left: The out-of-bounds fence following the old railway line

OLD COURSE
HOLE NO. 17
ROAD
461 YDS.
PAR 4 STR. 4

**D**ebatably the most famous single hole in the entire world of golf, the Road Hole for most golfers most of the time is a monster, and your first time on the 17th tee, even if you are a seasoned player, will induce a moment of terror. The hole is rated a par 4, yet for any club golfer it must be a 4.5, and in any conditions save quite still, it should be considered a par 5.

The siting of the tee and green, rather than any particular ground hazard, make the hole an absolute freak. Surely no one could imagine that a modern architect, even in a nightmare, could conceive of such a design. The point is that the 17th hole was not designed in the modern sense, but that like so much else on the Old Course, it 'happened'. It should be said, though, whether the

purists like it or not, that all these bunkers did not grow out of rabbit scrapes and sheep hollows; I'm sure that man has had much more of a hand in the development of the course than we sometimes allow.

Nevertheless, to make any sense of the present 17th, we must look back a little. In a course plan of 1821 for example, when the holes were played 'the other way round', the present ground was used for a perfectly straight, and dare I say normal, hole. Later in that century, when the railway came to St Andrews, sidings and sheds were built along the side of the 17th fairway. With the 17th tee hard by the 16th green, in the 'corner of the dyke', these black sheds impinged strongly on the fairway from the right, demanding a totally blind drive over them which became inevitably both famous and notorious. One wonders why the tee was not advanced to the corner of the sheds, making the hole shorter but at least allowing the player to see where he was going. On the other hand, not seeing the fairway or the green is not unusual on this course.

After the coming of the sheds, there were

many ploys among St Andrews caddies as to the line of the day, depending on the weather – slightly left, right, or directly over the gable of the sheds. In the late 1960s, when the railway and the sheds had gone and the present Old Course Hotel was built, the hotel people built an open trellis fence which maintained the profile and the roof outline of the black sheds, but at least gave the player some slightly better clue as to where he should go. A low stone wall and a path mark the edge of what was railway property, and which now belongs to the hotel.

The first problem, that of the drive, remains. From the corner of the 'sheds', the fairway turns to the right. The test is just how much, if any, of the corner should you cut off? Playing straight-away, or slightly to the left of the corner, you could well overrun the fairway and be in the rough between the 2nd and 17th fairways. You would certainly be left with a hopelessly long second shot. Playing too far to the right might leave you caught up in the grounds of the Old Course Hotel. The carry over the corner is in fact much less fearsome than it may look, even today. Indeed you could drive quite close to the hotel

building with a good shot and be well over the angle and into clear fairway. In all of this I have made no mention of wind or playing conditions, but you must be sure to apply them to your deliberations.

Given a decent drive into the fairway, you still must face a long shot – the hole is only 14 yards short of the regulation par-5 distance. And you will be looking a long way forward to the most infamous green in golf. It is set diagonally across the shot, built up into a very positive plateau three or four feet above the fairway, very long from left to right, very narrow from front to back. At the left centre, the viciously deep Road Hole bunker bites into the green so voraciously that there are putting surfaces on either side of it (and players of the very highest class have been known to putt into it). Immediately behind the back putting surface the green falls down a bank to a path and then a metalled road with a stone wall on the other side of the road. A pin position behind that bunker can be positively evil, and over the years this hole and this green have produced an endless series of triumphs

The approach to the green from the bunkers on the left of the fairway

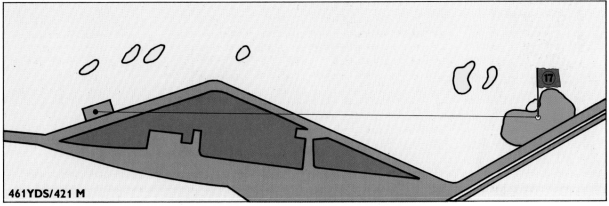

**461YDS/421 M**

and dread disasters.

In terms of modern thinking and modern techniques, the hole can be considered unfair in that such a green is positively not designed to receive a shot of 200 yards, which most players will be playing to it. However, the hole exists, you are not allowed to pass it by; it is a very powerful, challenging hole for anyone of ability, and we have to get on with the playing of it.

The tactics on the hole, despite all this, are straightforward. You must drive cleanly into the fairway, over the corner. You must hit your second shot quite deliberately short, as close as you can to the front-right corner of the green. At St Andrews they tend to water the approaches and the front fringes and this upslope, so you should have a soft bounce, and not much forward run on the ball. You must keep well to the right of the Road Hole bunker and you must *not* go over this green. If you do, you may never get back onto it. From that position, short right, you can chip or pitch along the length of the green (a shot which demands more than usual care because of the contouring) and be well content with two putts if you should need them.

This is a very, very powerful hole and a real cardwrecker. In any championship, there are more fives and sixes than fours scored here. In fact in the last round of the 1978 Open Championship, I believe there was not one single birdie made at the 17th hole.

### What's in the name?

A metalled road runs directly behind and beside the putting surface.

Viciously deep Road Hole bunker

Metalled road and wall immediately behind the green

*The 17th fairway from the corner*

OLD COURSE
HOLE NO. 18
TOM MORRIS
354 YDS.
PAR 4 STR. 16

Here you are at last, after all the sweat and effort, and no doubt many a new golfing experience, back at the world-renowned scene – the vast acres of the twin 1st and 18th fairways; the Swilcan Burn and its little stone bridge under your nose; Granny Clark's Wynd crossing 220 yards out; the houses and clubs and hotels behind the white fence along the right side, and the mass of the Royal and Ancient club-house looming ahead.

You have two things to think about. First, you may well be tiring, the legs feeling heavier, the reflexes a little duller. Second, you may again be influenced by the immediate surroundings, by the history of the place and the scatter of people leaning over the rails by the green – they are always there – with their implied criticism of everyone coming up this last fairway. So first of all relax, take a couple of deep breaths on the tee, and swing a shade more easily. And second, I would say, find a bit of swagger, have a bit of confidence in your own game and to hell with anyone around the green – you are just as likely to be better than they are at 'the gowff'.

And I have some cheer for you. This is not a difficult hole. It is an easy hole. If you drop a stroke here, it is not a stroke lost, but a stroke squandered. On the drive, the one thing that can go wrong is a slice out of bounds, over the fence. That is un-thinkable. Aim for the clock on the Royal and Ancient clubhouse and let it fly out there. Granny Clark's Wynd is approximately 120 yards from the centre of the green, and if you are in the general area of her metal path, you will be pitching the ball. Be bold.

The 18th green, scene of many famous victories

The 18th from the swil

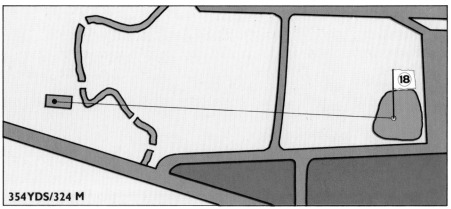

354 YDS/324 M

Go for the centre of that huge green. This hole is at its most difficult played downwind, with the pin cut at the very front of the green.

On the second shot, you have to handle the only real problems on the 18th – the green itself, and perhaps the Valley of Sin. This is a wide hollow immediately in front of the left half of the green. If you are hitting a full pitch to the green, it is no problem. Fly the ball over it. If you have

driven the ball rather a long way over Granny Clark's Wynd, you may want to play a running shot to the green. In that case you must give the ball enough weight to run through that sinful valley, and up onto the putting surface.

The green is enormous, sloping from right to left and down from back to front, with the back right-hand corner very much higher than the rest of it. It is the biggest single green

on the course, and putting it and its impish borrows will demand your final effort of concentration on this extraordinary Old Course. There it is – you have done with it. Only one thing is certain from your experience. You will want to come back, and play it again, for any one of a hundred different reasons.

### What's in the name?

He was the famous old R & A professional and greenkeeper.

Granny Clark's Wynd runs through the fairway at 220 yards

Enormous green with its own hazard – the Valley of Sin

Since Prestwick relinquished its exclusive grip on the Open Championship, the Old Course at St Andrews has been dominant, from Tom Kidd in 1873 to Jack Nicklaus in 1978. It remains the dominant name in world golf, the place where all the great champions love to win.

---

## Course Record (Old Course)
### 65 Neil Coles
(Open Championship 1970)

---

## Open Championship

| | | | |
|---|---|---|---|
| 1873 Tom Kidd | 179 | 1921 Jock Hutchinson (USA) | 296 |
| 1876 Bob Martin | 176 | 1927 R T Jones (USA) | 285 |
| 1879 Jamie Anderson | 169 | 1933 Densmore Shute (USA) | 292 |
| 1882 Bob Ferguson | 171 | 1939 Dick Burton | 290 |
| 1885 Bob Martin | 171 | 1946 Sam Snead (USA) | 290 |
| 1888 Jack Burns | 171 | 1955 Peter Thomson (Australia) | 281 |
| 1891 Hugh Kirkaldy | 166 | 1957 Bobby Locke (S Africa) | 279 |
| 1895 J H Taylor | 322 | 1960 Kel Nagle (Australia) | 278 |
| 1900 J H Taylor | 309 | 1964 Tony Lema (USA) | 279 |
| 1905 James Braid | 318 | 1970 Jack Nicklaus (USA) | 283 |
| 1910 James Braid | 299 | 1978 Jack Nicklaus (USA) | 281 |

---

## Alcan Golfer of the Year Championship
1967 Gay Brewer (USA) 283

---

## Alcan International Championship
1967 Peter Thomson (Australia) 281

---

## Dunlop Masters' Tournament
1949 Charlie Ward 290

---

## Martini International Tournament
1962 Peter Thomson (Australia) 275

---

## PGA Championship
1979 Vicente Fernandez (Argentina) 288

---

## PGA Match Play Championship
1954 Peter Thomson (Australia)

---

## Scottish Open Championship
1973 Graham Marsh (Australia) 286

---

## Spalding Tournament
1947 Henry Cotton    1948 Norman von Nida (Australia)

---

## Amateur Championship

| | |
|---|---|
| 1886 H G Hutchinson | 1930 R T Jones (USA) |
| 1889 J E Laidlay | 1936 H Thomson |
| 1891 J E Laidlay | 1950 F R Stranahan (USA) |
| 1895 L M B Melville | 1958 J B Carr |
| 1901 H H Hilton | 1963 M S R Lunt |
| 1907 J Ball | 1976 R Siderowf (USA) |
| 1913 H H Hilton | 1981 P Plojoux (France) |
| 1924 E W E Holderness | |

## Commonwealth Tournament
1954 Australia

## Eisenhower Trophy
1958 Australia

## European Amateur Team Championship
1981 England

## St Andrews Trophy
1976 Great Britain

## Walker Cup

| 1923 USA 6 | GB 5 | 1938 USA 4 | GB 7 | 1971 USA 11 | GB 13 |
|---|---|---|---|---|---|
| (One match halved) | | (One match halved) | | | |
| 1926 USA 6 | GB 5 | 1947 USA 8 | GB 4 | 1975 USA 15 | GB 8 |
| (One match halved) | | | | (One match halved) | |
| 1934 USA 9 | GB 2 | 1955 USA 10 | GB 2 | | |
| (One match halved) | | | | | |

## Ladies' Amateur Championship

| 1908 Miss M Titterton | 1965 Mlle B Varangot (France) |
|---|---|
| 1929 Miss J Wethered | 1975 Mrs N Syms (USA) |

## Commonwealth Tournament (Ladies)
1959 Great Britain

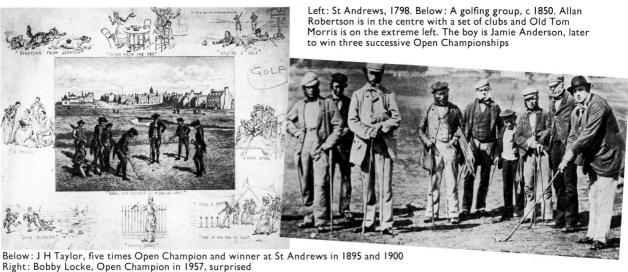

Left: St Andrews, 1798. Below: A golfing group, c 1850. Allan Robertson is in the centre with a set of clubs and Old Tom Morris is on the extreme left. The boy is Jamie Anderson, later to win three successive Open Championships

Below: J H Taylor, five times Open Champion and winner at St Andrews in 1895 and 1900
Right: Bobby Locke, Open Champion in 1957, surprised everyone by breaking into song at the presentation ceremony

Top left: Peter Thomson ends his first round with a long putt on his way to the 1955 Open Championship. Top right: The only time two trophies have been presented to the Open Champion – Kel Nagle winner of the Centenary Open in 1960 received a replica trophy to mark the occasion. Centre left: Open Champions gather at St Andrews in 1970. Back: Arthur Havers (1923), Gene Sarazen (1932), Dick Burton (1939), Fred Daly (1947), Roberto de Vicenzo (1967), Arnold Palmer (1961, 1962), Kel Nagle (1960), Bobby Locke (1949, 1950, 1952, 1957), Henry Cotton (1934, 1937, 1948), Peter Thomson (1954, 1955, 1956, 1958, 1965). Front: Denny Shute (1933), Bob Charles (1963), Max Faulkner (1951), Jack Nicklaus (1966, 1970), Tony Jacklin (1969), Gary Player (1959, 1968). Gary Player (1974) and Jack Nicklaus (1978) have both won the Open for a third time since this gathering. Centre right: The victorious Great Britain team, winners of the 1971 Walker Cup. Standing (l to r) Warren Humphreys, Rodney Foster, Michael Bonallack (capt), David Marsh, Charles Green, Hugh Stuart, Roddy Carr. Front: Geoff Marks, Scott Macdonald, George Macgregor. Above: USA get their Walker Cup revenge at St Andrews in 1975. Back row (l to r) Gerry Koch, Jay Haas, Dr Edward Updegraff (capt), Bill Campbell, Dick Siderowf, George Burns, Curtis Strange, Craig Stadler. Front: John Grace, Jerry Pate, Marvin Giles. Right: Peter Thomson gets a little too close to the Swilcan Burn

**Playing the course** The Old Course, like the other three courses at St Andrews, is a public course, open to all. However, the tremendous demands made on the course have required some restrictions. The course is closed on Sundays. Members of the Royal and Ancient Golf Club have priority on the tee at specific times in August and September. From April to October, a ballot system is applied for starting times. And from time to time the Old Course may be entirely closed for a few weeks in the late winter or early spring.

Applications for reserved tee times should be made to the Secretary, Links Management Committee of St Andrews, Golf Place, St Andrews KY16 9JA, tel St Andrews (0334) 75757, not less than eight weeks in advance of the date of play. Reservations are not made for Saturdays and Thursday afternoons. Single players may not reserve a starting time or enter the ballot, although they may be allowed to play at the Starter's discretion. Fourball medal play is not permitted and applications for reserved times and entry to the ballot are accepted only on this understanding. There are no restrictions on ladies' play.

**Adjoining courses** These are the New, Jubilee, and Eden. All of them maintain to some degree the character of the Old – many people consider the New to be at least as difficult – and together they make a marvellous golfing complex.

New 6604 yards SSS 72   Eden 5971 yards SSS 69   Jubilee 6284 yards  SSS 70

**Recommended courses in the surrounding area** There are many first-class courses in Fife; strongly recommended are Lundin Links, Ladybank, Elie and Crail. The Carnoustie and Gleneagles courses and Rosemount are also within reasonable reach of St Andrews.

Lundin GC, Golf Road, Lundin Links, Fife; tel Lundin Links (0333) 320202.
Ladybank GC, Annsmuir, Ladybank, Fife; tel Ladybank (0337) 30320.
Golf House Club, Elie, Fife; tel Elie (0333) 330327.
Crail Golfing Society, Balcomie Clubhouse, Crail, Fife; tel Crail (03335) 278.

**Where to stay** St Andrews and the surrounding area offers plenty of accommodation, and if possible visitors should spend at least one night in this splendid old university town.

Old Course Hotel, Old Station Road, St Andrews, Fife KY16 9SP;
tel St Andrews (0334) 74371, telex 76280.
Rufflets Hotel, Strathkines Road, St Andrews, Fife; tel St Andrews (0334) 72594.
Scores Hotel, The Scores, St Andrews, Fife; tel St Andrews (0334) 72451.
Rusacks Marine Hotel, St Andrews, Fife; tel St Andrews (0334) 74321.

Simon Owen in trouble at the 17th in the final round of the 1978 Open. At the end he finished two strokes behind his playing partner and the eventual winner, Jack Nicklaus

The Carnoustie Medal course is one of the wonders of the world of golf. The great Walter Hagen deemed it the best course in Britain, and one of the three best in the world. It should also be said that the course has been damned as 'evil', 'monstrous', 'brutal', etc, and no doubt the truth lies somewhere between.

It is certainly true that, for the ordinary player from the medal tees, *and* for the expert from the championship tees, Carnoustie is a very big golf course. Flat, and totally exposed, it stands by the sea (although you will see precious little of that). At no point do more than two holes run in the same direction. There are only three short holes, one of which is cripplingly long for a par 3. Every single hole is different in character and challenge, and I think it is correct to say that the course is without a single identifiable weakness, which may make it unique. It is stern, forbidding, a Presbyterian test; all the same, there is no reason for you to be afraid of it. Put some planning into your play and approach it with a positive attitude; even a slightly cavalier approach might be worth trying.

As with so many of the older Scottish links, the history of Carnoustie is not particularly well recorded. Parish records of 1560 refer to 'gowff' being played on the Barry Links adjoining the present ground. The game has certainly been played along this coast for centuries, and in the early years of the reign of Queen Victoria, a period of major expansion in golf with the formation of many clubs, the foundations of the Carnoustie Golf Club and course were laid. The original club is certainly the oldest 'artisan' club in the world, and the date of its formation is given as 1839. At first there were 10 holes, laid out by Allan Robertson, the greatest golfer of his time and generally regarded as the first professional. The course was extended by Tom Morris to 18 holes in 1867, which year also apparently marked the début of his son, Young Tom Morris, who 'beat all comers' there at the age of 16.

# Introduction

The artisan nature of golf at Carnoustie persists. As at St Andrews, the present courses are public, and are played over by six clubs – Carnoustie, Caledonia, Dalhousie, Mercantile, New Taymouth and Carnoustie Ladies.

The famous James Braid altered and modernized the course in 1926 so successfully that it was able to stage its first Open Championship five years later. There is another figure critical to the Carnoustie story, less well-known than those great professionals, but happily placed in history. He is James Wright, a Dundee chartered accountant, chairman of the Carnoustie Golf Courses Committee in the Thirties. Wright had extensive land and cattle interests in the United States, and was a man of broad international vision. Following that first Open Championship, he set about improving and extending the course, eliminating the bunkers and other hazards which the steel-shafted game was making obsolete. The outcome was a flexible course which, in Wright's words, 'can be adjusted to any length within reason, but we do not attach much importance to length as such. Quality rather than pure length has been our objective.' The altered Carnoustie was ready for the 1937 Open Championship, and has remained on the rota of courses ever since.

The town, founded in the 1880s and still little more than 6,500 in population, grew with the golf course and produced hundreds of fine players and teachers who became something of an export industry in themselves, spreading around the world as they did. Some became famous, and at least one became immortal, if anonymously. This was the gentleman who declared that he was off to make his fortune in South America, but was discovered next morning, no doubt feeling no pain, in the general area of the 10th hole, which is now named – South America. Of those who became famous, Willie, Alex and Macdonald, the Smith brothers, were the most successful of the Carnoustie exports. Willie and Alex became Open Champions of the US and Macdonald Smith was runner-up in the Open Championships of 1930 and 1932. Stewart Maiden, teacher of Bobby Jones, was a Carnoustie man, and it has been said that at one time or another Carnoustie men have won the Open Championships of Britain, USA, Canada, South Africa and Australia, and held every state title in America.

Probably the roster of Carnoustie's Open Champions demonstrates the quality of the course as much as anything. It is:

| | |
|---|---|
| 1931 | Tommy Armour |
| 1937 | Henry Cotton |
| 1953 | Ben Hogan |
| 1968 | Gary Player |
| 1975 | Tom Watson |

Meanwhile, you too can get enormous pleasure from playing this great golf course, though you would do well to take a few very simple precautions. These are, to warm up properly before you tee off; to take a local caddie first time round; to remember Wright's words about length and don't smash your way around the place, and above all remember that golf is a point-to-point game, to be played up to the limits of your capabilities, but *not* beyond.

Clubhouses for two of the six clubs that play over the Carnoustie courses: far left, Dalhousie Golf Club and, below, Caledonia Golf Club

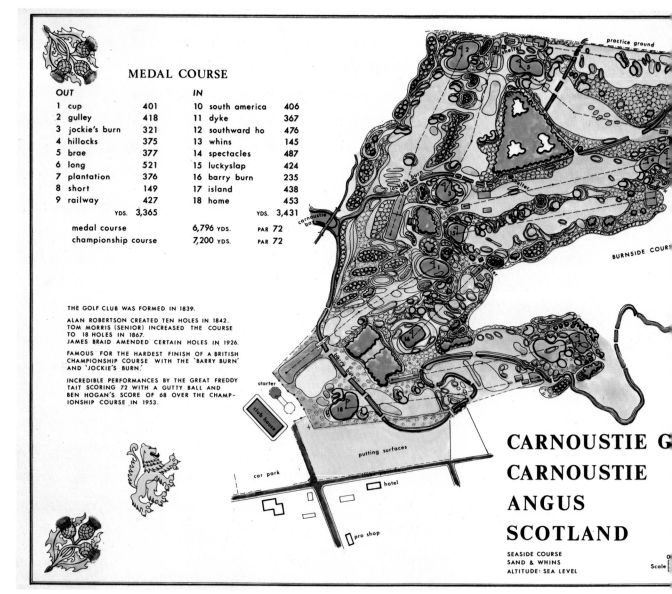

## MEDAL COURSE

| OUT | | | IN | | |
|---|---|---|---|---|---|
| 1 | cup | 401 | 10 | south america | 406 |
| 2 | gulley | 418 | 11 | dyke | 367 |
| 3 | jockie's burn | 321 | 12 | southward ho | 476 |
| 4 | hillocks | 375 | 13 | whins | 145 |
| 5 | brae | 377 | 14 | spectacles | 487 |
| 6 | long | 521 | 15 | luckyslap | 424 |
| 7 | plantation | 376 | 16 | barry burn | 235 |
| 8 | short | 149 | 17 | island | 438 |
| 9 | railway | 427 | 18 | home | 453 |
| | YDS. | 3,365 | | YDS. | 3,431 |

medal course      6,796 YDS.    PAR 72
championship course   7,200 YDS.    PAR 72

THE GOLF CLUB WAS FORMED IN 1839.

ALAN ROBERTSON CREATED TEN HOLES IN 1842.
TOM MORRIS (SENIOR) INCREASED THE COURSE
TO 18 HOLES IN 1867.
JAMES BRAID AMENDED CERTAIN HOLES IN 1926.

FAMOUS FOR THE HARDEST FINISH OF A BRITISH
CHAMPIONSHIP COURSE WITH THE 'BARRY BURN'
AND 'JOCKIE'S BURN.'

INCREDIBLE PERFORMANCES BY THE GREAT FREDDY
TAIT SCORING 72 WITH A GUTTY BALL AND
BEN HOGAN'S SCORE OF 68 OVER THE CHAMP-
IONSHIP COURSE IN 1953.

**CARNOUSTIE G**
**CARNOUSTIE**
**ANGUS**
**SCOTLAND**

SEASIDE COURSE
SAND & WHINS
ALTITUDE: SEA LEVEL

Simpson's Golf Shop has
stood beside the course
since 1883

The railway line and Grant's
warehouse are both
prominent features over the
closing holes on the Medal
Course

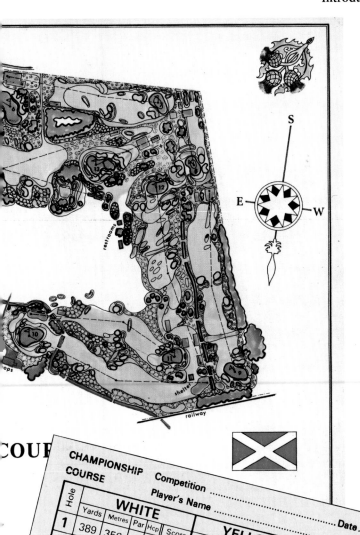

S
E ⊕ W

## CARNOUSTIE GOLF LINKS

# Championship Course

Player ..........................................................

Event ..........................................................

Class ............................ Date .........................

Total for 18 holes ...........................................

Less Handicap ................................................

..........................................................

Net score .....................................................

### HOLE NAMES

| | | | |
|---|---|---|---|
| 1 | Cup | 10 | South America |
| 2 | Gulley | 11 | Dyke |
| 3 | Jockie's Burn | 12 | Southward Ho |
| 4 | Hillocks | 13 | Whins |
| 5 | Brae | 14 | Spectacles |
| 6 | Long | 15 | Luckyslap |
| 7 | Plantation | 16 | Barry Burn |
| 8 | Short | 17 | Island |
| 9 | Railway | 18 | Home |

### CHAMPIONSHIP COURSE

Competition ..........................................

Player's Name ..........................................

Date .........

| Hole | WHITE | | | | | YELLOW | | | | | GREEN | | |
|---|---|---|---|---|---|---|---|---|---|---|---|---|---|
| | Yards | Metres | Par | Hcp | Score | Yards | Metres | Par | Hcp | Score | Yards | Metres | Par |
| 1 | 389 | 356 | 4 | 7 | | 377 | 345 | 4 | 7 | | 383 | 350 | 4 |
| 2 | 439 | 401 | 4 | 3 | | 414 | 379 | 4 | 3 | | 429 | 392 | 4 |
| 3 | 336 | 307 | 4 | 15 | | 311 | 284 | 4 | 15 | | 321 | 294 | 4 |
| 4 | 373 | 341 | 4 | 11 | | 429 | 392 | 4 | 11 | | 357 | 326 | 4 | 15 |
| 5 | 376 | 344 | 4 | 13 | | 360 | 329 | 4 | 13 | | 392 | 358 | 4 | 11 |
| 6 | 517 | 473 | 5 | 1 | | 487 | 445 | 5 | 1 | | 497 | 454 | 5 | 13 |
| 7 | 379 | 347 | 4 | 9 | | 389 | 356 | 4 | 9 | | 364 | 333 | 4 | 9 |
| 8 | 162 | 148 | 3 | 17 | | 150 | 137 | 3 | 17 | | 135 | 123 | 3 | 17 |
| 9 | 414 | 379 | 4 | 5 | | 405 | 370 | 4 | 5 | | 467 | 427 | 4 | 5 |
| OUT | 3385 Yards 3096 Metres | | OUT 36 | | | 3322 Yards 3037 Metres | | OUT 36 | | | 3345 Yards 3057 Metres | | OUT 36 |
| 10 | 414 | 379 | 4 | 2 | | 444 | 406 | 4 | 2 | | 400 | 366 | 4 | 2 |
| 11 | 360 | 329 | 4 | 12 | | 342 | 313 | 4 | 12 | | 352 | 322 | 4 | 12 |
| 12 | 476 | 435 | 5 | 6 | | 407 | 372 | 4 | 6 | | 416 | 380 | 4 | 6 |
| 13 | 143 | 131 | 3 | 18 | | 130 | 119 | 3 | 18 | | 160 | 146 | 3 | 18 |
| 14 | 482 | 441 | 5 | 4 | | 456 | 417 | 4 | 4 | | 440 | 402 | 4 | 4 |
| 15 | 428 | 391 | 4 | 8 | | 460 | 421 | 4 | 8 | | 420 | 384 | 4 | 8 |
| 16 | 218 | 218 | 3 | 16 | | 215 | 197 | 3 | 16 | | 228 | 208 | 3 | 16 |
| 17 | 401 | 401 | 4 | 10 | | 419 | 383 | 4 | 10 | | 391 | 358 | 4 | 10 |
| 18 | 406 | 406 | 4 | 14 | | 416 | 380 | 4 | 14 | | 402 | 368 | 4 | 14 |
| IN | IN 36 | | | | | 3289 Yds. 3008 Metres IN 34 | | | | | 3209 Yds. 2934 Metres IN 34 | | |
| | Metres | | | | | TOTAL 6611 Yds. 6045 Metres | | | | | TOTAL 6554 Yds. 5991 Metres | | |
| | S.S.S. 74 | | | | | Par 70 | | | | | S.S.S. 73 Par 70 | | |

### LOCAL RULES FOR CHAMPIONSHIP COURSE

1 MARKING POSTS
a White posts indicate out of bounds.
b Red posts indicate 'Lateral Water Hazard.'
c Yellow posts indicate "Water Hazard."

2 OUT OF BOUNDS (Rule 29 : Definition 21)
a All ground beyond any fence bounding the Course.
b In or over spigot trenches marking course boundaries.
c At 1st hole to left of black and white posts on banks of burn.
d In flower bed behind 1st tee and 18th green.

3 WATER HAZARDS (Rule 33 : Definition 14)
The Barry Burn, Jockie's Burn and all ditches, except those defined below as Lateral are Water Hazards. Lateral Water Hazards are as follows:—
a That part of ditch on left of 4th hole marked by red posts.
b That part of ditch between 9th and 12th holes marked by red posts.
c Those parts of the Barry Burn to the left of the 16th hole, left of the 17th hole, between 17th and 18th holes, and on the left of 18th hole, marked by red posts.

4 OBSTRUCTIONS (Rule 31 : Definition 20)
All coverings of water supply hydrants and telephone cables throughout the Course and the cavity at drainage grating short of burn at 18th hole are defined as obstructions.

5 BALL ON A WRONG PUTTING GREEN (Rule 35)
The 4th and 14th greens are deemed a double green and Rule 35 — 1j does not apply to these two greens.
(Revised Carnoustie, 1st April 1981)

### HANDICAP RULES

Strokes are taken at the hole which has the players handicap opposite it, and at all holes which have a lesser number than the player's handicap.

Acorn Press, Carnoustie. Telephone (0241) 59496

## Carnoustie

### CUP

**389 YDS 356 M
PAR 4
STROKE 7**

**Y**our first impression at the first hole, first time out at Carnoustie, might tell you that you are in for another spell of golfing purgatory, of not knowing the driving lines, of facing an assortment of blind shots and hidden hazards. You have an immediate introduction to the famous Barry Burn, which crosses some 40 yards in front of the tee, then rather inconsiderately runs along the left side of the fairway, making an out-of-bounds line, and is handily placed to receive a well-executed hook off the tee. You will not see the green. A white post in the distance, positioned above and behind the green, is the only directional indication you are offered. There are no bunkers in view. The fairway is wide and rising, with a good deal of undulation in it. All told, you might imagine that hole and course are like the Old Course at St Andrews.

Fortunately, this is not in fact typical of Carnoustie. There is a big gouging dip out on the right side of the fairway, feeding down towards insidious pot bunkers, and the left side of the fairway is where to

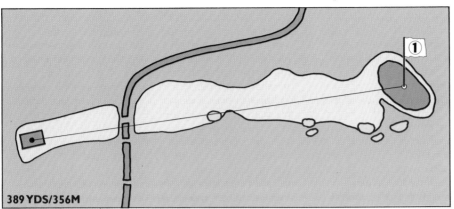

**389 YDS/356M**

be to get a better crack at the green. There is an altogether more reasonable area on the left of the fairway, known locally as The Battery, which is where to be for your second shot, but it is of course backed by that burn.

The green is quite large, slightly sunken in a hollow, and it is protected at the back and right side by a ridge covering all approaches save from the left front

corner. So drive to the right and you have a blind second. Drive to the left, and you can see at least half of the green, and the flagstick. There is no trouble over the green, save for a bit of heather here and there on the ridge, and I'd say it would take a bad shot to get up there.

Played downwind in reasonable conditions, this can be a not-unfriendly starting hole, perhaps like the first at

Troon, but into a strong west or south-west wind it will be as powerful a start as, say, the first at Muirfield. In the first round of the 1953 Open Championship, in such a wind, Ben Hogan needed a 2-iron second shot to reach the green.

### What's in the name?

The cup is the hollow in which the green lies, the sunken effect enhanced by the ridge at the back.

Left:
The undulating fairway with the tall marker post behind the green

Drive to the left of the fairway

Dip in the ground on the right falling away to two pot bunkers

*The First Fairway from the Right-hand Rough*

# GULLEY

### 439 YDS 401 M
### PAR 4
### STROKE 3

The second hole is quite different. There is a pleasant view from the tee up a narrow valley, on the line of the fairway, with ridges along either side. The one on the right is higher and comes down into the fairway quite sharply. You will see little of the green – just a few bunkers in the distance, at the end of the rising fairway. The first problem is Braid's Bunker, positioned in the centre of the fairway, with a supporting bunker perhaps 50 yards past it on the left. These bunkers look quite close and innocent. They are neither. They are very deep – a sand iron will be your only shot out. Braid's Bunker dominates the drive absolutely. It is 200 yards from the medal tee, and you must decide how to handle it, depending on your ability and on the conditions that day.

Before you drive the ball anywhere, accept the fact that this hole at any time will demand two very good hits to bring you anywhere near the green, so I would be inclined to play it as a par 5. In the driving zone the left side of the fairway, between these two bunkers, is the better side tactically, but the ground there is rather uneven, almost rutted. The right side is better ground, but the perfect place I suppose is past Braid's Bunker, in the centre of the fairway.

As you look ahead for your second shot, you will have the impression of everything funnelling into the green. The ridge persists almost all the way along the right. The ground rises somewhat, and about 80 yards short of the green there is rough ground on the right, which should be carried. There are two bunkers on the right, just past this, perhaps 50 and 30 yards short of the green, and the green itself is very long from front to back, two-tiered, and nipped in at the waist. This is a demanding second shot.

If you cannot make the distance, I think you should be aiming for that patch of fairway just to the left of the two right-hand traps, with a line on the centre or front right of the green. From there you would have an

The fairway running down the valley

*Approach to the 2nd*

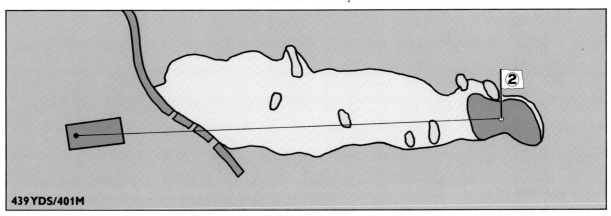

**439 YDS/401M**

open pitch or chip up the length of the green. The left side of this green is quite dangerous, particularly if the pin is at the back left. There is a bunker at the left front, not much more than 10 yards from the putting surface, and an evil little trap in the left side of the waist, cutting boldly into the putting surface.

In the Open Championship of 1975, I was caddying for Martin Poxon when he hit his second shot to the front-left edge of the putting surface, and with the flag at the back-left corner, he had no putt – the bunker intervened. He had to chip the ball over it from the putting surface.

The ground to the right of the green is rather mounded, and in general this is a powerful hole to meet so early in the round, and calls for careful, accurate shots.

**What's in the name?**

If gulley reminds you of drains, it would be better to think of the 2nd fairway as having the shape of a narrow valley.

Evil bunker cutting into the putting surface

Ridge runs down the right side of the fairway

# 3

## JOCKIE'S BURN

**336 YDS 307 M
PAR 4
STROKE 15**

A view of the green from the two bunkers to the left of the fairway

**B**y contrast with that muscular second hole, the third is a short par 4 which the professionals in a championship would consider a prime birdie hole. There is no reason why you should not do the same. Positioning the drive is the most important single task on this hole.

We are now playing in the opposite direction along the other side of the ridge that runs down the right side of the 2nd. The third fairway is rather narrow, moving out to the left slightly then turning back to the right. From 100 yards or more along the left side is a very pretty wood and in the rough on that side, about 180 yards out but well wide of the fairway, are two big bunkers. They should never be in play since you should favour the right side if any, where there are no hazards save the ground itself, coming down unevenly from the ridge.

The driving line should be on the centre of the green, or exactly on a fairway bunker placed precisely in the middle, 280 yards from the medal tee. Jockie's Burn comes in from the left side and crosses

## The 3rd – Jockie's Burn

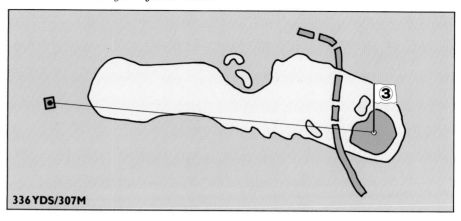

**336 YDS/307M**

Jockie's Burn runs through the fairway in front of the green

Fairway bunker 50 yards from the green

*2nd shot at the 3rd*

immediately in front of the green. You can just see the bank of this burn from the tee. So the very good player might not require a drive when playing downwind – he may elect to hit a 3-wood or even a 1-iron to stay short of that bunker. The important thing for any player is: be in the fairway! The second shot can never be anything but a straightforward pitch. The burn itself is a bit of a nuisance, but the

nuisance is mainly psychological. It crosses quite close to the green, 10 yards or so from the putting surface, perhaps 25 yards from the centre, but it will be a hazard only for the player who completely mishits, or dribbles the ball about a bit.

Fly the ball over the burn. As you would expect on the shortest par 4 at Carnoustie, the green is quite small. If you must miss it with

your pitch, miss to the right. There are grassy hollows there, but the greenside bunker on the left is deep and dangerous, and can hypnotize some players.

### What's in the name?

Jockie's Burn is the stream that runs across the front of the green, some 10 yards short of the putting surface.

## HILLOCKS

**373 YDS 341 M
PAR 4
STROKE II**

The central fairway bunker
dominates the view from
the tee

Bunker just in the right rough
at 200 yards

*Approach to the 4th from the Right-hand rough*

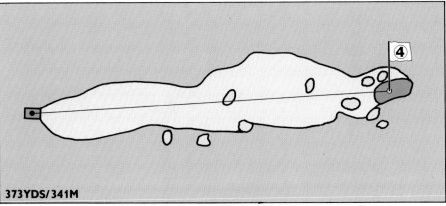

**373YDS/341M**

Three bunkers to the right of the green

This hole is rather misleading from the tee. It is not the easiest of holes for first-timers seeking the right driving line. There is some high ground on the right, separating you from the 15th fairway, and from the medal tee a mound prevents you from seeing the green. However, the hole plays towards the left and out there, near the end of the triangular wood which sits inside the 3rd, 4th and 5th holes, there is fair ground. The driving line is to the left of the bunker which you can see towards the end of the wood, or directly over it if you feel you can make the carry (200 yards). The fairway in that general area is flat and true, rather untypical of a links fairway.

The hole then dog-legs slightly to the right. In the angle are three separate bunkers, reaching into the fairway from the right and in the range 180–215 yards from the tee. In still air, or downwind, the drive is not frightening, the hole is a straightforward par 4, and you may be persuaded you can knock it past all these bunkers. Into wind it is a different proposition, obviously, and you might think of keeping well left of the bunkers. In that case, please note that a ditch runs along the line of the wood, and continues along the left side of the hole beyond the green. You need not beware of this – just be aware of it.

The second shot can be rather deceptive. You will be playing to a large green with lots of flat ground in front of it. The green is twinned with the 14th green, which is behind rather than beside it, as at St Andrews, and a slight ridge divides them. However, the 4th green itself is big – the flagstick can be 30 yards back from the front edge. This, plus the flat ground in front, means that club selection on this shot is important. Even from a decent drive, you might still be 150 yards from the flag. Two bunkers close up at the left front, and three slightly further out on the right, protect the green and suggest that the best angle of attack is from the left side of the fairway, underlining again the need to get your tee shot into exactly the right position.

### What's in the name?

This refers to the hillocky, broken ground along the right side of the fairway.

# 5

## BRAE

### 376 YDS 344 M
### PAR 4
### STROKE 13

This is a hole of very strong character. It is only three yards longer than the 4th, but from the tee it looks three miles longer. It dog-legs to the right, and the first commanding visual feature is the wood which runs down the left side, parallel to the entire length of the second shot, and which, because of the dog-leg, seems from the tee to lie across the line of the drive.

In the corner of the dog-leg, swells of heather close out that angle. This is an area of very heavy rough from which you have no hope of reaching

Above:
The open ground is to the left towards the woods

Jockie's Burn crosses the fairway at 270 yards

2nd Shot at the 5th

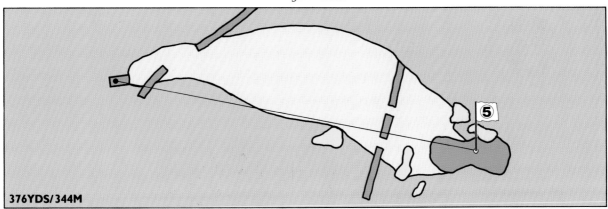

**376YDS/344M**

the green. You would simply have to swallow your medicine and get back to the fairway somehow, somewhere. There is one key bunker in that angle, on the right side of the fairway, at 225 yards. Beyond it, Jockie's Burn crosses the fairway some 270–280 yards from the tee and is therefore a danger to very long hitters playing downwind.

To get the best line into a very long, two-tiered green (there are very few such greens at Carnoustie), particularly if the flag is set on the upper level, you really ought to be on the right side of the fairway. That would mean carrying beyond the angle bunker, or flirting with the heather and gorse in the angle. Tactically, you may have to go on the defensive with this drive, and concentrate on being in the fairway. The line therefore would be on the end of the wood, and to the left, but only just, of that key bunker.

Position A in the fairway in that area would leave you say 140 yards to the centre of the green. The fairway here is reasonably wide, but uneven. There is a big fairway bunker on line 40 yards short of the putting surface, and another smaller one off to the right. Broken ground beyond them means that you cannot see the front of the green very well. It is very long, looks as though it narrows slightly halfway up, slopes upwards very positively from the front, and has a pronounced ridge, perhaps three feet high, across the middle. Hogan's Bunker, close to the putting surface, presses in from the left. (The great champion holed a recovery shot from that bunker in the 1953 Open Championship.)

This green must be 50 yards from front to back, and the problem is in deciding what club will get you to the back if you have to be there. If the flag is at the top, and you stick at the bottom front, you face a very difficult, dangerous putt. So be up there if you can.

### What's in the name?

The Brae is aptly named, for it's uphill to the green which itself slopes positively upwards.

Green runs up onto a higher level

Large fairway bunker 40 yards from the green

# 6

## LONG HOLE

### 517 YDS 473 M
### PAR 5
### STROKE I

From this tee, the prospect can be good or bad, either rather pleasant or quite terrifying. Thus the state of mind you bring to this hole and your thoughts on how you might play it are possibly the overriding factors.

The hole stretches nicely before you and below you, straight, flat, running evenly away to a distant green. Quite innocent. On the other hand, this is debatably Carnoustie's most severe, most demanding hole, and certainly one of the greatest and most famous long holes in golf, and the barriers that stand between you and a par score are exacting in the extreme. But, as ever, for the rational golfer playing a great golf hole, there is always a common-sense way of overcoming such barriers.

An out-of-bounds ditch marked by white posts runs hard down the entire left with the new Buddon Links course on the other side. The first consideration for the tee shot is the classic, if architecturally rather old-fashioned, central fairway bunker which presents itself like Braid's Bunker on the 2nd, or the Principal's Nose on the 16th at St Andrews. At Carnoustie's Long Hole, there are in fact two fairway bunkers, placed at 200 and 220 yards from the medal tee, one directly behind the other. There is another bunker on the right side of the fairway,

Above:
It is 300 yards from the deep fairway bunkers to the green

Gap of 25 yards between the end of the ditch and the out-of-bounds fence

Approach to the 6th

The 6th – Long Hole

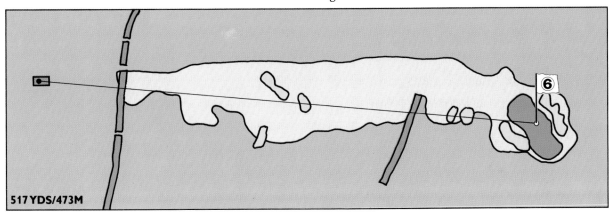

517 YDS/473M

level with the nearer central bunker. This leaves narrow passages, one between the fence and the central bunkers, another between the central bunkers and the right trap and rough. The hole runs almost directly west, so it is likely to be into wind.

The first decision is to select a driving line. If the conditions will allow you to carry these central bunkers, do so. Go smack over them. If not, I think it is better to take a line slightly to the right of them. You cannot afford to flirt with that out-of-bounds area. All the same, I have to tell you

that is exactly what the second shot will ask of you. The average player, perhaps afraid of the central bunkers, will go right, but the more right he goes, the more blocked and thwarted will be his second shot.

The ditch that marked the left side of the 4th hole comes in here diagonally from the right, entering the fairway and ending at a yellow marker-post in the centre of the fairway, about 200 yards on from the central bunkers. Over that ditch, there is fairway on the right side, but there are also two bunkers in line ahead, 60–80 yards short

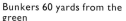

Bunkers 60 yards from the green

of the green and just past the end of the ditch – and, alas, one huge greenside bunker; all of this blocks out the entire right-side approach to your ultimate destination. So, on the second shot, everything points to a left incline. The gap between the fence and the end of that ditch is no more than 25 yards. That is the 'peak' into which your second shot should be directed, with a line on the red shelter behind the 7th tee. The entrance to the green is best from that left side, so you are now asked to go as far left, as close to the fence, as you dare.

Depending on how far you can hit the ball, you can of course carry the ditch and take a more direct line to the green. There is fair ground over it. But staying down that right side on this second shot is a real gamble for anyone but a first-class player. You can be in stiff rough, or a bunker, if you take a direct line, since you have diminished very sub-stantially your potential landing area.

The flat ground makes it difficult to see clearly, or to know, exactly what is ahead on the second shot. Having a good local caddie, or at least a hole plan, will give you a better idea, but for a very long hitter difficult decisions have to be made. Short hitters might be wise to keep short of the ditch, even if it means a 5-iron third shot. On this shot, too,

decisions have to be made. It must go to a flat green protected, as we have said, at the front and right by sand, and also at the back and left by another dangerous bunker. The line of an approach shot coming anywhere from the right will be into the narrowest sector of the green, with the back bunker even more dangerous. Neither of the greenside bunkers may be seen by the short hitter. Even on his third shot, the only place to be really safe is short – just short of the putting surface, then go for a chip and one putt.

I know that no golfer enjoys being short on a third shot, but you have to be sensible. If you get up level with the end of the ditch (90 yards from the centre of the green) or beyond it in two, then you are in good shape for a pitch. But remember, this is an extremely powerful hole and any system you employ to score 5, especially in any kind of wind, is the right one.

**What's in the name?**

At 517 yards, the 6th is the longest hole at Carnoustie, and possibly the most demanding.

# PLANTATION

**379 YDS 347 M
PAR 4
STROKE 9**

The first strong and persistent feature of this hole is that same out-of-bounds ditch running all down the left side. Along the right, a wood or 'plantation' extends for a good 100 yards, which gives you the impression of driving out of a funnel. Two hundred yards out, rather close to the fence, is the first bunker and a line directly over it would no doubt be perfect. At the same time, that seems altogether too adventurous.

The 7th hole is in general flat, and the tee certainly is, but all you may see of the green is the flagstick. There is not a great deal of definition about this hole – some critics might call it nondescript – and I think you may come to see it as a 'breather' hole after the rigours of the 6th.

Beyond that first bunker and to the right side of the fairway, set at 250 yards, is a pair of bunkers which makes the perfect line for the average player. Longer hitters should keep left of them. Such tee shots should leave fairly open approach shots. There is a bit of undulation in the ground in all the driving zones, but nothing which should make for a very uncomfortable lie or stance.

There are two bunkers in the area of the green, one covering the left approach, 20 yards from the front. You must fly over that. The other, as you would suspect, covers the right front corner, making any shot from the right side of the fairway that much more difficult. The green remains slightly hidden, and you may still see only the flagstick. However, the green is essentially flat (slightly hollowed in the centre), and the best entrance is at the centre and left centre, so you must simply put your faith in the yardage and

be long rather than short with the shot. The hollow in the centre of the green should gather the ball in nicely, and the surrounds of the green are fresh and clean. These should pose no problems. The out-of-bounds ditch is close, but not desperately close, on the left side – all of which amounts to a reasonable, medium-length par-4 hole.

## What's in the name?

Along the right side of the fairway a plantation of trees runs for 100 yards or more, helping to 'funnel' the view from the tee.

The out-of-bounds posts line the left side of the fairway

Out-of-bounds fence along the left

*2nd shot at the 7th*

## The 7th – Plantation

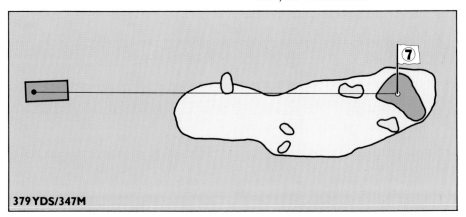

**379 YDS/347M**

Two bunkers at 250 yards

# SHORT HOLE

**162 YDS 148 M
PAR 3
STROKE 17**

The out-of-bounds posts leave little space to the left of the green

The 8th tee is about the furthest point from the clubhouse, and the most south-westerly point on the course. From the 7th green, we make a smart right turn and play towards the north-west. Unfortunately, that out-of-bounds fence comes with us and runs hard along the left side of the 8th hole, and indeed the 9th hole, which continues in the same direction. It also comes rather too close for comfort to the left side of the 8th green.

The 8th is the first par 3 at Carnoustie, and a pretty hole it is, with great banks of heather between tee and green. The tee shot should be straightforward, although the hole will play quite long directly into wind. This is one of Carnoustie's bigger greens, slightly waisted, with a bunker at the centre left, in the waist, another at the back left, and two very big, strong bunkers short of the right-front corner. There might be a good case for having another bunker at the left-front corner – the entrance is quite wide – but the out-of-bounds fence is so close to that left-hand centre trap that in a right-to-left wind, the

## The 8th – Short Hole

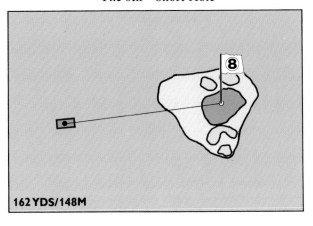

**162 YDS/148M**

tee shot might be even less attractive to a habitual hooker.

This green slopes nicely upwards to the back and therefore should help hold the shot. There are no particular problems over the back, but there is a wide, deceptive hollow immediately in front of the green which you will not see or appreciate from the tee, and which

could take a good deal of sting out of your shot. So, yet again, the thing is to be up, well up, on that putting surface.

### What's in the name?

The first short hole on the course. The trick here is not to be short yourself and get into that awkward hollow in front of the green.

Wide hollow in front of the green

Large bunker at the right front

*From the 8th Tee*

# 9

## RAILWAY

**414 YDS 379 M
PAR 4
STROKE 5**

The 9th is a strong, straight clear-cut par 4, the longest we have tackled since the 2nd hole, and one which requires two firm and positive strokes. A ditch running along most of the right side is a lateral water hazard, and is the boundary with the 12th hole. The out-of-bounds fence runs straight up the left side but is well-protected and screened by bushes and trees – an attractive variety of conifers – all the way beyond the green. Neither ditch nor fence cramps the hole unduly. There is a good sprinkling of heather and gorse, as everywhere at Carnoustie, particularly on the right side of the hole.

Some 200 yards out are two bunkers on the right side of the fairway, side by side. On the left side of the fairway at 225 yards is a single bunker. Just past this bunker and slightly to the right, a lovely island of perfect fairway, about 60 yards long and 20 yards across, fills out the right half of the fairway, and somewhere on that island you really must be to give yourself the best possible shot at the green. It calls for a driving line exactly between the left-hand bunker and the 'inside' trap of the pair on the right.

If you do reach the front of that island, you

Above:
The tree-lined fairway

Bunker on the left side of the fairway at 225 yards

The 9th Fairway

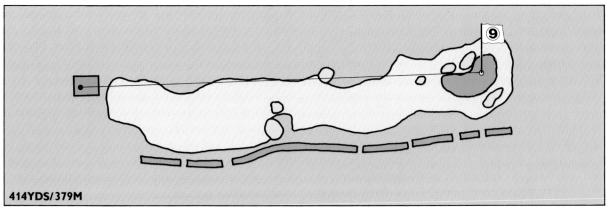

**414YDS/379M**

will be 180 yards from the centre of the green. If you reach the far end of it, where a path crosses the fairway, you will be about 130 yards away, which would represent an exceptionally fine drive. Either way, you will have an open sight of, and approach to, the green. The final 120 yards of ground to the green is again good and even fairway.

There is a tactical element to be considered at the Railway hole, where the main Dundee–Aberdeen railway line runs behind the trees at the back of the green. Even a first-class player will not, I think, consider it as a hole to be birdied very often. And the average player may not quite reach that island in the fairway – after all he is being faced with covering 400 yards in two shots to make an orthodox par. He should therefore think of being short of that left-hand bunker, driving with a 3-wood if he has to, even if it means facing a longer second shot. What is of the greatest importance here is to keep out of these fairway bunkers – Carnoustie bunkers are just as tough as any.

There is one small bunker short and left of the green, two on the left-hand putting surface, one at the back right. These bunkers are rather flat, and not too easily seen from the fairway. The trees framing the back of the green make it an attractive target, but the green is quite big. It is important to get the ball well up to the flag-stick, either on a long second or short third shot. The average player would do well to think of this as a 4.5 par – for him, this is a strong hole.

## What's in the name?

The railway line from Dundee to Aberdeen, though hidden by trees, runs along the back of the green.

Small bunker 40 yards short of the green

## SOUTH AMERICA

**414 YDS 379 M
PAR 4
STROKE 2**

At 414 yards, South America is exactly the same length as Railway, and is equally strong but quite different in character, probably because of the approach to the green. I would say it is certainly just as difficult. Our friend the Barry Burn re-enters the scene, running wide along the left side of the hole, then looping across in front of the green. The hole runs reasonably straight, with a hint of dog-leg-to-the-left about it, but you can see the flag in the distance, across the burn and into the trees.

Since the hole does turn slightly left, the ideal position for the drive would be out to the right side, but as you may well suspect, out there is a mess of trouble. A line of three bunkers enfilades the fairway from the right. The nearest of these is 160 yards out, the most distant, the one on the left, is 200 yards out. Forty yards beyond and behind them, unseen, is one big supporting bunker tightening that line. Across the fairway, left of the line and at the end of a slight rise, is a single long bunker at a range of 245 yards. The fairway beyond all these bunkers is true.

The line of the drive ought to be on the wooden tea hut behind the green. This will take you to the right of the left-hand single trap, and to the left of the left-hand bunker of that trio. A good solid hit will be required, and if you must slice here, make it a big one – that will take you clear of everything and put you on the 11th fairway, out of trouble. As at the 9th, a very positive second shot is required, demanding a firm act of will on your part to go for the green. It is none too large for the length of shot that it must receive, and, lying quite flat beyond the burn, it is framed by trees at the front, and these can be very inhibiting.

There are two bunkers at the left front and another at the right-centre back which you will not see behind the trees. However, between that loop of the burn and the green itself is perhaps the flattest piece of ground in all Carnoustie, a lovely piece of fairway perhaps 50 yards long. So the challenge is: should you carry the burn, perhaps 140 yards ahead, and go for the green a further 50 yards on, or do you lay up short of the burn and hope to get close to the pin with an 80-yard pitch shot? In spite of the bunkering and the trees, the burn is the barrier – and a major challenge it is, as physical as it is psychological. Incidentally, the side on which to miss this green is the left – the burn turns and runs up the right side of

Two bunkers at the front left

*The 10th Green from the Barry Burn*

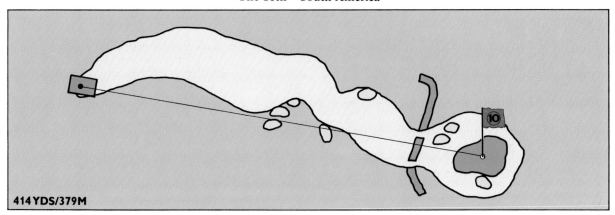

**414 YDS/379M**

the green towards the hut – and there is a pleasant piece of ground to the left of the left-hand bunkers.

This can be a difficult hole; into wind I would certainly think of it as a par 5 for most club players.

## What's in the name?

A local citizen set off one night to take golf to South America, but by morning had got no further than a point on the 10th hole.

The three bunkers lie in wait on the right

Refreshment hut

# 11

## DYKE

**360 YDS 329 M
PAR 4
STROKE 12**

This hole is a drive and a pitch, the shortest par 4 on the course, and after 9 and 10 a place of respite. Professionals would definitely consider it a birdie hole. For all that, there is nothing very clear about it, certainly from the tee. The mathematically direct line from there to the green goes directly over the centre bunker of yet another trio, placed on what seems the right side of the line. Carry these bunkers on that line and you would be left with a little flick of some 80 yards to the middle of the green. But carrying

Above:
The Barry Burn runs in front of the tee

More space at the back of this pear-shaped green

*Approach to the 11th*

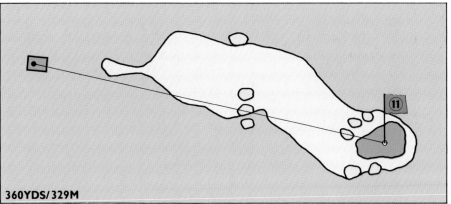

**360YDS/329M**

them means hitting the ball a good 240 yards through the air!

Perhaps you should look for another way. A single bunker on the left, 200 yards out, is perhaps the initial focal point and it makes a good marker. Your driving line could be just to the right of that, but at first sight the hole and the ground ahead of you is confusing. The problem is in knowing exactly where to go. In fact, if I had the opportunity to do anything with this hole, I would certainly think of raising the tee about six feet. That would let the player see where to

go, perhaps show a bit of the green, and make it all the more attractive.

Depending on conditions, you might think of using a 4-wood from this tee. You want to be right of that left-hand bunker, but definitely short of the other three unless you can carry them or pass them. If you get into any of these bunkers, you have no chance of being on the green in two.

From the centre of the fairway, in the driving area, you can see the green and the flagstick. The green is shaped like an inverted pear, with the broad bit at the back, and all the defences

clustered at the front. There are three bunkers along the left front, two at the right front, leaving by Carnoustie standards a rather narrow entrance. The green is flat and exposed and offers no particular putting problems. A shot that catches the back of any of these greenside bunkers will be thrown to the middle of the green – and any shot that finishes where you want it is a good shot. If you have birdie ambitions here, be in the fairway, do not get into a bunker, and pitch boldly and confidently to the flat.

## What's in the name?

The dyke, mercifully, is no longer present, and you can concentrate on the main problem of where to place your tee shot.

Three cross-bunkers at 240 yards

# SOUTHWARD HO

**476 YDS 435 M
PAR 5
STROKE 6**

By any standards, this is one of the greatest and most powerful holes in golf. Many critics talk of the 14th being the beginning of Carnoustie's big and punishing finish, but I prefer to think it starts here, for here is where you will need all your energy, resolution and powers of concentration. Now is the time to get really wound up!

On yet another flat tee, you look out on what seems a wilderness, a mass of heather and gorse stretching out for what seems like eternity, but in fact is some 200 yards. We are paralleling the 9th hole, and that same ditch runs along the right-hand side. In the far distance you will see a flagstick but not a green – mounds and ridges short of the green disguise it. The fairway (at this point you have not seen it) is narrow and undulating, and the entire hole has an Old Course feel about it. It is very demanding, with a second shot no less difficult than the drive, even from the very front tee, when the hole becomes a par 4. Although it is only a yard above the regulation par length from the medal tee, I think that, for the average player from either tee, it plays more honestly as a par 5.

Your target is a rectangular patch of fairway about 60 yards long but not much more than 25 yards across. To get there, you will have to drive the ball at least 200 yards down the line of the path through the heather in front of the tee, keeping left of a line on two big bunkers at the end of the rectangle, 250 and 270 yards out. You have a fair chance, but no more, of getting a lie and stance on that island, but in general this fairway never stops rolling.

To encourage you, I should say that the back of the more distant of the two fairway bunkers is 200 yards from the centre of the green. On the second shot, from wherever, you will still not see the green. The screening mounds and ridges have a pair of bunkers on the right, 40 yards short of the front, another pair on the left 20 yards short, but off the direct line. I should ignore them if you can make the yardage, and let fly at the green and carry past them. If not, stay well short of them.

The green is a rather odd type, very wide across and narrow from front to back. There is a rather high bank behind it which will check the ball, or even return it to

A daunting prospect from the tee

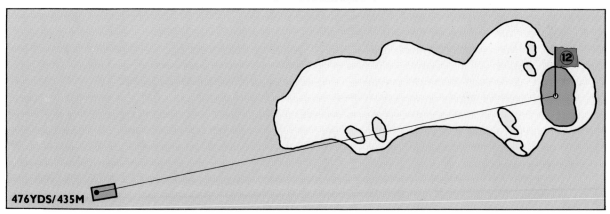

**476YDS/435M**

the putting surface. The green acts partly as a kind of basin, with the front part sloping down towards the centre. But there is a ridge running smack through the centre which divides the green into two equal parts, the right half higher than the left; the ridge also slopes towards the left, that is,

towards the centre of the green.

This gives you plenty of margin to miss the true line either to right or left, but it does mean that your length of shot must be accurate. The green is probably 45 yards across. So you must make sure that your yardage is correct, that

you have the right club and put your faith in your stroke. Whether it is your second or your third, your shot to the green must fly positively over the ridge at the flagstick. Either way, these frontal bunkers are too far out to be seriously in play.

This is a very difficult

hole. If you do not 'bring it to its knees', fret not – very few people have done that!

## What's in the name?

From the west-facing 11th green you turn almost through a right-angle and head south, or nearly so.

Bunkers on left and right are well short of the putting surface

Ridge at the back of the green

The 12th green

# WHINS

**143 YDS 131 M
PAR 3
STROKE 18**

The final third of the Carnoustie Medal course is about as severe a sequence of holes as any you will find, anywhere in the world.

The Whins, the shortest par 3, superficially at any rate might seem to be the one relief hole in this stretch, simply because it is rather short. But like any hole on the great championship course, you must not take it too lightly, you must not take it for granted.

It is a pretty hole, the green wholly in view and

The roofs of Carnoustie make an attractive background

Wide central bunker with space behind

*The 13th green*

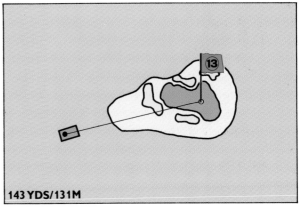

**143 YDS/131M**

sloping up from the front, making an attractive holding slope towards you, and a rather long target area. However, it is none too wide. The green is hourglass in shape, with strong bunkers right and left, nipping in the waist. There is another bunker at the back left, rather wider, and a very large bunker closing out most of the front of the green. It is quite a few yards in front, however, so if you only just carry it, you are likely to do no more than stagger on to the putting surface.

Accuracy of line, and the correct club selection for the wind conditions are obviously important here. If you must miss this green, probably the best area would be off the right half; over the back there are whins and downslopes that you would do well to keep away from.

## What's in the name?

Whins equals gorse, and that's what you'll see before you from the tee. (There's more over the back of the green.)

Deep bunker eats into the green on the right

## THE SPECTACLES

**482 YDS 441 M**
**PAR 5**
**STROKE 4**

Once more you are faced with a very difficult driving hole, and once more it is a question of line – from the tee there is virtually nothing to be seen of the fairway.

The Spectacles is the ultimate at Carnoustie, the classic links hole. It is a short par 5, a dog-leg to the left, with the green completely hidden by a ridge that, some 50 yards short of the putting surface, crosses the entire fairway. Two bunkers are set side by side on this ridge, glaring back up the fairway. These are The Spectacles. On every single shot on this hole, no matter the conditions, no matter how you play it, there are problems to be solved, decisions to be made.

The first problem is on the tee, which is fronted by a mass of heather and gorse, with no fairway to be seen. Beyond this you will see a wood, marking the right side of the first leg of the hole. As good a line as any for the drive is along the path leading away from the tee through the gorse bushes. Alternatively, and on much the same line, you could aim on the far end of that wood on the right. There is a good fairway area on that line, but you will not be surprised to know that out there lurks a sneaky little bunker, 240 yards from the medal tee. Beyond that bunker, the valid fairway narrows progressively – a problem

for very long hitters downwind.

The drive is critical. A line too far to the left can be gobbled up by a trio of one small and two large bunkers. You must somehow drive the ball into the fairway, which means a carry of only 150 yards. That would not make much impression on the hole. If you do get out somewhere in the region of that right-hand bunker (240 yards), you are still 250 yards from the flag, including a carry of some 170 yards to pass the Spectacles ridge. Here comes the second

point of decision. Beyond the ridge is 50 yards of ground to the putting surface. You may see the flag beyond the ridge, and think it only just past the ridge. It isn't. However, although the ground up there is a little uneven, in general it will move the ball forward, and if you do carry the ridge, you have a very good chance of being at least on the very front of the putting surface.

This was the precise situation facing Gary Player in the last round of the 1968 Open Championship. Paired

with Jack Nicklaus and battling with him for the title, Player hit a 3-wood shot which flew like a rifle bullet directly between The Spectacles, finishing a couple of feet from the hole, giving him an eagle and the cushion he needed to win. If ever one single shot won an Open Championship, that was it.

If you feel that such a shot is beyond you, you can always pop the ball along just short of The Spectacles, where you will be little more than 100 yards from the flagstick; after walking

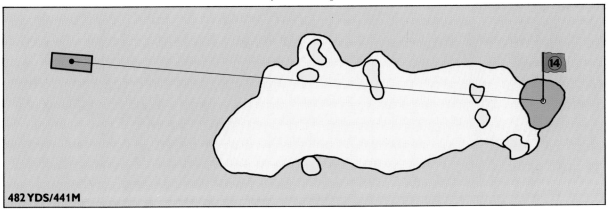

482 YDS/441M

forward and taking a comprehensive look at the land, you can then pitch straight to the flag. Although this hole is only just a par 5 in terms of yardage, in almost all conditions it plays like a par 5. So make that your aim, and be content if you achieve it.

### What's in the name?

The twin Os of these famous bunkers stare at you from a fairway ridge, some 50 yards short of the putting surface.

*The 14th from the left hand Rough*

Trio of bunkers on the left at 220–260 yards

The Spectacles

50 yards from the Spectacles ridge to the green

# 15

## LUCKYSLAP

**428 YDS 391 M
PAR 4
STROKE 8**

Y ou will have decided already that one of Carnoustie's principal defences is the way that often, perhaps too often, it does not let you see where to go, and so you do not get a view of some greens until it seems too late. As far as glimpsing the green is concerned, this hole is no exception. Here we look at a very strong par 4 with the ground sloping down from left to right, from banks along the left, to a fairly wide fairway. The fairway turns to the left, so that the whole 'camber' of the ground is wrong, rather like the 17th on the King's Course at Gleneagles Hotel, if not quite so extreme. There is a scatter of bunkers wide of the fairway on

Above right:
The broken ground on the left will trap any hooked tee shot

Fairway slopes from the left

2nd shot at the 15th

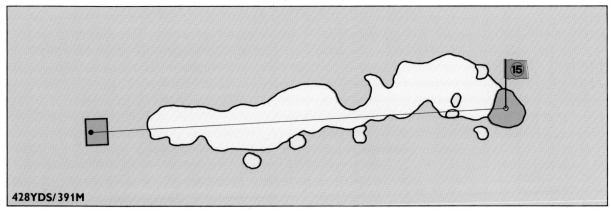

428YDS/391M

the right in the range 200–240 yards, but they apply rather more to the parallel 4th hole.

Although the green is not visible from the tee, you will see a flagstick in front of a distant copse of trees. The ideal driving line should be on the centre of that copse, where the church steeple pokes above the trees (provided they do not grow much higher). This is probably a shade left of the 'geometric' line from tee to green, but the sloping ground should bring you down into the fairway quite handily. Don't overdo this. If you go too far left, you will be in some tough areas which will stifle and stop your ball and leave you with a very difficult recovery.

The left side of the fairway, if you can hold the ball there, is the place to be for the second shot. All you will see, again, is the flagstick, a lot of tumbling ground, and a rise to the right of the green with three bunkers in it. If you pitch short, you may well break right into one of them. Fifty yards short of the green is a quite strong procession of ridges and bumps coming in from the left, with a bunker covering the line of the second shot. You must carry over this ground.

The best entrance to this green is left centre, so you should take aim on the Bruce Hotel, which is slightly left, and let it fly. The ball should break right and go into a rather basin-shaped green. It slopes down from the front, and if the pin position is near the front, it may be difficult to get the ball close. Don't worry about that – if you are on this green in two, you have hit two excellent shots. The green is quite generous, and being low is likely to be more lush, more holding, than the average Carnoustie green. It may therefore putt a shade more slowly, too.

### What's in the name?

Given that you won't see the green for a while, some canny chartwork may be better than a random smash.

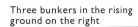

Three bunkers in the rising ground on the right

## BARRY BURN

**238 YDS 218 M
PAR 3
STROKE 16**

**M**any a professional player has stood on this tee and gasped. And sworn, I don't doubt. Carnoustie's 16th is a monster par 3 of 238 yards; in terms of yardage this may sound a non-sequitur, but it isn't. You are being asked to carry the ball the entire distance (even first-class players will have to use a driver in some circumstances) to a green which is something of an up-turned saucer, built up but falling away in all directions, ringed around by bunkers and with a pronounced gully in front. It is a long green, a long slog, played by the expert with anything from a 5-iron to a driver, depending on wind and weather.

The green is undulating as well as long, but at least it does slope towards you. There are six bunkers around it: a pair short, one right and one left, another wider to the left, then two together at the right-front corner, and another past them at centre right. None of these bunkers is close to the putting surface, and this is where I think the hole is a little unfair in that it would be just as good a test if it were 50 yards shorter.

The shape of the green is such that it will throw the errant shot well clear, as much as 15 or 20 yards to the left, and 10 yards or so to the right (although there is a patch of rough in that area as well as the bunker to stop it). This can mean

*Approach to the 16th*

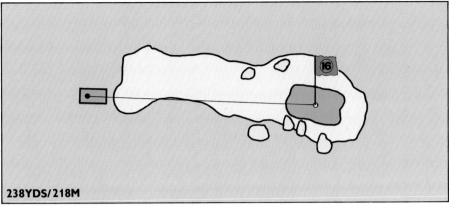

**238YDS/218M**

a very difficult second shot. I think it is too tight a hole, too stiff an examination for the distance. When the golfer is asked to hit more than 200 yards to an unreceptive target, heavily bunkered with steep traps which are not too close to the green and will thus demand very long sand shots (possibly the most difficult shots in the game), then I think the green's surface and contouring should be more sympathetic to the reception of the ball. Those left-hand traps are a good 30 yards from the putting surface. That means you would have to play exceptional recovery shots.

My advice to you is that nine times out of ten you should take a wood from the tee, consider the hole as a par 4, and try for the gulley in front of the green. If you get past these front, bracketing bunkers, you are in a good chipping position. The essential thing is – be straight!

## What's in the name?

The burn runs along the left side but shouldn't threaten you – as it does on the two final holes.

Left:
A very long short hole

Green slopes up at the back

Two steep bunkers on the right

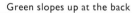

Bracketing bunkers 40 yards short of the green

## ISLAND

**439 YDS 401 M
PAR 4
STROKE 10**

You now come to the climax of the round on this great course, a little tired no doubt, but girding up your concentration for the final examination over the two big closing holes.

To get yourself into a position to attack the 17th green, very great care is needed with the drive. You can see the pin in the distance quite clearly, but the first complication is that the Barry Burn swirls around everywhere in this fairway. It enters the scene from the right about 180 yards out, runs back more or less directly towards the tee for about 100 yards then crosses in front of you. It turns back to cover the left side of the hole, then loops and makes a diagonal crossing of the fairway at about 240 yards on the left side to about 320 yards on the right. This creates a huge loop, a near-island effect, and inside the loop, which is your first target, is as perfect a piece of fairway as Carnoustie can offer, guaranteeing an excellent lie and stance.

How to get there and where to be is the first task. A shot hooked to the left will be devoured by the burn, which spells trouble all the way along that side. The driving line therefore should be slightly to the right of the green. There is much more room to the right, the further you go. A solitary bunker stands 220 yards out, but is placed fairly wide. If you get well out to the left of that bunker, perhaps a little past it, you have broken the back of the hole. Position A would be beyond that, in the general area of the bridge that crosses the burn at 260 yards – say about 20 yards short of it. You would then be 200 yards short of the centre of the green.

The next requirement is to shoot for the left-front corner of the green. The right front is closed out by three rather strong bunkers. There is a left-hand bunker about 40 yards short of the putting surface which you would have to pass or carry with a shot of at least 140 yards. Local wisdom is that the ground behind and beyond that bunker will turn the ball and direct it towards the centre of the green. This ground poses yet another of the demands which this 17th hole – one of the great holes in golf – will make of you. There is a very positive down-

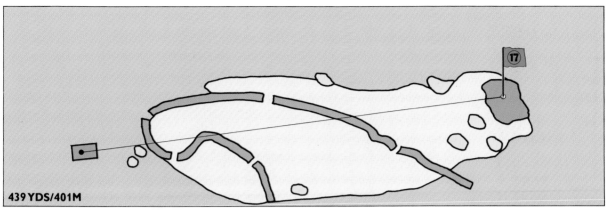

**439 YDS/401M**

slope in front of the green. If you have decided to play short of that bunker and are left with a pitch of some 80 yards for your third, have a care. That downslope could give you a forward, flying bounce to take you all the way to the back of the green – and you may not want to be there.

The green is rather basin-shaped, gathering from the left. If you do carry the left-hand bunker, you are likely to be on the putting surface. With the pin set on the right, behind the three traps as it were, this really is a very difficult hole. The drive and the second shots need very

careful study and good shot-making alike, as indeed would a third shot. It is an outstanding par 4. Should you encounter a strong wind against, however, the questions in this examination are entirely different, and vastly more taxing. Mercifully, this is unlikely to happen.

### What's in the name?

The island is the sanctuary across the burn where you will want to be with your first shot.

*Approach to the 17th from the Barry Burn*

Bridge is 180 yards short of the green

The green is well protected by bunkers on the right

Left:
Some of the danger threatening an approach from the right

## HOME

**444 YDS 406 M
PAR 4
STROKE 14**

**B**arry Burn is again all over the territory on this final hole, but is not quite the brow-beating influence it is on the 17th. It crosses 130 yards in front of the tee, stretches up the left side of the fairway, then crosses back 20 yards short of the green. Just as important as the burn on the left side, which you may be favouring, is the out-of-bounds fence which runs the entire length of the hole and in fact squeezes it uncomfortably towards the left side of the green.

There is a line of three bunkers on the right side, the first 235 yards from the medal tee,

the third at 270 yards. Drive to the left of them, without forgetting the presence of the burn and the fence. The line should be on the clubhouse, favouring the left end of the building, the end towards the green. This is an excellent driving hole. You must carry 150 yards to cross the first stretch of the burn. There is an area of excellent fairway 200 yards out on

a line to the left of these bunkers, providing an ample, friendly target area. Remember, however, that with a strong wind behind, from the south-west, the bunkers may well be reachable.

In the 1975 Open Championship, at the 72nd hole, Johnny Miller from one of these bunkers hit one of the bravest golf shots I could imagine. With a chance

to tie, or even win, he had driven it there, and failed to get out first time. He then hit the most prodigious shot which carried the burn and almost reached the green. I thought it was one of the greatest of all golf shots, first to attempt to make the carry, second to succeed.

Since the average player is not, alas, Johnny Miller, he has somewhat

Deep bunker on the left

20 yards between the Barry Burn and the putting surface

The 18th Green from the Barry Burn

94

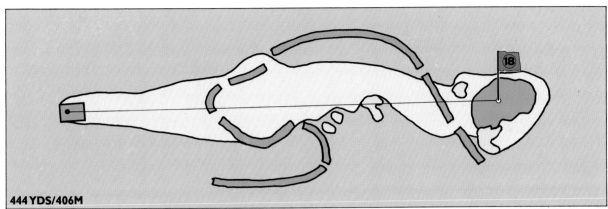

**444 YDS/406M**

different problems to face. If we assume that he has moved the ball nicely out from the tee, say to 225 yards, and is well positioned, he will now, also alas, have a frightening second shot to cope with. The target is a smallish green, strongly trapped at front left and front right with the Barry Burn crossing the fairway only 20 yards short of the putting surface. To get anywhere near the green, indeed to carry the burn, he will have to hit a shot of at least 200 yards through the air, and almost certainly will need a wood to do it, whereas the first-class player,

from a strong drive, might play no more than a 7-iron.

The drive, then, remains the key shot, governing entirely the option on the second shot. The average player might be wise to play short of the burn, and pitch a third shot in from there. Into a strong easterly wind, that would be a good plan, since two strong shots simply would not carry the burn.

Again, you might sensibly think of this as a par 5, before you leave the tee, and rate a score of 4 a birdie and a bonus. No matter what, you have now finished with Carnoustie. It is a very

great golf course, but you may be understandably thankful to get that last putt of your first round behind you. Next time round, it will be better – it always is, isn't it?

### What's in the name?

Home is the classic name for the final hole on a Scottish course – and after the other 17 at Carnoustie you may be glad to reach it!

Above:
The right-hand bunkers
eat into the fairway

While golf at Carnoustie goes back over several centuries, it was not until 1931 that it staged its first Open Championship, following the improvements made by James Braid in the Twenties. It produced a series of great championships and great champions, but by the Seventies its ability to continue staging the Open became doubtful – not because of the quality of the course, but because of the lack of off-course facilities and accommodation which a modern championship now requires to cope with both spectators and the media.

## Course Record (Medal Course)
65 Jack Newton (Australia)

(Open Championship 1975)

## Open Championship

| | | | | |
|---|---|---|---|---|
| 1931 Tommy Armour (USA) | 296 | 1968 Gary Player (S Africa) | 289 |
| 1937 Henry Cotton | 290 | 1975 Tom Watson (USA) | 279 |
| 1953 Ben Hogan (USA) | 282 | | |

## PGA Match Play Championship
1950 Dai Rees

## Amateur Championship

| | |
|---|---|
| 1947 W P Turnesa (USA) | 1971 SN Melnyk (USA) |
| 1966 R E Cole (S Africa) | |

## Home Internationals
1964 England

## Ladies' Amateur Championship
1961 Mrs A D Spearman    1973 Miss A Irvin

Left: Tommy Armour, winner of the Open at Carnoustie in 1931
Above: Henry Cotton, Open Champion in 1937
Below: Ben Hogan driving at the 7th during the 1953 Open

Top: Bobby Cole blasts out of
a bunker on his way to the Amateur Championship in 1966.
Above right and left: Gary Player plays his second shot at the 1st
in the final round of the 1968 Open watched by Jack Nicklaus
whom he eventually beat by 2 strokes. Left: Steve Melnyk,
Amateur Champion 1971

**Playing the course** The Carnoustie courses are public courses, and open to all. But, as with all of Scotland's great courses, traffic is heavy at certain times of the year, and advance reservations for tee times should be made by calling the Starter on Carnoustie (0241) 53249. There are no restrictions on ladies' play.

**Adjoining courses** The Burnside course is tucked inside the Carnoustie Medal course, and is less demanding, but again the Barry Burn comes into play on several holes. The new Buddon Links course runs outside the Medal course, between it and the sea, and is possibly the 'newest' links course in the UK.

Burnside 5935 yards   SSS 69

Buddon Links 6445 yards   SSS 71

**Recommended courses in the surrounding area** Monifieth and Panmure courses are attractive links between Carnoustie and Dundee. Downfield is probably the most celebrated Dundee city course, and Carnoustie is not much more than an hour's drive from the famous Rosemount, Gleneagles and St Andrews courses.

Monifieth GC, Princess Street, Monifieth, Tayside; tel Monifieth (08263) 532767.

Panmure GC, Barry, Tayside; tel Carnoustie (0241) 53120.

Downfield GC, Dundee, Tayside DD2 3QP; tel Dundee (0382) 825595.

Blairgowrie GC (Rosemount), Blairgowrie, Tayside; tel Blairgowrie (0250) 2383

Gleneagles Hotel Golf Courses, Gleneagles, Auchterarder, Tayside;

tel Auchterarder (07646) 3543.

St Andrews Golf Courses, St Andrews, Fife; tel St Andrews (0334) 75757.

**Where to stay** In Carnoustie itself, accommodation is perhaps somewhat limited, but there are numerous hotels in Dundee. Many golfers prefer to use Carnoustie as a 'day trip' from other centres such as St Andrews or Gleneagles.

Bruce Hotel, 1 Links Parade, Carnoustie, Tayside; tel Carnoustie (0241) 52364.

Glencoe Hotel, 8 Links Parade, Carnoustie, Tayside DD7 7JF;

tel Carnoustie (0241) 53273.

Left: Ann Irvin, Ladies Champion 1973. Below: Jack Newton plays a recovery shot at the 5th during the final round of the 1975 Open. Right: Tom Watson sinks his putt at the 18th to tie with Newton. Below right: Watson and Newton pose together for photographers but Watson won the play-off the following day

# ROYAL TROON

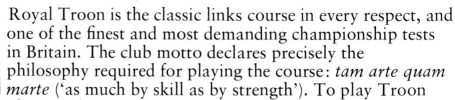

## Royal Troon

Royal Troon is the classic links course in every respect, and one of the finest and most demanding championship tests in Britain. The club motto declares precisely the philosophy required for playing the course: *tam arte quam marte* ('as much by skill as by strength'). To play Troon well, to the limits of your talent, you need an abundance of both.

The setting is almost without compare. Only the Ailsa at Turnberry, slightly more dramatic, surpasses it. They share the same wide vista of the Firth of Clyde; Arran and Kintyre stand beyond; there are flaming sunsets and in the far distance, to the south, lies Ailsa Craig. It is indeed a place of beauty.

The formation of the club came as part of golf's great expansion in the second half of the 19th century, spreading first from Scotland to England and the other home countries, then to Europe, North America, and all the lands of the British Empire. This expansion was made possible partly by the invention of the cheaper, truer 'guttie' (gutta-percha) ball in the middle of the century, which superseded the 'feathery', and also by the coming of the railways, which had such an extraordinary influence on all Victorian life.

One of the first railways in Scotland ran from Kilmarnock to Troon Harbour. That was in 1811, when Troon was an important seaport in the Firth of Clyde trade. In 1840, this railway line was followed by the Glasgow–Ayr route, which ran via Troon and Prestwick. An entire stretch of coast was opened up to the merchants of Glasgow, Paisley and Kilmarnock, and soon Prestwick had a golf club, formed in 1851.

The Troon club was in being by early 1878, founded by a group that included a doctor, bank managers and ministers from Glasgow, Barassie, Kilmarnock and Prestwick. The annual subscription was one guinea. Land was leased from the sixth Duke of Portland, and five holes, which shortly became six, were laid out in the area separating Craigend Farm, which lay between the present clubhouse and the Marine Hotel, and the Gyaws Burn. This general area now embraces holes 1, 2, 17 and 18. In the classic manner, the course was extended along the shore. By 1883, there were 12 holes; by 1888, there

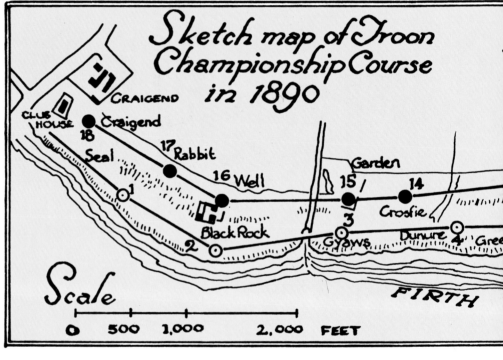

Sketch map of Troon Championship Course in 1890

| | | |
|---|---|---|
| Seal ... ... ... | 285 | yards |
| Blackrock ... ... | 335 | yards |
| Gyaws ... ... | 332 | yards |
| Dunure ... ... | 425 | yards |
| Greenan ... ... | 280 | yards |
| Ailsa ... ... ... | 292 | yards |
| Turnberry ... ... | 257 | yards |
| Tel-el-Kebir ... | 342 | yards |
| Monk ... ... | 322 | yards |
| Sandhills ... ... | 447 | yards |

were 18. The clubhouse was extended and improved, and by 1895 the club had become so successful that a 'relief' course, now Troon Portland, was necessary.

Proud men, they were, those early Troon members, and anxious to make of their course one comparable with any in Scotland. In 1882, for

example, the 'North Berwick pattern' of having tees separated from greens and built up on elevated plateaux was invoked, and the 'St Andrews pattern', of tees intrinsic with greens, abandoned. By 1904 the club was regarded highly enough to stage the Ladies' Championship. The ladies returned in

1925 and 1952. The Amateur Championship was played at Troon in 1938, 1956, 1968 and 1978, the club's Centenary Year. And Troon was chosen for the Open Championships of 1923, 1950, 1962, 1973 and 1982.

Royal Troon is a grand club. Its clubhouse is spacious and

The Smoke Room

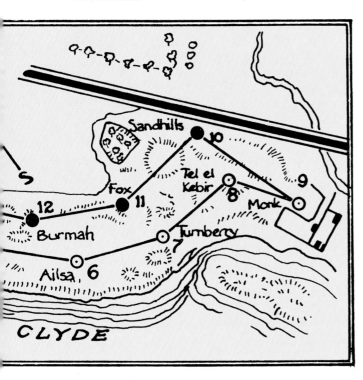

| | | | | | | | |
|---|---|---|---|---|---|---|---|
| ... | ... | 327 yards | Well ... | ... | ... | 345 yards |
| ... | ... | 350 yards | Rabbit | ... | ... | 197 yards |
| ... | ... | 208 yards | Craigend | ... | ... | 267 yards |
| ... | ... | 450 yards | TOTAL | ... | ... | 5656 yards |
| ... | ... | 195 yards | | | | |

comfortable, and has retained an air of privileged masculinity from times when the membership was not much inclined to let ladies, or lowlier males, across the threshold. However, those ideas belong in the past, and Troon is now as up to date as the next club and has, so I understand,

excellent arrangements for the ladies.

The course is very fine. It is quite difficult, and falls into clearly defined segments. The three opening holes are not really intimidating, and happily allow players to warm up, relax and get into some kind of stride for the challenges to come. The next three

holes are a good deal less benevolent – two big, taxing par fives straddling a powerful par three. The 6th, from the championship tee, is the longest hole in British championship play.

From the 7th through to the 11th, the course surges and plunges through a huge range of sandhills, and includes the shortest hole in championship golf, the 8th, by which hang many tales. The present hole was designed in the winter of 1909–10. It had formerly required a blind shot to a green behind the hill to the left of the present green, and the new hole was not universally acclaimed. The then golf correspondent of the *Glasgow Herald* was most affronted, quoting a 'golfer of some experience' as having called it 'the worst golf hole I have ever seen'. He went on: 'Some months ago we indicated that this hole would be likely to meet with some adverse criticism, because the destination of a well-hit tee stroke is so very much a matter of chance . . . the green is shaped like a dining-

room table . . . it is ridiculously small . . . without attempting to depreciate in the slightest degree the golfing ability of the members of the Troon club, one may fairly suggest that not many of them find much pleasure in playing the new 8th hole. It is a pity when golf, which on a fine course like that of Troon is a difficult game, is made painful.'

However, in the spring of 1910 Messrs Vardon, Braid, Taylor and Herd played an exhibition on the course, including the new hole, and all subsequently wrote to the club saying how much they had enjoyed it, and approved of the hole.

In the 1950 Open Championship Hermann Tissies, a German amateur, hit his tee shot into a bunker on the left of the green. He played five shots in there, the fifth into a bunker across the green, where he took a further five shots. Including another visit to the original bunker, he at last got on the green and holed his single putt for a . . . 15! In the last round of the same championship, Roberto de Vicenzo hit his tee

**Royal Troon Golf Club**

THE FIRST TEE IS RESERVED FOR
MEMBERS AT THE UNDERNOTED TIMES.

MON - FRI.  UNTIL 9·30AM AND FROM
1·30 TO 2·15PM
(WEDNESDAY 12·30 TO 2·30PM)

SUNDAY  UNTIL 10·30AM AND FROM
12·30 TO 2·30PM

Above: Briefing for visitors,
left, and Royal Charter, right,
awarded in centenary year
(1978)

Right: Clubs displayed in the
Smoke Room, believed to date
from the 17th century

shot into a bunker and was plugged. As the rule at the time permitted, he declared his ball unplayable (loss of distance only), went back to the tee, hit a second tee shot onto the green and holed the putt. Score 3! The rule, which had been experimental, was quickly dropped by the R & A.

In the 1973 championship Gene Sarazen, at the age of 73, made a nostalgic pilgrimage back to the course which he had last seen 50 years earlier. He had played there in the 1923 Open, having already won the US Open and PGA Championships. At Troon, however, he was caught in a gale and had failed to qualify, going home no doubt with a slender opinion of the Troon course. Half a century later he came to the Postage Stamp, as the 8th was then known, and holed in one in front of the television cameras. Next day, at the same hole, he hit his tee shot into a bunker and holed out with his second shot, directly from the sand.

From the 11th hole to the finish, with the possible exception of the 12th, which you might think is not an unreasonable hole, Troon is a very severe and demanding golf course. It will stretch you to the limits of your concentration, shot-making and self-control, although these are no more than the demands that any great golf course should make on any golfer.

# Introduction

## ROYAL TROON GOLF CLUB (Old Course)

**COMPETITOR'S SCORE ONLY MUST BE MARKED ON THIS CARD**

**MEDAL COURSE S.S.S. 73**

Player ....................................    Date.........................19....

| OUT Name | Metres | Yards | Holes where Strokes taken | Par | Mark Won 1 Lost x Halvd 0 | Score | IN Name | Metres | Yards | Holes where Strokes taken | Par | Mark Won 1 Lost x Halvd 0 | Score |
|---|---|---|---|---|---|---|---|---|---|---|---|---|---|
| 1. Seal | 326 | 357 | 16 | 4 | ...... | ...... | 10. Sandhills | 352 | 385 | 10 | 4 | ...... | ...... |
| 2. Black Rock | 348 | 381 | 7 | 4 | ...... | ...... | 11. The Railway | 385 | 421 | 1 | 4 | ...... | ...... |
| 3. Gyaws | 339 | 371 | 11 | 4 | ...... | ...... | 12. The Fox | 390 | 427 | 6 | 4 | ...... | ...... |
| 4. Dunure | 477 | 522 | 4 | 5 | ...... | ...... | 13. Burmah | 376 | 411 | 12 | 4 | ...... | ...... |
| 5. Greenan | 177 | 194 | 14 | 3 | ...... | ...... | 14. Alton | 160 | 175 | 15 | 3 | ...... | ...... |
| 6. Turnberry | 497 | 544 | 2 | 5 | ...... | ...... | 15. Crosbie | 407 | 445 | 3 | 4 | ...... | ...... |
| 7. Tel-el-Kebir | 348 | 381 | 9 | 4 | ...... | ...... | 16. Well | 487 | 533 | 8 | 5 | ...... | ...... |
| 8. Postage Stamp | 113 | 123 | 18 | 3 | ...... | ...... | 17. Rabbit | 192 | 210 | 13 | 3 | ...... | ...... |
| 9. The Monk | 354 | 387 | 5 | 4 | ...... | ...... | 18. Craigend | 342 | 374 | 17 | 4 | ...... | ...... |
|  | 2979 | 3260 |  | 36 |  |  | In | 3091 | 3381 |  | 35 | In | ...... |
|  |  |  |  |  |  |  | Out | 2979 | 3260 |  | 36 | Out | ...... |
|  |  |  |  |  |  |  | Total | 6070 | 6641 |  | 71 | Gross | ...... |

*In Bogey Competitions Competitors must enter their actual Score for all Holes Won or Halved*

Handicap

Nett

Marker ....................................

Player ....................................

## ROYAL TROON GOLF CLUB

### OLD COURSE

#### SCORE CARD
#### LOCAL RULES

1. **OUT OF BOUNDS (Def 21, Rule 29-1)** is defined by
   (a) Any fence wall or hedge bounding the course. Note Angled struts are part of a boundary fence (i.e. not obstructions).
   (b) The fence at the 6th hole.
   (c) Any part of the Clubhouse including the gravel paths.
   (d) The greenkeepers house and garden—demarked by white posts.
   (e) All houses and gardens on Crosbie Road. (Ball driven into gardens is not recoverable).
   (f) The white posts defining the path from the Marine Hotel to the Clubhouse.

2. **IMMOVABLE OBSTRUCTIONS (Def 20, Rule 31-2. 31 (b))** Immovable obstructions include the road behind the 16th green and in front of the 17th tee. A ball lying on the road or the sides of the road dividing the two courses may be lifted and dropped on the east side of the road and not nearer the hole without penalty.
   POP UP SPRINKLER HEADS
   All pop up sprinkler heads are immovable obstructions and relief from interference by them may be obtained under Rule 31-2. In addition, if such obstruction intervenes between the ball and the hole the player may obtain relief without penalty in the following circumstances:—
   (a) If the ball lie on the putting green, it may be lifted and placed, not nearer the hole, at the nearest point at which intervention by the obstruction is avoided.
   (b) If the ball lie off the putting green (but not in a hazard) and is within two club-lengths of the intervening obstruction, it may be lifted, cleaned and dropped as in clause (a) above.

3. **WATER HAZARDS (Def 14b, Rule 33-2)**
   The burn at the 3rd and 16th holes.

4. **GENERAL (Local Rules appendix 1f)** Ball lying on patches recently sown and where grass is not properly rooted must be lifted and dropped but not nearer the hole (Rule 22-2b).

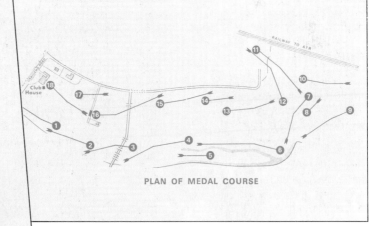

PLAN OF MEDAL COURSE

# 1

## SEAL

**357 YDS 326 M
PAR 4
STROKE 16**

The 1st green showing the
right-hand bunkers

Bunkers at 250 yards

*From the 1st Tee*

This is not an inhibiting start to the round. The hole is quite flat, running hard by an open beach, and turns only slightly towards the green. There is ample fairway space, and you should drive to the middle right of the fairway. There are bunkers set out on the left side, more in the rough than in the fairway, and your best line will take you to the right of them. A good 250 yards out, they should be out of range except in a following wind.

The prevailing wind here, and at the first

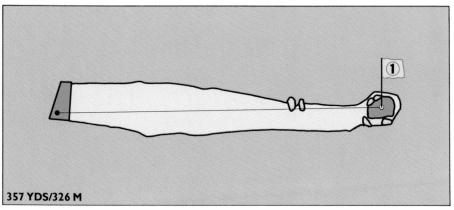

**357 YDS/326 M**

half-dozen holes, will be right to left, from the sea, from the west or south-west, which is another reason for favouring the right side of the fairway. The hole will play appreciably longer, of course, into a headwind, which would be more southerly. The first requirement on the hole, particularly downwind, is simply to be in the fairway. The second requirement, on the approach shot, is – be straight.

The green is more or less flat, and although there are four bunkers it is not an unfriendly place. The bunkers are quite sharply defined, at front right, front left, middle left and back right, and there is a clear entrance a good 20 yards across and quite unprotected. So if your approach shot is not your absolute best, as it may not be this early in the round, you can still hope to bumble the ball on. There is no serious trouble at the back of the green, but you must keep straight. You must not miss the green on the left, especially if you miss beyond or wide of the left-side bunkers. Then you would have to tackle a rather delicate chip shot, or short pitch, possibly over a bunker. All told, a fair and gentle start to your Troon adventure, and a hole on which you should certainly expect to make an opening par, and, with good shot-making, why not a birdie? This assumes that you have followed my perennial advice and have hit some balls on Troon's ample practice ground, and are warmed up properly!

**What's in the name?**
This hole is named after the reef in the bay on which seals used to bask.

Plenty of room for the drive

## BLACK ROCK

**381 YDS 348 M**
**PAR 4**
**STROKE 7**

A closer view of the green
over the fairway bunkers

This hole has a touch more character to it than the 1st. In fact, although I have described the first three holes at Royal Troon as being fairly relaxing, you should consider this only in terms relative to the other 15! You will also find that the 2nd and 3rd are each slightly more difficult than the previous hole, which makes for an interesting progression.

Black Rock is a more positive dog-leg than the 1st, this time going to the right, but again is fairly flat. Your first responsibility on the tee is to check the flag position. If it is well to the left of the green, you will have to hold your tee shot on the right side of the fairway to get the best approach line. For the average player, the driving line will be directly on the centre of the green. There is a little bunker on the right, just where the fairway starts, which is invisible from the tee. It is 150 yards out, so should pose no problems, but you should be aware of its existence as you fly the ball over it!

You will see a bigger bunker on the left, at 220 yards. Your line must certainly be to the right of that. At the same time you should certainly not miss on the right, where there is some punishing rough. In fact, on any hole of any course, you should always identify where the 'rubbish' – the heavy rough or strong hazards – lies, and establish the best place to 'miss' either fairway or green, if there is a chance that you might miss.

The distraction on the second shot is a set of cross-bunkers, set out some 40 yards short of the good-sized green. Two in the fairway cover the right and centre, and the third is set only just in the left rough. The greenside defences are strong – two bunkers covering the right front and centre, one covering the left front. All these bunkers are beautifully defined, the banks revetted, the edges clearly cut, with excellent sand. The left

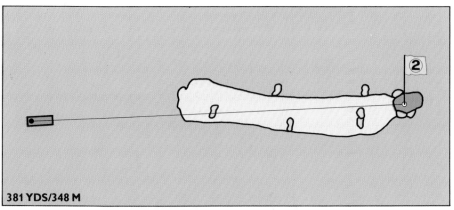

**381 YDS/348 M**

bunker turns round the front of the green slightly, but there is still a wide flat entrance, so if you carry the cross-bunkers you have a chance to run the ball on. All the trouble is clearly at the front of the green, and the thing to think about is to be up – even past the flag.

### What's in the name?
**Black Rock takes its name from the prominent reef between the 2nd and 3rd tees.**

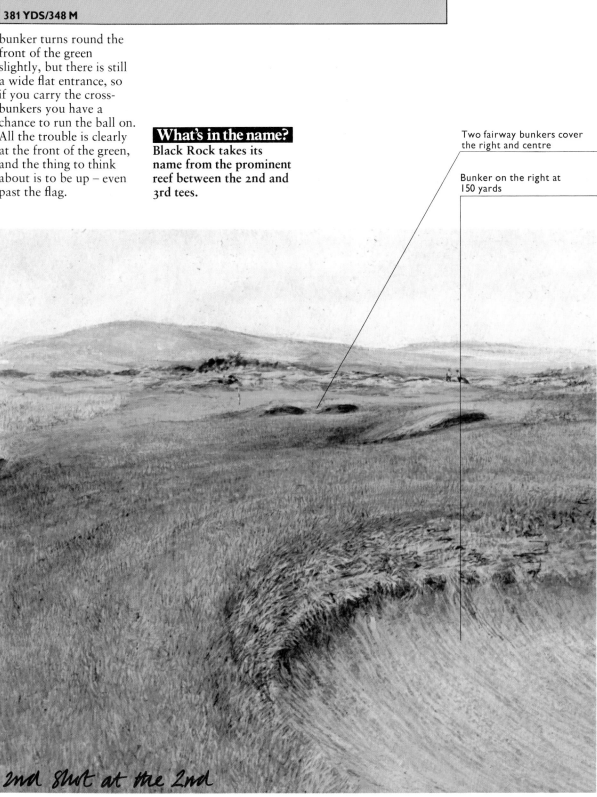

Two fairway bunkers cover the right and centre

Bunker on the right at 150 yards

2nd shot at the 2nd

# 3

## GYAWS

**371 YDS 339 M
PAR 4
STROKE 11**

As you can see from this tee, the holes are becoming tighter. This one follows a pattern repeated at Troon, where there are several par-4 holes, not quite 400 yards long, dog-legged one way or the other, with heavy rough, bunkering or sand dunes in the inside angle, and, on the outside of the angle, selective bunkering across the fairway in the driving zone. These holes require carefully considered, carefully placed tee shots.

This fairway is narrower than the 2nd, and turns to the right. The bunkers on the left are certainly reachable by the amateur player. And this time the right side of the fairway is much more heavily guarded, with rough ground in front of the tee. The main object yet again is to drive into the fairway, but if you must miss, do so on the left. Your driving line then is to the right of the two bunkers on the left side.

The next feature of the hole is the Gyaws Burn. This crosses the fairway in front of the green, some 50 or 60 yards short of the

Approach shot must be well up to the flag to avoid trouble

### What's in the name?

A gyaws is a channel or drain or hollow with a spring flowing from it, and here refers to the burn that crosses the 3rd and 16th fairways.

*The 3rd from the Gyaws Burn*

## The 3rd – Gyaws

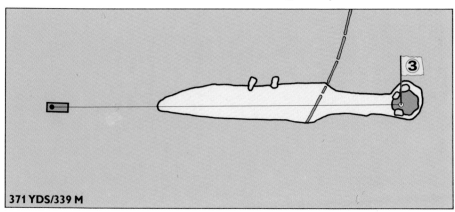

371 YDS/339 M

putting surface and the best part of 300 yards out from the tee. So the thing for you to do is: forget it. It will be in play only from a mishit second, or the second shot of a rather poor player.

The green is well bunkered, with two on the left side, one on the right. It slopes slightly away at the front, but broadens out rather

A net is provided to fish your ball from the Gyaws burn

attractively to the back. A shot pitching just short of the edge of the green might break appreciably to the left and so get you into trouble. One pitched halfway up on the right side might run away from you. There is no trouble at the back, but quite enough at the front, so get your approach shot well up to the flag. The green itself is medium in size, though none too large. So, to summarize: ignore the burn and hit a positive, careful, high approach shot right at the centre of the green. This I judge to be the most difficult second shot you will have faced so far.

## 4

# DUNURE

**522 YDS 477 M
PAR 5
STROKE 4**

This is the first of Troon's difficult tests, the beginning of a stretch of three holes, 4, 5, and 6, which embraces two big par 5s and a rather strong par 3. You look out over an area of about 100 yards of rough and marram grass and your first problem might be: find the fairway. It can all seem a little off-putting, but it is really just another lesson in not letting what you see frighten you too much. You will need only a straightforward drive to get into the fairway landing area.

The hole clearly dog-legs to the right, but it is not a severe and sharply defined angle, and there is a good initial focal point – a sizeable bunker at the corner, 210 yards out, set only just in the rough. Unless you are sure you can carry the ball directly over it, keep left. Up to about 250 yards, the fairway is reasonably wide, and unprotected on the left. The left rough here is much more gentle than that on the right. All this serves to reinforce the wisdom of an old links-course adage, which in recent years had no greater devotee than Peter Thomson. Peter, the greatest of Australian champions – and no man ever played links courses better – always had one simple but critical piece of advice for any young Australian golfer coming

to tackle British links courses for the first time. 'At all costs,' said Peter, 'keep the ball in play.'

At approximately 250 yards, the fairway narrows and stays narrow all the way. But there is a good second focal point, a bunker on the left side, just in the rough, 240 yards on from that first right-hand bunker and therefore about 80 yards from the front of the green. You may not quite be able to reach it, and if so, you can aim directly at it. The left side of the

fairway is better for the third shot. If you feel you might reach the bunker, keep right. By this time you will have noticed that the fairway of Dunure has much more movement in it than the three opening fairways, and you may be faced with some awkward stances.

Having advanced up the fairway to, say, 100 yards from the green, take a long close look at what lies before you. The split-level green is no more than medium-sized, and closely

guarded by two bunkers at right front and centre, and another at left front. The entrance to the green is quite adequate, and there is good fairway space just short of it along the right side. If you have come this far successfully, you would still be doing well to pitch anywhere around the middle of the green, and take a two-putt par. This is a testing hole, as much because of the narrow, undulating fairway as it is because of the man-made hazards.

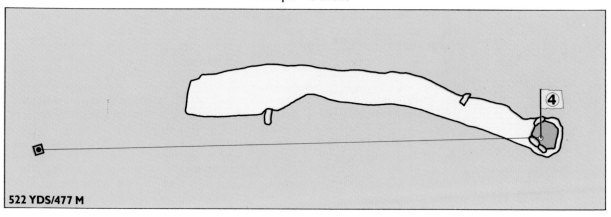

**522 YDS/477 M**

*The 4th from the Dog-leg*

Narrow undulating fairway
from 250 yards onwards

Avoid deep rough on the right

## What's in the name?
Another local reference,
this time to a fishing
village across the bay,
just south of the Heads
of Ayr.

Left:
The green from
the right-hand rough

## 5

## GREENAN

**194 YDS 177 M
PAR 3
STROKE 14**

### Royal Troon

Lined straight along the escarpment above the beach, this, the first of the short holes, is very nasty indeed. It is all fairly flat, or rather on the same level, and from the tee you do at least have a good view of the green. Immediately in front of the tee, extending apparently all the way to the green, is a wasteland of marram grass; this in fact stops about 30 yards short of the green.

There is a large and deep bunker short left of the green, but acceptably wide of it. There is a menacing bunker hard by the right front, blocking off the right half, and along the left side of the putting surface is what looks like one bunker, but is really two pots with only a yard between them.

Visually, this is not the most beautiful or inspiring short hole you have ever seen, nor does it have any great humps or dips to carry, or ridges to avoid. In that respect, it is not unpleasant, but it is not a particularly sympathetic hole. What you need here is your very best shot, a clean, confident

Long menacing bunker hard
by the right front

Tee shot must be straight

Large deep bunker short-left
but wide

### What's in the name?

The Kennedy family, who later became the Earls of Cassilis, and the Marquesses of Ailsa from 1831, built Greenan Castle to the south of Ayr; it is now a ruin.

## The 5th – Greenan

and positive strike at the ball to the heart of the green – and that applies to players of all standards.

The green is quite big – it has to be to accept the kind of shot that is called for. On the other hand, you could be just short of the green and run on, but you must be absolutely straight. The questions posed and decisions required have

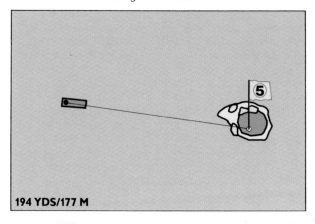

**194 YDS/177 M**

to do with choice of clubs, with judgment of distance and, of course, wind. It will prevail against you, or from around 2 o'clock, and you may well be playing a wood from the tee. You can be more than pleased if you dispose of Greenan in three strokes.

A closer view of
the bunkers on the left

The 5th Green

# TURNBERRY

### 544 YDS 497 M
### PAR 5
### STROKE 2

Here we have the second of Troon's outward par fives, at 577 yards the longest hole in championship golf. Even at its medal length, 544 yards, it will take a good deal of digesting. The hole is named Turnberry because, on a clear day of course, away to the south-west, across the bay of Ayr and behind the headlands called the Heads of Ayr, can just be seen the Turnberry lighthouse. At this hole begins the first set of holes, running through

to the 10th green, which have to wrestle with a great tumble of high sand dunes; these, if not quite Himalayas or Alps, might be considered at least as Grampians.

Along the right side of the hole, and screening us from the beach, is a sand ridge which rises progressively towards the green, which is set slightly into it behind the putting surface. On top of the ridge is some rather dramatic close fencing put there to stop what the architects call 'sand blow'. During the Second World War, Special Service troops

used an area of the beach, just short of the green, as a hand-grenade school, and this whole stretch of beach was used for tank landing practice. But all that is long gone, the club will assure you. The hole is almost straight, the fairway set slightly to the right from the tee shot, and the prevailing wind will be against, or fractionally from the right, from about 2 o'clock. In still air, and in good conditions, the best professionals will have thoughts of birdies here, and in the Open Championship of 1973 some people reached the

green in two shots, even at 577 yards.

The average player must consider it no less than a par five. It will require two very good wood shots and a firm pitch, perhaps even a mid-iron, to cover the distance, and into any kind of headwind this will be a severe test of your patience, good sense and careful shot-making.

Play this hole conservatively. Make sure you stay in the fairway and accept that there is simply no point in breaking your back to get an extra 10 or 20 yards on your shots. In

Two deep bunkers guard the left side of the green

Wide bunker 80 yards from the green

2nd shot must pass through the funnel

2nd shot at the 6th

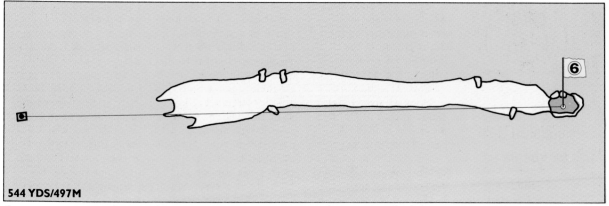

**544 YDS/497M**

that way, you can take some of the sting out of the hole.

From the tee, your marker is a pair of bunkers on the left, perhaps 230–240 yards out. There is a bunker about the same distance on the right, but in the rough. Your driving line should be just inside, or to the right, of these left-hand bunkers. The fairway is narrow and uneven, in true links style.

On the second shot, the fairway appears to have a funnel-like effect as it marches along a shallow valley towards the green, which looks a long way away – it is! Your second shot may well be the most critical on the hole, given a reasonable drive. On the left side of the fairway, around its narrowest point (it does broaden somewhat from there to the green) there is a wide bunker, about 80 yards out from the green. Behind these is a long dip or swale, running on towards the left side of the green, with troublesome rough. There are two quite deep greenside bunkers closing the left side of the green.

Then on the right side of the fairway, perhaps 30 yards short of the green, is a deep and important bunker. Since you must be on the right side of this fairway to attack the green and the flag, let this bunker be your target, and try to come up just short of it. This can be an exacting shot, since the wind may well be from the right, the rough on the right is particularly severe, and the bunker itself may seem intimidating. But you must approach the green from the right side. Anything to the left will mean pitching over two very deep greenside bunkers and across the line of the green, which is comfortably long from front to back, but rather narrow.

Turnberry is not a hole for heroics. It is a hole for sensible, conservative play, emphasizing yet again that golf is above all a point-to-point game.

## What's in the name?

**Turnberry – lighthouse and golf course – marks the furthest point south that is visible from Troon.**

# 7

## TEL-EL-KEBIR

**381 YDS 348 M**
**PAR 4**
**STROKE 9**

Tel-el-Kebir is one of the most magnificent holes in all the world of golf. The tee is set above the 6th green, where the long sand ridge along the shore turns into a mass of high, dramatic dunes which dominate the entire landscape at the southern end of the property and embrace holes 7, 8, 9, 10 and 11.

The view is spectacular, even to landward, taking in the shore, the Pow Burn, part of the revered Prestwick course to the south, Prestwick Airport, the main road and railway, and, it should be said, a caravan park. All around the end of the course is a heaving mass of dunes, heather and gorse, awesome bunkers and, happily, beautiful islands of emerald-green tees, fairways and greens.

Turn now to Tel-el-Kebir itself, and you may shiver in your spikes. The hole is a dog-leg which turns quite sharply to the right. Inside the angle is a great rampart of sandhills which contain the par-3 8th, clearly seen. Also in the angle are two powerful fairway bunkers. On the left side of the fairway at the same distance – 220/240 yards – are two more bunkers, just as sinister. It would be an act of very cold courage for you to try to carry that right-hand corner.

But the first detail likely to hypnotize you from the tee is the mass of dead ground falling away in front of you. The second is the big bunker placed on the left, just where the fairway starts, 160 yards out. So you have five traps to consider on this drive, and from the tee you will have the impression that the fairway slopes upwards quite noticeably. This means you must carry more than 160 yards, avoid the bunker on the left, and get between those two sets of two traps. Easy. Go as far left as you can, and when you get up there and look back, as so often happens, it will not look

*The Glasgow–Ayr Express hurries behind the green*

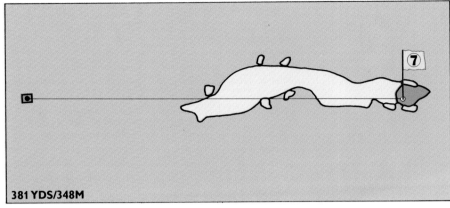

**381 YDS/348M**

so severe from the other viewpoint.

The green makes a gap in a huge sand ridge, rather tucked away, and you will have to drive fairly long and to the left side to (a) make the carry and pass the first trap, and (b) have an open sight of all the green. At the same time you must keep out of the fairway bunkers. It's not much to ask. Once again, though, you simply must be in the fairway; fortunately, there is plenty of it.

After all that, a dramatic shot to the green is still required. The green is narrow,

sunk beneath the ridges. It falls off into nothing at the back, with a rather steep downslope, so your shot must not be too long. The bunkers, one left, two right, are wicked, man-deep, but

the front of the green is quite unguarded and you can scuffle the ball on if you choose or have to. All told, this is an exceptional golf hole, one which will make you plot and plan all the way.

## What's in the name?

Tel-el-Kebir commemorates the battle fought in the Sudan in 1882, just before the hole was made.

Target area for the drive

Two powerful fairway bunkers

*From the 7th Tee*

119

## POSTAGE STAMP

**123 YDS 113 M
PAR 3
STROKE 18**

This is the shortest hole on the course, and indeed the shortest hole in championship golf. It is entirely penal – in fact it might as well be surrounded by prison walls, or be an island in the ocean for all the help it will offer you.

The green is set into the side of a high sandhill which rises to the left, and it is comprehensively protected by a bunker at the front and two at each side. These side bunkers are very deep and utterly 'straight-faced'. The two on the right are down a steep bank and very much below the level of the green, which is reasonably flat, quite long, but little more than a dozen yards wide, with a steep downslope to the back. The front bunker is deep, broad, close in, and virtually covers the entire front of the green. Ponder all that and you will quickly see that you have only one option. Hit the ball on to the putting surface, and hold it there.

The green is set slightly below the level of the tee and, at least before you play the hole, offers a pretty prospect. It certainly proves that a par 3 does not have to be 200 yards long to be testing. The shot can be anything from a pitch to a full shot with a wood, and there are times when it will play as long as you could imagine. The story is told of how Colin Maclaine, a club member and a first-class player, hit a 2-iron shot here into the teeth of a winter gale. The ball pitched past the flag and was blown back. At that moment, the wind blew the flagstick out of the hole, and the ball hit the pin, ran along it and plopped into the hole – score 1! (Maclaine survived all this and in the 1970s became captain of Royal Lytham

Deep bunker covers the entire front of the green

*The Postage Stamp*

## The 8th – Postage Stamp

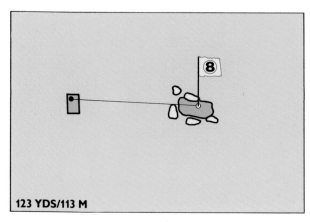

123 YDS/113 M

and chairman of the Championship Committee of the Royal and Ancient.)

As I mentioned in the introduction to the course, this hole is famous indeed, with such names as Braid, Vardon, Taylor, Sarazen, de Vicenzo and the luckless Herr Tissies having tasted its delights. I'm sure, too, that in retrospect you will look back on the 'wee Ailsa' as a memorable hole.

### What's in the name?

Once it was known as the Ailsa because of the fine view of the rock from the tee. Then in 1923 Willie Park said it had 'a pitching surface skimmed down to the size of a postage stamp'.

Hard work in the right-hand bunker

The tee shot must pitch on the green and hold to make par

# THE MONK

### 395 YDS 361 M
### PAR 4
### STROKE 5

The green is tucked away behind the ridge

This hole is fairly similar to the 7th, though somewhat less spectacular, in that it is played to a rising fairway that dog-legs to the right and to a partially-hidden green. First time round, you are not quite sure what you will find after either drive or approach shot. It's something of a mystery hole, but a neat par 4 for all that, with a quite generous fairway area.

A ridge comes in from the right side, short of the green, blocking off a good sight of it, so you are obliged to drive left. To compromise that, needless to say, there are two bunkers positioned on the left side, in driving range, and in the centre of the fairway in the same general area is a mound, with a rather sharp upslope. The first challenge is to handle these bunkers, which are about 240 yards out. Can you fly over them, squirt past them, or place yourself just short of them, at all costs on the left side? The wind and weather as much as anything will provide the answers.

### What's in the name?

**The Monk is the village of Monkton, and the 9th hole runs towards it.**

If you drive into a good initial position, you should be able to see the bottom of the flagstick and a good slice of the green, but even from the highest point of the fairway you will not be able to see all of the green. The ground from this point is deceptive, and the closer you get to the pin, the more it undulates in all directions and the narrower the fairway becomes. There is one little flat approach area just short of the green, to the right, which might be kind to a 'missed' shot, but if your approach shot pitches anywhere else, it will bounce anywhere else!

The green is small, but built up, leaning towards you and therefore holding, but you must really be thinking of nothing but flying your second shot

From the 9th Tee

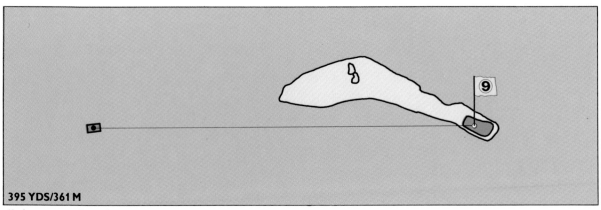

**395 YDS/361 M**

all the way and pitching
on the putting surface.
Thus The Monk puts as
much pressure on your
mental processes and
control as it will on your
shot-making, and for
that reason you will find
it an intriguing hole. Its
qualities are underlined
by the fact that it does
not need any greenside
bunkers – if you miss you
will always have the
chance to save the par
with a little chip or pitch.

Two bunkers to avoid at
240 yards

Green hidden around the
corner

# SANDHILLS

**385 YDS 352 M**
**PAR 4**
**STROKE 10**

There are two tees for this hole, widely separated, and the first one, nearer the 9th green, I would dismiss out of hand since I do not care for blind tee shots. I do like to see where I am going, and I suspect you will feel the same. This tee calls for a drive over a high ridge right in front of your nose, and when you play the hole for the first time from this tee, you can do no more than put your faith in the marker on top of the ridge, and crack the ball right over it. From that tee the line of the second shot follows a half-left turn.

The other, the 'railway' tee, is much further on and closer to the railway tracks which

The blind tee shot from the lower tee

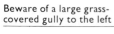
Beware of a large grass-covered gully to the left

*The Approach to the 10th*

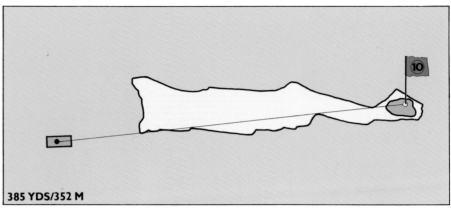

**385 YDS/352 M**

run along the right side of the hole. A slight right turn is required on the second shot, which makes it altogether a better golf hole. It may also make the prospect a little frightening for the average player. The tee is rather flat, and a strong expanse of heather stretches out some 70 yards in front of it. This is common to almost all the remaining holes on the course. The dominant feature is again the landscape itself. Ahead is a great sand dune with the green cut into the side of it, beyond a rolling, rising fairway. To the left of this dune, in a dip between it and another sand hill, you should see the Marine Hotel in the

distance. That should be your driving line. All of this makes a lovely picture because between and beyond the dunes is a hint of the Firth of Clyde, with the mountains of Arran forming a striking backcloth.

Sand dunes dominate the entire left side of this hole, heather and gorse the right, between fairway and railway lines. Keep away from the right side. In fact on all links courses you must keep out of heather and gorse – it's better to be in a bunker. Heather or gorse destroys you. You just cannot get the blade of the club through it with any certainty, and if you do get caught in either or both your one

concern should be to return to the fairway.

On this hole you should try to get about 220 yards out, using a 3-wood if you have to; this should take you down the left side, beneath the sand dune and more or less level with the 7th green, which you will see. That will give you a long or middle iron down the length of the green. Do consider taking one club more than you think, since the green is above you. There is plenty of fairway to work with on that left side.

You will see the green quite comfortably. There is a big bank behind the left half, but the right half is skylined. There is nothing at all behind it,

which can make problems in assessing the depth of your shot. As at the 9th, there are no greenside bunkers and the ground around the green, with little dips and swales beneath the sand dune, is fair, since with a long approach shot you may well be faced with a little chipped third from just off the putting surface. Beware of a large grass-covered gully to the left and beneath the green, about 20 yards short.

I would say that this is a difficult but reasonable hole. Play it as a par 4.5, and if you make par count that as a reasonable bonus.

Avoid heather and gorse on the right

### What's in the name?

No ambiguity here – all along one side are sand dunes; even the green is cut into the side of one.

## THE RAILWAY

**421 YDS 385 M**
**PAR 4**
**STROKE I**

The solitary bunker narrowing the entrance to the green

**A**gain, two tees are in use here, making a pronounced difference to the playing of the hole. The first, the medal tee, is high in the dunes, between the 10th and 7th greens, and offers a striking prospect down a very narrow fairway. The other tee, the championship tee, is on the other side of the 10th fairway, hard against the railway line, and it lengthens the hole by as much as 60 yards. A shot from this lower tee requires a drive to carry perhaps 200 yards across a prairie of rough to hold a narrow fairway which runs diagonally from left to right 'across the shot'. The hole then plays away from the railway, then back to the railway. Given a choice of tees, it becomes no choice at all!

This is a very powerful hole. Henry Cotton has described it as one of the most difficult holes in championship golf

'anywhere in the world'. In Open Championship play, Jack Nicklaus has scored 10 on the hole, Max Faulkner 11; on the other hand, Arnold Palmer, in winning the championship of 1962 in fulminating style, played the hole in one par, two birdies and one eagle. So be of some cheer.

From that first high, sand-hill tee, you see a very narrow fairway compressed by rough on both sides. However you do it, you must get on that fairway, and stay on it. There are no bunkers; with all that heather, gorse and rough, none is needed. As you assess the second shot and its demands, you will notice that the fairway seems to narrow towards the green. It does in fact do so slightly, some 100 yards from the green, but then it widens out again. You will nevertheless have the impression that the 11th hole is cramping you.

The green is pressed

hard against a stone wall along the railway line, and its only hazard defence is a small bunker at the left-front corner, but which heightens even more the narrowing effect. If you think of this hole rationally, you will conclude that fear is its greatest single defence: the fear that is implanted in the mind of the player by the narrowness of the fairway; the severity of the rough on either side; the narrowing effect on the second shot; the crowding presence of that out-of-bounds wall and the railway line, squeezing in from the right; the length of the second shot into what looks like a hopelessly tight target area, and the fact that if the prevailing wind is blowing, it will be pushing you ever closer to the wall and that cursed railway.

In time, though, you will come to know that there is an area, beginning about 100 yards short of the

green, in which the fairway widens much more than you could have imagined, and persists to the green. So, tactically, you might well think of playing slightly short of the scary 'funnel' with your second, and attacking the green and the hole with a chip and one putt. The Railway hole can be a card-wrecker. You will do well to score five on it. But don't be afraid – emulate, this time, Arnold Palmer, not Jack Nicklaus.

### What's in the name?

The Glasgow-Ayr railway runs hard by the hole; the out-of-bounds wall is uncomfortably near as you approach the green.

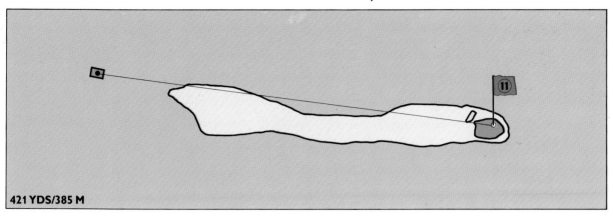

**421 YDS/385 M**

*The Railway Hole*

Severe rough

Railway line and wall

# THE FOX

**427 YDS 390 M
PAR 4
STROKE 6**

Having followed a northerly line for a couple of holes, we now turn back towards the south-west and the sea, and although it is half a dozen yards longer than the Railway hole, the Fox looks to offer much less of a battle, to be more of an unassuming, straightforward golf hole. There are no hazards visible from the tee, and up ahead is what looks like an open driving zone. Your line should be the tall chimney-stack in Ayr (provided it is visible).

The fairway is quite wide at 200 yards, but narrows appreciably at about 230 yards. You may not want to drive too far. You will need two substantial shots in any event to cover the distance, and into wind this hole will play quite long. There are no fairway bunkers to distract you. The second

A view of the fairway showing the angle of the dog-leg

Fairway narrows

*2nd shot at the 12th*

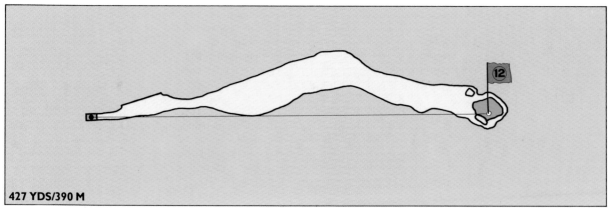

**427 YDS/390 M**

shot is rather attractive, clean and clear to a wide, slightly raised green. There is one pot bunker on the left, some 30 yards short, which I am sure you will ignore. There is one very deep greenside bunker at the right front, and a big dip or downslope to the left of the green, which could be irritating, but the green leans agreeably in towards you.

Some low sand dunes behind the green are silhouetted against the skyline and make an attractive horizon which will give a good feel of depth on the second shot. In retrospect, you might come to think of this as an essentially honest hole – the last place where you were able to draw an even, relaxed breath before you were plunged into the terrors of Royal Troon's fearsome finish.

### What's in the name?

No cunning traps are hinted at here. The simple explanation is that once there was a wood, by the present tee, which harboured foxes.

Pot bunker 30 yards short

## BURMAH

**411 YDS 376 M
PAR 4
STROKE 12**

I find this a very confusing hole, certainly one of the most difficult on the course. The view from the tee presents a jumble of hillocks like a lunar view, particularly on the right of the narrow fairway which is quite difficult to see. You certainly cannot tell, from the tee, which side of the fairway is which, and I suspect that it is one of those golf holes that needs to be played half a dozen times before the player really knows what it is about. The right side looks very forbidding, with exceptional movement in the ground and lots of heavy heather close by the fairway. The rough on the left looks a touch lighter. You can see the flagstick in the far distance.

In driving range, at 200 yards and on, the fairway is very narrow, not more than 20 yards across. And since the ground here is a mass of humps and hollows, many of them quite sharp, I believe that the average player should be given, at 200 yards, a fairway twice as wide, to give him an even chance of reaching the green. For him, there is no proper, flat, definable area into which he can drive safely. He will need luck to keep the ball in the fairway.

You may say that this is the essence of links golf, and I suppose it is, but I find myself wondering quite seriously if this hole isn't unfair. Even if, when you drive the ball in the fairway, you risk the more dangerous right side to have a better chance of reaching the green, you may then face a blind second shot, the left side of the green being screened off by a ridge of rough. And on this second shot, even the better players who have driven the ball further may well find a lie in which the ball is beneath their feet on a downslope, with a sharp upslope only five or six feet in front of them, and they still have to hit

Typical Troon rough – and plenty of it on this hole

### What's in the name?

This hole was laid out just after the British annexed Burma in 1886.

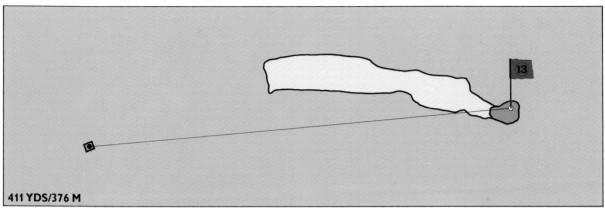

**411 YDS/376 M**

quite a long shot. This is without considering the wind and weather.

I know very well the game is 'not supposed to be fair'. I know the hole was laid out with the best of intentions. It has no bunker, and I know it certainly does not need one. I know that thousands of golfers have played it, and some, for all I know, may even have enjoyed it. And it exists. It is there, so it has to be played. But I do think the average player should get more help than he will presently find here. The green, by the way, is slightly raised, and waisted, broadening out at the back. But this is essentially in my opinion a 'hit-and-hope' hole, on both shots, and you will be well advised to do your best to keep the ball in play, and expect nothing better than a five.

*From the 13th Tee*

Narrow fairway – the driving range approximately 20 yards wide

Jumble of hillocks on the right

# ALTON

**175 YDS 160 M
PAR 3
STROKE 15**

The tee here is elevated just enough to let you see the green, and give some indication of its three guarding bunkers, which remain at least partly hidden. The green is none too big for the shot, being pear-shaped with a rather narrow entrance and broadening out towards the back. It slopes slightly from left to right, and anything pitching just short will break to the right and be gathered towards the right-hand bunker.

There is one very big bunker on the right, some 15 yards short of the putting surface; another, quite deep, lies at the left front of the green, and the third is hard by the right side. Together they make this a well-defended and very strong par 3. It is certainly not what I would call a 'ladies-type hole', since there seems to be no way you can run the ball into the green. The hole demands a shot carried all the way, perhaps a good 170 yards, no doubt with some kind of wind against; in other words, you are facing a long iron, or perhaps a wood shot if dead into wind.

There is no trouble at the back, so you should motivate yourself on the tee to 'think past these bunkers' or even 'think past the flag'. If anything, my inclination would be to over-club. The

*From the 14th Tee*

**175 YDS/160 M**

bunkers in themselves
are not too frightening –
their siting is their real
danger. Although this
hole does not quite have
the glamour of the
Postage Stamp, I would
think of it as being
almost as demanding,
and I would even think
that, for the average
player, the classification
would be 'par 3.5'.

## What's in the name?

The 14th takes its name
from part of the
Fullarton estate, situated
on the north side of the
railway.

A closer view of the
right-hand defences

No easy approach – the tee
shot must carry the bunkers
and stop on the green

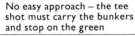

## CROSBIE

**445 YDS 407 M
PAR 4
STROKE 3**

This is a very powerful hole, and certainly must be accepted as a par 5 by the average player – before he tees off. It is one of the most sinister holes in Troon's very demanding finish. Your driving line will be on the white house in the distance (named, oddly enough, Black Rock House). From the tee you will not see the green, only the flagstick. There is a drive over more than 100 yards of rough to reach a very narrow fairway. Two bunkers in view out on the left side, just past 200 yards, look particularly nasty and the fairway yet again is nothing but humps and hollows and continuous turbulent movement.

Under almost any circumstances, the hole demands a big second shot, and you may well be hitting two woods here. Perhaps two-thirds of the way up the fairway are what can only be described as grass-covered 'bomb-craters', five or six feet deep, caused I understand by mine workings and certainly to be avoided.

They should not be in play, except from bad mishits, but they are very distinctive features of the hole, and very difficult places to be. Fifty yards from the centre of the green, bunkers on either side cause the fairway drastically to narrow, and just past them a ridge crosses the fairway.

The green is quite small, rather too small I would say for the length of shot it has to accept. It has one bunker, at front left. In fact the only concession this hole will make to you is around the green. If you can carry that ridge – which means covering 400 yards in two shots – the downslope behind it should carry you forward to the green. And the green itself is basin-shaped and will gather the ball to the centre from either side.

Playing this hole for the first time may turn out to be a unique and certainly unnerving experience unless you produce two of your prime, super-effective shots.

The 15th Fairway

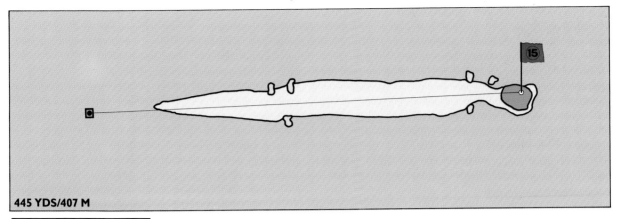

**445 YDS/407 M**

## What's in the name?

Crosbie is an ancient fortress near Alton, for centuries the home of the Fullarton family.

Black Rock House

Nothing but humps and hollows

Far left:
The narrow neck of the fairway

## 16

# WELL

**533 YDS 487 M
PAR 5
STROKE 8**

Now you are at the heart of the matter, facing the longest hole on the very difficult inward half of a very big course. These last half-dozen holes have been tough, you have probably been fighting some kind of wind, and it has been a long slog. So you are tired.

This is a time for being sensible, for pausing a little, and working on your concentration. You will know that tiredness affects your game in one way or another. I find that when I am tired, I don't quite get my normal extension through the ball after impact, so I stand just a little closer to it, and take a shade more care with my swing. It's a move that you also may find useful.

The view from the tee – a long way to the flag

### What's in the name?

The well lies halfway along the 16th fairway, near Gyaws Cottage, itself named after the burn that crosses the fairway at about 300 yards.

Target area for the second shot

*The 16th from the Gyaws Burn*

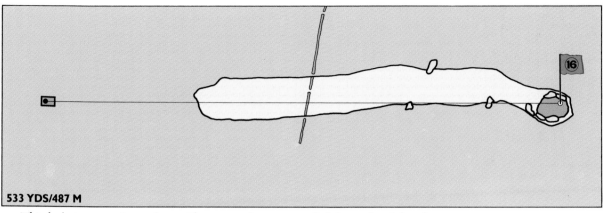

**533 YDS/487 M**

This hole is a genuine par 5, and you should play it that way. If a birdie comes, accept it graciously, but don't press for it. And if you go over par, don't worry about it. Your first task here is to get the ball on the fairway, no more, carrying over perhaps 150 yards of rough. The fact is, elderly golfers may be doing well to reach this green in four shots, so relax.

There are no bunkers in the driving area. The Gyaws Burn crosses the fairway at about 300 yards and is virtually unreachable for almost all players. The fairway in the driving area is reasonable in width and for stance, but even after a good drive the green both looks and is a long way off. Don't fret too much about the burn. If your strokes are good, it will not be in play. From the burn to the green, the hole is strongly protected by rough on the right side. Approximately 100 yards past the burn, there is a big bunker on the right side, with another touching the rough on the left, 20 yards on. These narrow the fairway somewhat. The bunker on the right is almost exactly 400 yards from the tee, which gives you an indication of what you must do with two shots. Beyond this bunker, 80 yards on, is another, clearly in the right side of the fairway. Fifty yards or so past that is the green, closely screened by bunkers, three on the right, two on the left.

On the second shot, you should aim on or slightly to the right of the left-hand fairway bunker, since you want the attacking line to the green on your third shot to be from the left side. If you get up into that general area with your second shot, you will now be some 125–150 yards from the green. Although it is a well-defended green, the entrance is fair, and you should be aiming for the left-front half of the putting surface.

The 16th is a very fine par 5. It is quite difficult, but totally honest and one of the very best of Royal Troon's many fine holes.

Bunkers on the left and right narrow the fairway 400 yards from the tee

# 17

## RABBIT

**210 YDS 192 M**
**PAR 3**
**STROKE 13**

The last of Troon's par-3 holes is thought by many to be the most testing, although I must say I think they are all quite difficult. The green is built up, with quite positive slopes falling away from it. The prevailing wind is from left to right, which is clearly why three deep bunkers range along the right side, at the foot of the slopes. Two bunkers, set short of the green to the left, perhaps 15 and 30 yards short of the putting surface, are very important – they must be missed!

For a hole of 210 yards, you are asked to play a fairly long shot, and I would rate the hole as a par 3.5. Apart from the traps it has no particularly outstanding feature. The bunkers to the left are quite big, and very deep. If you land in there it will be impossible to reach the green with a second – to get the ball up and forward and on will be more than you can hope for. All things considered – and one of these may well be the fact that you are tiring – I would say that, rather than flogging away with perhaps a 2-iron, it might be sensible to be short – past the left-hand bunkers by all means – but just short of the front of the green. Although there is an upslope, there is a reasonable entry, and you could even thin a shot and scuttle up quite nicely. If you are short and on the upslope, you still have a chance with a very open chip shot and one putt. That would be as good a plan as any.

### What's in the name?

As with The Fox (12th), there is no golfing connotation here; the rabbits are merely those who live in nearby warrens.

*From the 17th tee*

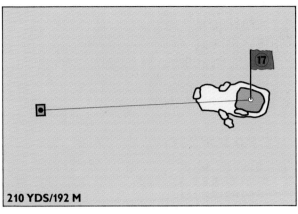

**210 YDS/192 M**

A very testing short
hole – the only hole at
which Jack Nicklaus
dropped a stroke when he
broke the course record

Aim left but be sure to carry
the left-hand bunkers which
are short of the green

Prevailing wind will push the tee
shot to bunkers on the right

# CRAIGEND

**374 YDS 342 M**
**PAR 4**
**STROKE 17**

This closing hole is quite flat, and looks almost innocent from the tee. It is certainly not as difficult as other championship finishes, Muirfield, for example, or Carnoustie, but it is not without subtleties and does require some respect, as well as one final effort of concentration.

There is a bunker on the left side of a straight fairway, some 210 yards out. Thirty yards on, bunkers straddle the fairway, and each encroaches slightly into it. Your driving line could be on the club flagpole, slightly to the right of that first bunker, and the trick with the drive is to be in the fairway (of course), and perhaps past the left-hand bunker but avoiding the other two. From the left-hand bunker to the front of the green is 150 yards.

The one major subtlety of this hole emerges as you shape up to your second shot. There are two bunkers up the fairway, covering the centre: the first is 30 yards short of the front of the green, and the second, placed a touch to the right, is perhaps 10 yards short of the front. These are effectively on your line, and they have a definite foreshortening effect on the shot. You must realize that there is plenty of room beyond these bunkers, two or three clubs in fact to the middle of the green, so

There is plenty of room beyond these two bunkers

The 18th Green

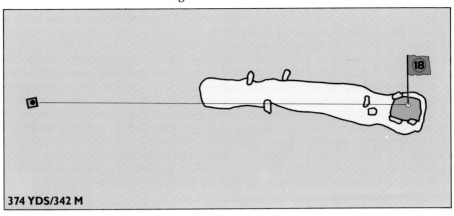

**374 YDS/342 M**

you must have the confidence to fly the ball well over them.

The green is quite big, and flat, and the really important thing on this approach shot is to believe in your yardage and let go with a bold shot. The path at the back of the green is out of bounds, but Royal Troon is a friendly club – they won't be too upset if you knock one right through the clubhouse window. Will they?

### What's in the name?
The last hole is named after the farm, long vanished, on which the Old Troon and Portland courses are laid out.

Five bunkers lie in wait for the wayward approach shot

A generous green but the path in front of the clubhouse is out of bounds

The championship 'career' of the Troon course, known for so long as Old Troon before it became Royal Troon in its centenary year, 1978, had a rather odd start in that the ladies made it a championship course in 1904. The first Troon Open was staged in 1923, and with the passing of Prestwick as a modern venue in 1925, Troon became the premier Open Championship course in the West of Scotland. It remained so until Turnberry came to share that title in 1977.

## Course Record (Old Course)
65 Jack Nicklaus (USA)
(Open Championship 1973)

## Open Championship

| | | | |
|---|---|---|---|
| 1923 Arthur Havers | 295 | 1962 Arnold Palmer (USA) | 276 |
| 1950 Bobby Locke (S Africa) | 279 | 1973 Tom Weiskopf (USA) | 276 |

## Amateur Championship

| | |
|---|---|
| 1938 C R Yates (USA) | 1968 M F Bonallack |
| 1956 J C Beharrell | 1978 P McEvoy |

## Home Internationals
1932 Scotland    1952 Scotland    1972 Scotland

## Ladies' Amateur Championship
1904 Miss L Dod    1925 Miss J Wethered    1952 Miss M Paterson

Left: The gallery at the 7th
following Arthur Havers,
winner of the 1923 Open.
Above: Miss Joyce Wethered,
four times winner of the
Ladies' Amateur
Championship, playing to the
6th green during the 1925
final. Right: Bobby Locke won
the 1950 Open at Troon with
an aggregate of 279 to become
the first player to break 280
in the Open Championship.
Below: James Braid, five times
winner of the Open
Championship, playing at
Troon in 1923

Above: John Beharrell, winner of the Amateur Championship at Troon in 1956. Above right: Tom Weiskopf receives the trophy as 1973 Open Champion. Left: Michael Bonallack (left) and John Beharrell (right) with Charlie Yates, Amateur Champion (1938), at Troon for the 1978 Amateur Championship. Below: Arnold Palmer driving at the 7th during the 1962 Open

**Playing the course** As with all private clubs, some formalities are required for visitors. As a matter of politeness, you should check in advance with the Secretary, Royal Troon GC, Troon, Strathclyde, tel Troon (0292) 311555, and be able to show him some evidence of your own club membership and handicap. Ladies may play on Mondays, Wednesdays and Fridays by similar prior arrangement. You must not simply turn up and hope to play.

**Adjoining course** The adjoining course, Troon Portland, is a deceptive companion to Royal Troon. Without the dramatic duneland out at the turn of the 'big' course, nevertheless it is a fine test of golf in the classic links manner.
Troon Portland    6274 yards    SSS71

**Recommended courses in the surrounding area** Prestwick Golf Club is the original home of the Open Championship. It is now considered by many people as an 'ancient monument' and, as such, it must be preserved, and it must be played by anyone interested in golf as it was. Also in the area are three outstanding courses well worth playing – Western Gailes, Glasgow Gailes, and the Kilmarnock GC course at Barassie. All these courses have been used for major competitions and as qualifying courses for the Open Championship.
Glasgow Gailes GC, Gailes, Strathclyde; tel Irvine (0294) 311347.
Western Gailes GC, Gailes, Strathclyde; tel Irvine (0294) 311357.
Kilmarnock GC (Barassie), Barassie, Troon, Strathclyde; tel Troon (0292) 311077.
Prestwick GC, Links Road, Prestwick, Strathclyde; tel Prestwick (0292) 77404.

**Where to stay** Troon itself is a marvellous base for playing many of these fine West Coast courses, with a variety of accommodation available. Prestwick and particularly Ayr also offer a wide range of accommodation and are within a few minutes' drive of Royal Troon.
Marine Hotel, Troon, Strathclyde; tel Troon (0292) 314444, telex 778215.
Sun Court Hotel, Troon, Strathclyde KA10 6HF; tel Troon (0292) 312727.
South Beach Hotel, Troon, Strathclyde; tel Troon (0292) 312033.
Caledonian Hotel, Dalblair Road, Ayr, Strathclyde KA7 1UG;
tel Ayr (0292) 69331, telex 76357.
Savoy Park Hotel, Ayr, Strathclyde; tel Ayr (0292) 66112/63469.

Left: Michael Bonallack, 1968 Amateur Champion, on the tee at the Postage Stamp. Below right: Jack Nicklaus established a new course record in the final round of the 1973 Open

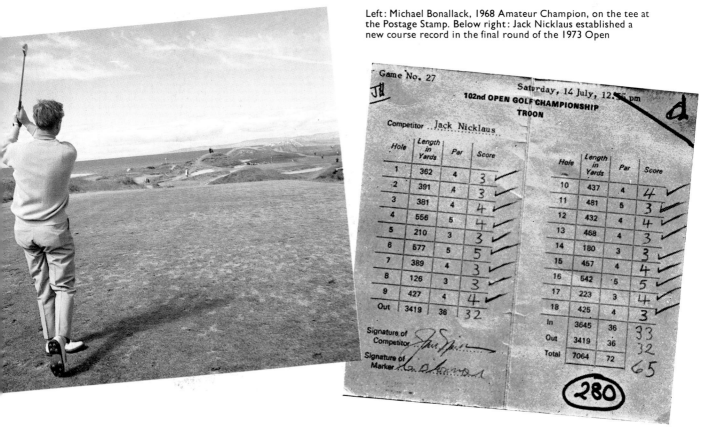

# TURNBERRY

## Turnberry

Of all the great Scottish links, the Ailsa Course at the Turnberry Hotel is the most dramatic, the most spectacular and the most compellingly beautiful. Set along a rock-bound coast, above the golden sweep of the sands of Turnberry Bay, the Ailsa is a fine championship course made doubly magnificent by the surrounding landscape. Across the water to the north-west stands the great bulk of the Island of Arran with its towering peaks; beyond it to the west lies the long, low peninsula of Kintyre; to the south-west is the massive granite outcrop of Ailsa Craig, marking the southern end of the famed Firth of Clyde; and to the east are the rich, ripe, rolling farmlands of Carrick. All of this makes the Ailsa a marvellous place of blinding sunsets and sea mists and long Scottish gloamings, and, it should be said, from time to time – storms.

There are two Turnberry courses. The Arran, slightly less testing, flatter and running through avenues of gorse, lies 'inside' the Ailsa. Jointly they have had an uneven history. Originally the third Marquis of Ailsa commissioned Willie Fernie to design 13 holes, for the use no doubt of his local tenants. Willie Fernie was professional at Troon from 1887–1924, and his son Tom became the first professional at Turnberry. The third Marquis combined landowning with being a director of the Glasgow & South-Western Railway Company and, in 1899, captain of Prestwick Golf Club. At the turn of the century he leased land at Turnberry to the railway company. By 1905, Fernie had designed and laid out a second course of 13 holes, and the hotel had been completed as possibly the first hotel/golf complex in the world.

With the amalgamation of the railway companies into four main groups in 1926, Turnberry became the property of the London, Midland & Scottish Railway Company, and before British Railways chairman Dr Beeching came along in the 1960s with his celebrated 'axe', it was possible to board a sleeping car at London's Euston Station and emerge next morning in the hotel, virtually untouched by the weather.

The courses scarcely had time to settle before World War I, when the Royal Flying Corps used the ground as a pilot training station, with much resultant damage. After the war, the newer 'number two' course became the major course, and was named after the third Marquis. Between the wars an experienced architect, Major C. K. Hutchison, who had worked on the newer Gleneagles Hotel courses, was engaged to lengthen the Ailsa and eliminate some blind shots, changes which had been completed by 1938.

World War II was a disaster for golf at Turnberry. RAF Coastal Command constructed an air base on the courses – many thought unnecessarily! – and littered the area with enormous buildings and concrete runways, some of them 18in thick. So convulsed was the ground that many Whitehall mandarins, and indeed some of the hotel company's directors, were convinced that Turnberry was finished as a golfing centre. However, Frank Hole, managing director of British Transport Hotels Ltd, by then the owners, thought otherwise. After a bitter and perhaps bloody-minded battle, he extracted from the government of the day enough financial compensation to underwrite the entire rebuilding of the courses. Jimmy Alexander, BTH's superintendent of grounds and golf courses, with Suttons of Reading as contractors, re-made golf at Turnberry to the designs of Mackenzie Ross, the golf architect. Between them, they produced a masterpiece: the present Ailsa course.

By June 1951 the courses were completed, and over the next two decades the Ailsa was to stage an Amateur Championship, two PGA Match Play Championships, two Scottish Professional Championships, the Home Internationals, a Walker Cup match, and many professionally sponsored tournaments. The final accolade came with its first Open, the 106th Open Championship of 1977, and perhaps the most astonishing of all in modern times. That year Jack Nicklaus and Tom Watson scored three identical rounds of 68, 70, and 66, and were paired in the final round, when Watson scored 65 and Nicklaus 66. In the quality of their stroke-making, and in the valour of their temperaments, Watson and Nicklaus fashioned one of the greatest battles ever known in championship golf. And oddly, although the championship was played in generally fine conditions, only one other player, Hubert Green, was under par for the week.

For the professionals, from the championship tees, the Ailsa Course is difficult. For amateurs, from the medal tees, the Ailsa Course is still difficult! Yet it is not harshly or brutally difficult, and I believe it is essentially fair. The fairways are reasonably generous and provide few awkward stances, and on the whole I make it one of our finest links courses. Your only problem at Turnberry may be that the dramatic beauty of your surroundings will distract you from the work at hand.

Top left: The main entrance
to the Turnberry Hotel
Top right: Evening sun on the
Ailsa Course

Above: Turnberry Hotel from
the course and, left, the
Dormy House, the course and
the lighthouse from the hotel

# Turnberry Hotel Golf Courses

## AILSA COURSE Local Rules

1. **Out of Bounds**
   A ball is out of bounds if it lies:
   (a) Beyond any fence bounding the course (as at the 1st, 3r[d] and 18th holes).
   (b) Over the garden wall at the 9th hole.

2. **Water Hazards**
   The beach at the 9th hole and the burn at the 7th, 16th an[d] holes are ordinary water hazards. (Rule 33/2 applies).

3. **Lateral Water Hazard**
   The beach at the 10th hole is a lateral water hazard. (Ru[le] applies).

4. **Roads and Paths**
   (a) The Lighthouse Road crossing the 9th hole and on the ri[ght] 13th and 14th holes is an obstruction. (Rule 31/2 applie[s])
   (b) A ball lying on or within one club length of the footpa[th] 18th hole may be lifted and dropped without penalty ke[eping] point from which the ball was lifted between the playe[r] hole, but not nearer the hole.
   (c) A ball lying on the gravel surface surrounding the clubh[ouse] be lifted and dropped without penalty within two club[ lengths of] the gravel, but not nearer the hole.

5. **Obstructions**
   The direction stone at the 9th hole is an immovable o[bstruction] (Rule 31/2 applies).

6. **Tarmac Areas**
   All tarmac areas within the boundaries of the course are i[n play] of the course.
   **Note:-** The ball must be played as it lies or be declared [unplayable] (Rule 29/2).

7. **Pop-up Sprinkler Heads**
   All pop-up sprinkler heads are immovable obstruction[s and relief] from interference by them may be obtained under R[ule In] addition, if such obstruction intervene between the ball [and the hole] the player may obtain relief without penalty in th[e following] circumstances:
   (a) If the ball lie on the putting green, it may be lifted an[d placed, not] nearer the hole, at the nearest point at which such in[terference by] the obstruction is avoided.
   (b) If the ball lie off the putting green (but not in a [hazard) and] within two club lengths of the intervening obstruc[tion it may be] lifted, cleaned and dropped as in clause (a) above.

Left: The Championship tee at the 9th and, inset, a spectacular view to the south

| Hole | | CHAMPIONSHIP LENGTH IN YARDS | PAR | MEDAL S.S.S. 71 LENGTH IN YARDS | PAR | STROKE INDEX (AND LADIES) | LADIES LENGTH IN YARDS | PAR |
|---|---|---|---|---|---|---|---|---|
| 1 | Ailsa Craig | 362 | 4 | 362 | 4 | 9 | 345 | |
| 2 | Mak Siccar | 428 | 4 | 378 | 4 | 13 | 367 | |
| 3 | Blaw Wearie | 462 | 4 | 393 | 4 | 5 | 381 | |
| 4 | Woe-be-Tide | 167 | 3 | 167 | 3 | 17 | 112 | |
| 5 | Fin'me oot | 477 | 5 | 411 | 4 | 3 | 393 | |
| 6 | Tappie Toorie | 222 | 3 | 222 | 3 | 15 | 219 | |
| 7 | Roon the Ben | 528 | 5 | 465 | 4 | 1 | 424 | |
| 8 | Goat Fell | 427 | 4 | 427 | 4 | 11 | 385 | |
| 9 | Bruce's Castle | 455 | 4 | 413 | 4 | 7 | 372 | 4 |
| **OUT** | | 3528 | 36 | 3238 | 34 | | 2998 | 39 |
| 10 | Dinna Fouter | 452 | 4 | 430 | 4 | 6 | 339 | 4 |
| 11 | Maidens | 177 | 3 | 137 | 3 | 18 | 130 | 3 |
| 12 | Monument | 391 | 4 | 391 | 4 | 8 | 358 | 4 |
| 13 | Tickly Tap | 411 | 4 | 379 | 4 | 14 | 338 | 4 |
| 14 | Risk-an-Hope | 440 | 4 | 400 | 4 | 2 | 395 | 5 |
| 15 | Ca Canny | 209 | 3 | 168 | 3 | 16 | 160 | 3 |
| 16 | Wee Burn | 409 | 4 | 381 | 4 | 10 | 343 | 4 |
| 17 | Lang Whang | 500 | 5 | 487 | 5 | 4 | 401 | 5 |
| 18 | Ailsa Hame | 431 | 4 | 377 | 4 | 12 | 374 | 4 |
| **IN** | | 3420 | 35 | 3150 | 35 | | 2838 | 36 |
| **TOTAL** | | 6948 | 71 | 6388 | 69 | | 5836 | 75 |

GROSS    HANDICAP    NE[T]

## Turnberry Hotel Golf Courses

TURNBERRY HOTEL

Practice Ground

Club House

ARRAN COURSE

AILSA COURSE

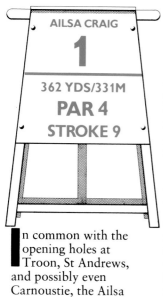

AILSA CRAIG

**1**

362 YDS/331M

**PAR 4**

**STROKE 9**

In common with the opening holes at Troon, St Andrews, and possibly even Carnoustie, the Ailsa start is fairly benign, as though to encourage you for the delights, or otherwise, to come. The hole should be a comfortable two-shot par 4, and I suspect its defences look slightly more daunting than they are. It dog-legs to the right at around the 200-yard mark, turning and appearing to narrow between two sets of bunkers set in the rough on either side. There is in fact a cluster of two large and two small bunkers on the right stretching from 210 to 250 yards. On the left are two bunkers which have recently been intentionally grassed over forming no more than awkward mounds at 200 and 220 yards. The rough on the right side can be quite severe and all the bunkers are reachable from the front tees unless you are driving into a particularly strong wind.

The ideal drive should put you in the left half of the fairway, giving you the optimum angle of attack on the green. Thus your line may well be dead-centre between the bunkers and the mounds on the left, if anything favouring the left side. If you are past the mounds and in the fairway, you are ideally placed. The front centre and front right of the green are closed off tightly by a very purposeful bunker. There is another to the back left. A slight dip occurs in front of the green, which is built up but quite flat with no major contours to worry about, either on the approach shot or in putting.

On the right side of the green, behind the front bunker, is a

**What's in the name?**
Ailsa Craig is named
after the famous Ailsa
rock in the Firth of
Clyde, visible from
almost every part of the
course.

Left:
A closer view of the green
shows clearly the large
front bunker and the
downslope to the right of
the green

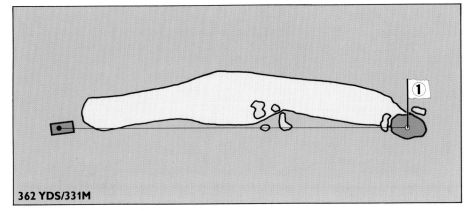

362 YDS/331M

Bunker guarding front centre
and front right of the green

Cluster of bunkers at
210–250 yards

*2nd shot at the 1st*

downslope, so if you
miss the green on that
side the ball can be
thrown right and scuttle
down into some bushes.
If you decide you cannot
carry the front bunker
and fly the ball all the
way to the putting
surface, think of playing
to the left of that
bunker, taking a line for
your second shot on the
bunker at the left back.
At the left end of the

front bunker, at the left
entrance to the green, is
an attractive patch of
fairway, from which you
might plan to chip (and,
of course, one-putt
home).

You must work hard
to make no more than
four on this opening
hole. On a course like
the Ailsa you are bound
to drop strokes, so drop
them at a hole which has
much stiffer defences

than this one. If I started
a championship with a
five, I would be very
disappointed.

If this makes the
opening hole sound
fairly routine, it remains
true that the first half-
dozen holes of the Ailsa
constitute a difficult
beginning, and it is
important to get into top
gear quickly. Allow time
to hit some balls on the
practice ground before

you start, and be
properly warmed to the
task. In the 1979
European Open, I
birdied six of the first
seven holes to give
myself an 8-shot lead,
having started the round
one shot behind. That
broke the back of the
round, and won me the
championship. The one
hole I didn't birdie was
the second.

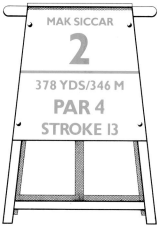

MAK SICCAR

**2**

378 YDS/346 M

**PAR 4**

**STROKE 13**

**W**hat I failed to do at the second in 1979 (see previous page) was 'mak siccar', or make sure, since I missed the green badly to the left, but managed to pitch up from the depths of the rough and hole the putt for a par.

The second I find an interesting hole which also has a good deal in common with the third. Neither hole needs a fairway bunker to compromise or direct the drive. At the second, you must drive up to a fairway set along a right-hand ridge. Your line could be slightly to the

right of the distant flag. The immediate rough on the right, in the driving zone, is not all that heavy, but along the entire left side, from there to the green, the ground falls quite sharply down to the parallel third fairway and these slopes have very telling rough. So keep away from the left side.

Having got into position, you find that the architect of the Ailsa is still not finished with you. In your line to the centre of the green is a big fairway bunker, some 60 yards from the front edge of the green and perhaps 80 yards from the flagstick; a secondary, supporting bunker lurks 20 yards behind it. The green is big, possibly 40 yards long. There is a bunker just short of the left front, with downslopes continuing to the left of it. There is a bigger bunker at the right front, with mounds and slopes around it, but there is a reasonably wide entrance to the green so that you can get at it from either

the left or right side of the fairway. But to have any chance at all with this hole, you must be on the fairway with the tee shot.

At best, the second

shot will be long, perhaps as much as 170 yards, and you must carry these two fairway bunkers. They have the effect of foreshortening the hole, and it is

Ground slopes steeply away on the left side of the fairway

If you are likely to be short, be short on the right

*Approach to the 2nd Green*

# The 2nd – Mak Siccar

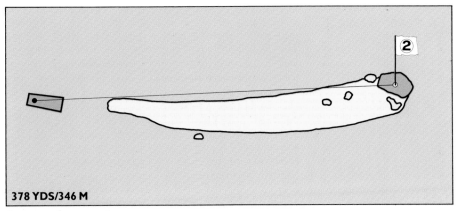

**378 YDS/346 M**

there are few worries past the pin and plenty of space beyond the central fairway bunkers. If you must be short, be short of the right, greenside bunker; from there you will have a clear and open chip or pitch to the flag. All in all, this hole is quite a testy par 4.

The larger bunker covering the right of the green

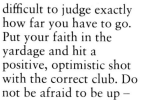

difficult to judge exactly how far you have to go. Put your faith in the yardage and hit a positive, optimistic shot with the correct club. Do not be afraid to be up –

## What's in the name?

**The name of the 2nd hole is its motto too – 'Make sure' with every shot you play.**

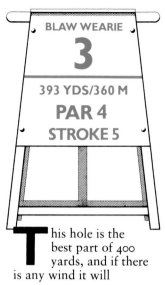

**BLAW WEARIE**

**3**

393 YDS/360 M

**PAR 4**

**STROKE 5**

This hole is the best part of 400 yards, and if there is any wind it will probably be dead against, so you have to face up to two quite long hits. As you stand on the tee, you will see that the hole takes you down a shallow valley, the fairway turning slightly right, and from the tee you can see virtually nothing of the green at all. The fairway is narrow, the green is narrow, and the third hole vies with the 9th and 14th as the toughest par 4 you will meet on this course.

Like the second, the third hole has no fairway bunkering in play for the drive. The right side of the fairway falls off, down towards the fifth fairway, in a sharp slope scarred with deep gullies covered in strong and dangerous rough. The left half of the fairway will give a better view of the green and the pin, and the rough on the left is possibly less severe; but you must keep away from that right side. The first demand this hole makes is that you get in one of your very best drives, in the middle of the fairway, and so leave yourself with a feasible second shot. The third on the Ailsa is indeed one of the most perfect 'natural' holes in golf, forcefully illustrating how the terrain can be just as hazardous as anything man-made.

From about 80 yards up to the green, the ground is very broken, with quite pronounced mounds to the right. There is a greenside bunker, left centre, which cannot be seen from the left side of the fairway. There are two rather sticky bunkers at

the right front which also cannot be seen too clearly, so we are talking of a rather narrow target entrance. The average player may well land the ball short, hoping to tumble it on to the putting surface. A better player might hope to fly the ball to the middle of the green for a safe par, but the less-than-good player will frankly have problems.

In a championship, a prime pin position would be tight on the right side, making it very difficult for anyone who has

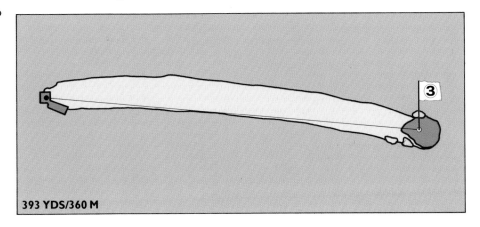

393 YDS/360 M

Keep left to open up the green

Ground falls away on the right into severe rough

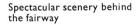

2nd shot at the 3rd

Spectacular scenery behind the fairway

driven on the right side of the fairway, with those two right-hand bunkers closing out the second shot. The latter would have to be a high, soft fade to keep the ball in control and get somewhere close to the flag, and we had better assume that not too many people have that shot in the bag. So, if you get Blaw Wearie behind you with not more than a five on the card, you may sigh with some relief and be well pleased with yourself.

## What's in the name?

**Blaw Wearie means 'out of breath', which will be your fate on a windy day, for the wind here usually blows dead against.**

# Turnberry

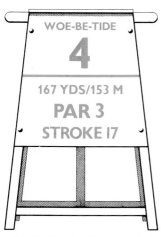

WOE-BE-TIDE

**4**

167 YDS/153 M

**PAR 3**

STROKE 17

The first of Ailsa's par-3 holes is the start of the most dramatically spectacular sequence of holes to be found anywhere in the world of golf. From the 4th to the 11th we play along the outer perimeter of the property, above the sweep of Turnberry Bay, through valleys behind the long, screening sand ridge with tees and greens high above and within sight of the ocean, to the rocky cliffs and coves of 'Bruce's Castle' and the Turnberry lighthouse, and beyond.

The fourth tee is at water level, hard by the beach, and the line to the green is along the shore, across the edge of a little bay. A pulpit green is cut into the left (seaward) side of a huge mound with a steep, tangled slope falling away to the shore on the left. On the face of the mound, apparently covering the right half of the green, is a vast bunker. We might call this a heroic hole, in the sense that there is nowhere you can miss the green without penalty. Success can only be bought with courage. To make a par or better, you must hit and hold the green with the tee shot, and you should find the green on

Small figures on the green emphasize the depth of the bunker

Steep, tangled slope to snare anything wandering to the left

*From the 4m Tee*

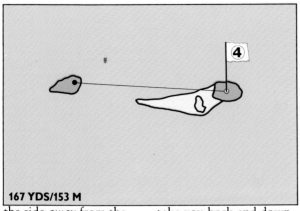

**167 YDS/153 M**

the side *away* from the pin. If the pin is cut on the left side of the green, shoot for the right side. If the pin is on the right, aim for the centre or left half of the green.

If you miss on the left with the pin on the left, you will go down a horrible bank. From there it will be a major achievement to get on in two, let alone arrive anywhere close to the flagstick. If you miss on the right, and find yourself tangled up on the mound, it will be quite difficult to get your second close to the pin. And if you carry that big bunker and are short of the green, the slope of the ground may well take you back and down into the bunker.

Over the back of the green is a slight downslope, perhaps not severe enough to be considered any kind of a hazard, and the essential requirement here is to be straight and go for the middle back of the green. The hole is totally exposed to the weather, so give some thought to that, also to pin position and to your yardage. Above all remember: there is no alternative to being on if you want the par. The hole does make one meagre gesture towards the player. The green is slightly saucered, and will tend to gather the ball into the centre.

**What's in the name?**
Woe-be-tide tells you playfully to watch out, or the lurking waters of the Firth could be your downfall.

High mound protecting the right side of the green

Vast bunker to catch the ball falling short and to the right

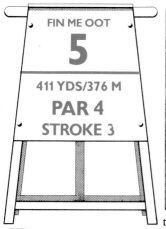

FIN ME OOT

# 5

411 YDS/376 M

## PAR 4

### STROKE 3

By contrast with the previous hole, the fifth runs along a lovely valley, sheltered on the left by that high sand ridge above Turnberry beach which runs a good mile or more all the way to the eighth. The fifth was originally a par 5, but for the Open Championship of 1977 the back tee was abandoned, a tee just over the mound from the fourth green was used, and the hole was reduced by some 70–80 yards to become a par 4. As a par 5 it required two straightforward shots up the fairway,

then a half-left turn and a pitch to an ample green. As a par 4, I think it is a rather better hole, with most of the emphasis on the second shot.

All along the left side of this hole, rising up the sand ridge, is heavy rough. Keep clear of this. The whole thrust of the design of the present hole will influence you to play down the right side all the way. And if there is wind from the sea, that will help force you right. I have to confess, however, that in the last round of the 1979 European Open I drove into the left rough,

advanced my second shot towards the green but still in the rough, and from there took a sand wedge and knocked the ball straight out, on to the green, and into the hole for a birdie! A birdie is a birdie at any time, but this is not the recommended route for the fifth hole.

Your driving line should be on the hut, up on the ridge by the 18th tee. There are two bunkers on the left side of the fairway, one at about 165 yards which is irrelevant and should not trouble you, another at around 215 yards which might. Keep to the right

of this bunker – there is ample fairway space. From that bunker, you are looking at a shot of some 170 yards to the centre of the green. The angle of approach for that shot is across the green (whereas the angle of the third shot when the hole was a par 5 was along the length of the green), and the front left has been closed off by two awkward little pot bunkers, nudging the putting surface, which must be carried.

There is a bunker at right front, rather wide, about 10 yards from the putting surface. Between that bunker and the two

Awkward pot-bunkers closing the front left

*Approach to the 5th green*

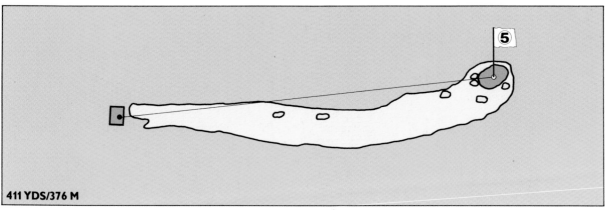

**411 YDS/376 M**

pots is a decent gap and it may be good tactics, if you are scared of making the carry, to target that space, then chip from there to the flag.

There is a substantial bunker 50 yards out, to the left, but I would think no longer really in play and another at the back right of the green, which is generously large. It slopes up from the front, levels off across the back half, and slopes down from the right through a flat central belly, then slightly up again on the left side. There is ample clear space through the green, which nestles in a huge arena or amphitheatre of sand dunes.

## What's in the name?
The 5th hole does not easily disclose its secrets, so: 'Find me out.'

Target area for those worried about carrying the bunkers

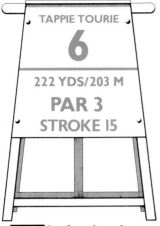

**TAPPIE TOURIE**

# 6

**222 YDS/203 M**

## PAR 3

### STROKE 15

The first thought you should have when you look at this hole, and the wisest decision you may make in the entire round, is to dub it a par 4 and play it accordingly. In harshness and severity it must rank with the 16th at Carnoustie. There is nowhere to go but the green, but you may find getting there very, very demanding.

The defences of the hole are threefold. First is the distance. A variety of tees can make it play anything from 190 yards to 250. You are playing across a valley to a green set into the sand ridge, and appreciably above you. Second are the fortifications – the bunkering, the slopes, the contours of the green and its surroundings. Third is the wind. If it is dead against, you must use a driver from the tee if you persist in thinking this can be a par 3; if from left to right, which is more or less prevailing, your shot will be drifted or thrown to the right, which is stiff with hazards, natural and man-made. So, by any judgment, you are facing a king-sized hole.

There is a very large bunker, set in the rough just left of a direct line, at 185 yards. Into a headwind it might well be in play. Short right of the green, on an upslope, there is a cavernous trap. Pitch in there, and you are likely to be plugged and have a fearsome task

to get out. The slope up to the green will gather any short shot towards that trap, and it will be a very difficult shot to advance the ball and to get it out and up to the green very much above the bunker. A little grassy swale to the left of the green was formerly a safety area, but that was sealed off by two tight, deep pot bunkers, put there for the Open Championship of 1977. So if you still insist that this is a par 3, there is virtually nowhere to go on Tappie Tourie but the putting surface.

The green is a decent size, sloping sharply up from the front to the centre, then only slightly up to the back. It slopes in to the centre from the left side, and if you were to carry the tee shot over and beyond the bunker, you could pitch slightly off the green, and see the ball break left, and on.

Pot-bunkers close the left side

*From the 6th Tee*

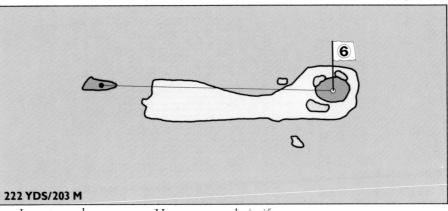

**222 YDS/203 M**

I must say, however, that if the weather conditions are against you or you have the slightest doubt about making the carry to the green, the sensible thing is to hit an iron shot to the bottom of the slope in front of the green, pitch up, look for a single putt but be well content with two.

However you do it, if you make three you can jump for joy. It is a very harsh golf hole.

## What's in the name?

A 'tourie' means a 'thing on top', such as a bobble on a cap, so the name probably calls for a 'hit to the top', ie the high green.

Playing from below that awesome bunker on the right

Cavernous bunker and steep slope protect the right

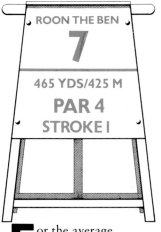

**ROON THE BEN**

**7**

**465 YDS/425 M**

**PAR 4**

**STROKE I**

For the average player, climbing up on this tee and surveying the prospect ahead, the first emotion could well be one of terror – and it would be entirely valid!

No matter what is said and written of the much-publicized and praised 9th and 10th tees, I suspect that this may be the most dramatic point in the course. High above the beach, the tee offers a stunning prospect, away to the left, of the wide Firth of Clyde, with islands and mountains and wheeling seabirds. But the hole itself surely dominates all. Falling away immediately in front of the tee is a tumbled broken valley with Wilson's Burn running through it. Beyond, the fairway starts and rises through a slight saddle in the dunes then dog-legs sharply to the left, continuing on up a long, rolling valley and climbing to a distant green. The initial carry over the valley is only some 150 yards, and to the saddle where the hole turns is perhaps little more than 200 yards. But it is the prospect that is disquieting.

So we should give it some sensible thought before we tackle it. Measured, I imagine very tightly, from the medal tee, it is listed at 465 yards, and you would do well, as at the previous hole, to make your own par – under almost any conditions call that five – and play the hole accordingly.

The first requirement is to drive up to and, if possible, over the saddle, the first decision whether or not you can carry or pass an evil bunker set in the left angle. It is 225 yards from the medal tee. There is space to the right of it, but if you should drive too far across the angle of the fairway, two bunkers on the far side, at 235 and 245 yards' range, will nail you. The rough inside the angle, and all along the left side, is very rough indeed. The left-hand bunker is penal, very large, very deep. If you are in that general area, you can call it a shot lost – all you can do is splash out of bunker or rough to the fairway, and still have 250 yards to go.

Position A from the tee might therefore be on or over the centre of the saddle, but not too far over, and if you can make that position with a 4-wood or a 3-iron, forget the driver. No matter where you find yourself here, the second shot will be a smash with the longest wood you have. In his final Open Championship round in 1977, having driven from the championship tee,

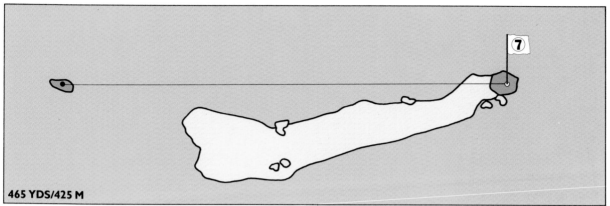

**465 YDS/425 M**

Tom Watson hit a driver from the fairway to make the green and a birdie, two astonishing blows.

This second shot demands some care and tactical thinking. About 150 yards on, some 100 yards from the green, is a bunker only just in the left rough, which perhaps should not be in play. There are two more by the green, slightly to the right and slightly short, amongst some mounds and slopes coming down from the right. The impression is of everything funnelling in towards the green. Beyond that bunker on the left is a very deep rough-strewn valley. Keep away. You could die down there and never be missed. If you are uncertain, make sure your shot goes right. You could be 50 yards wide to the right and still hit the green in three from light rough. The most sensible course for your second shot is aimed at the greenside bunkers, and short, whence you pitch on and make a relaxed five.

There is a good deal of movement in the back half of the green, with positive contouring. The front half is easier to putt, so pin position and some extra concentration on the green are important. Conservative positional play is the key to success on this hole. By all means make a birdie if you can, but do not seek to emulate Mr Watson on the second shot.

**What's in the name?**
'Round the mountain' is the intended drift here, not that you will need the attentions of a Strathclyde sanatorium.

Left:
Breathtaking view
of the fairway

Target area for the safety shot, but still a long way to go

Bunker and dangerous rough
on the left

More bunkers on the right

*The 7th Fairway*

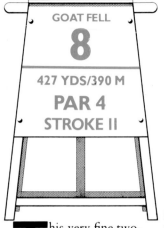

GOAT FELL
**8**
427 YDS/390 M
**PAR 4**
**STROKE 11**

This very fine two-shot hole presents a drive completely dominated by one single fairway bunker. This is the last of the set of holes screened on the left by the long sand ridge above the beach, and the entire fairway slopes down from it, from the left, as though pointing everything towards that solitary bunker. It is beautifully placed, 250 yards out from the medal tee, and some 10–15 yards in from the edge of the rough.

For a professional or first-class amateur, particularly downwind, the plan would be to carry that bunker, or at least get past it, for the best possible sight of the green. Without being a dog-leg, the hole does turn slightly to the left. The average player will probably not reach the bunker, so his plan should be to drive along the left side, even marginally off the fairway, since the contouring, even from the light rough, will bring the ball back down into play.

The second shot can

Closer in to the green, showing the treacherous left-hand bunker

Bunker and general danger area

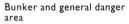

2nd shot at the 8th

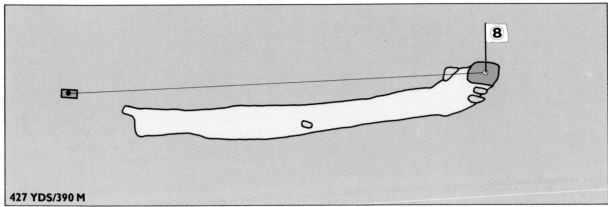

**427 YDS/390 M**

be deceptive. There is quite a large valley of 'dead' ground in front of the green which is set up high, and goes right back to the edge of a cliff. On the second shot, I would be inclined to take a club and a half, or even two clubs, more than you think at first glance, since you then have a chance to chase or scuffle the ball through the valley and up the slope to the green. Two large bunkers are set into the face of a big sand dune at the right front of the green, and there is one deep bunker 20 yards short on the left. The general area of that bunker is very dangerous – miss or be short if you must, but again favour the right side. The green is quite ample, with a slight ridge through it.

You will be asked for two big shots on this hole, quite possibly two woods, but it is an honest, open hole, asking only for honest, straightforward shot-making.

Dead ground makes distance deceptive

### What's in the name?

Goat Fell takes its name from the tallest peak on the Island of Arran, across the Firth to the north-west.

# Turnberry

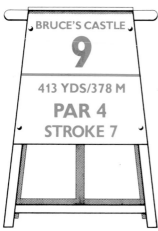

**BRUCE'S CASTLE**

**9**

413 YDS/378 M

**PAR 4**

**STROKE 7**

**T**he most photographed of all Turnberry's delights, and one of the most photographed tees in golf, the championship tee of the ninth hole on the Ailsa course, perched out on a rocky promontory of cliff with sheer drops of 50 feet or more to the shore below, is a paradox, and possibly a fraud. Mackenzie Ross, the architect of Ailsa, designed the hole to be played from the medal tee, and this championship tee, behind and slightly below, came later. It is entirely spectacular and marvellously theatrical, but the visual effects may not have much bearing on how you play the hole.

By all means, if you do not suffer from vertigo, stand on it and enjoy the prospect, and if you feel particularly resolute and indomitable at the time, by all means play from it. You will see very little of the fairway. You will be obliged to carry the best part of 200 yards, over an inlet of the sea, to a stone cairn marker set on the rise opposite. Put your faith in your Maker, the marker, and your swing, and go for it. If you are a long hitter, aim 10 yards left of the marker to get to the left side of the fairway, where the lighthouse will loom above you, and you will discover there an open shot to the green.

From the medal tee your carry will be some 150 yards to the marker, your line directly on it. You may see only the top of the flagstick from the tee, and the absolutely perfect line is on the war memorial behind the green.

There is a lot of movement in this fairway – some players believe too much – and it is not much more than 20 yards wide at its

The view from the medal tee

*From the Championship Tee at the 9th*

168

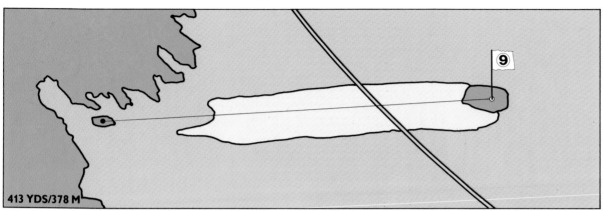

413 YDS/378 M

narrowest. Your ball can be rather thrown about. If you hook badly left of line, you can be in troublesome rough. Slice to the right, and there is even more trouble with the ground falling away From that side you will be blocked off from the green by some mounds protecting it on the right front – again Mackenzie Ross has produced a stiff, well-protected hole without using one single bunker.

The shot to the green, then, should come in from the left. From that direction you have a very reasonable target:

the green, if slightly narrow, is the best part of 45 yards long. The real challenge of the hole is the drive, and the anguish you may feel on the tee. You can overstress this to yourself. A positive, correct, firm strike at the ball from the tee, and you have broken the back of the hole.

## What's in the name?

**Bruce is Robert the Bruce, Scottish king from 1306–29. Remains of his castle lie between the 8th green and the 9th tee.**

The undefended green

War memorial behind the green

200 yards to the stone cairn

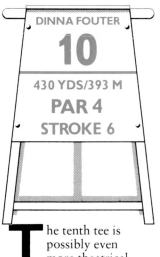

**DINNA FOUTER**

# 10

**430 YDS/393 M**

**PAR 4**

**STROKE 6**

The fairway, the bay and the Ayrshire hills

The tenth tee is possibly even more theatrical than the ninth. Before you lie the now familiar seascapes to the west and north, the lighthouse, the familiar symbol of Turnberry just behind, the ripe, rolling hillsides of South Ayrshire ahead, while beneath you, rolling round a bay of rocks and sand, is the marvellous tenth hole. It sweeps round what looks like a great semi-circle, with every hazard in view.

In the driving area, there are no fairway bunkers, giving ample

*From the Fairway Bunker at the 10th*

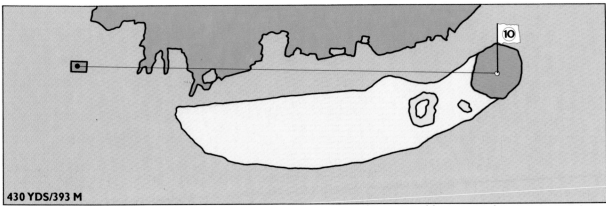

**430 YDS/393 M**

space to manoeuvre. All you need to decide is how closely you dare skirt the left side, and the beach, with your tee shot. As on so many other holes on the Ailsa, the architecture and the ground indicate that you should play to the right.

Dominating the hole visually, and certainly compromising the second shot, is a massive circular fairway bunker that fills almost the entire width of the fairway, with an 'island' of grass in the centre. Here more than anywhere is demonstrated a famous Ailsa signature – the 'bearded' or 'whiskered'

bunker, the long marram grass left growing round the fringes and giving that effect. This bunker is 25 yards from front to back. The back is 65 yards from the centre of the green, so you must seek to dismiss it completely by flying your second shot over it.

Since the best access to this green is from the right, another smaller bunker is set strategically beyond the big one, to defend that right side. But it is still 40 yards from the centre of the green, 20 yards from the front edge, so you have a margin there for your second shot.

Your biggest problem on this hole may well be this second shot, and the psychological block you may have in looking ahead to the bunkers and contemplating what you can do about them. Force yourself to ignore them and hit a full shot to the green. You could pitch as much as 20 yards short and run on. The green is very big. If you have driven anywhere on the left side of the fairway, you must shoot your second at the right half of the green. The green will be kind to you except on the left, where there is a rather quick slope down into

rough grass. So trend to the right, and let fly boldly at the green, even if you have a 4- or 5-wood. Don't worry about going past the flag. This is a hole where you must venture bravely if you are to succeed.

### What's in the name?
'Don't mess about' is the firm instruction for this hole, particularly when going for the green.

Ground slopes away to the left

Bunker defending the right-side approach

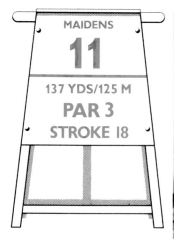

**MAIDENS**

**11**

**137 YDS/125 M**

**PAR 3**

**STROKE 18**

This is the last of that incomparable run of seaward holes which started back at the fourth. Again, it is worth having a look at the championship tee, a pulpit perched on a rocky outcrop rather like the back tee at the ninth, with the same wonderful vistas surrounding you. To the south, you look across the vast fields of gorse encompassing the Arran course to the Turnberry Hotel, with its dazzling white walls and red tiles, stretched along the ridge that overlooks the entire property.

The medal tee is 137 yards, the championship tee 40 yards further back, and if I were you, I would play the hole from the latter. It makes it much more challenging, particularly if you find yourself hitting into wind. From the medal tee, the hole is obviously just a short pop.

'Maidens' is a delightful and very attractive short hole. The green is reasonable in size for a par 3, with a good deal of width. There is one long bunker which closes off most of the left half at the front, and two more covering the right, centre and

back, but towards the right front of the green you have a good entrance, and on this hole you must certainly expect to make par, and have a fair shot at a birdie. The important thing to be sure of here is that you select the right club for the prevailing conditions.

The green is set just in front of a quarry, and many people believe it should be set further back, more into the quarry. I daresay that might make for greenkeeping problems, and I for one am content with things as they are. I see no reason to fiddle about with a very pretty and very friendly short hole.

Large bunker closing off the left side of the green

*The 11th Green*

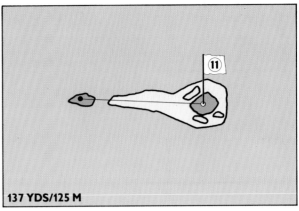

**137 YDS/125 M**

A panoramic view from the tee

### What's in the name?
Local geography is the key: Maidens is the village to the north of the course.

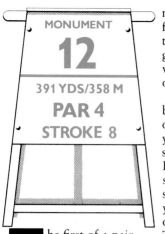

MONUMENT

## 12

### 391 YDS/358 M

## PAR 4

### STROKE 8

The first of a pair of holes which by Turnberry standards are flat, and form a respite from the preceding three or four holes and a breather before the big finish to come, the 12th is a straight par 4 down a fairly narrow fairway. I find it a rather oddly designed hole, and have the feeling that it has not quite kept pace with the modern game and the first-class player, as has the Ailsa course in general. That may not worry the average player overmuch.

There is a pair of bunkers on the left side of the fairway at 175–180 yards which normally should not be in play. Beyond them on the same side is a good-sized bunker at 250 yards which will be out of range for most Turnberry players and in certain conditions would be difficult even for professionals to reach. The right side of the fairway is completely unprotected. This you must use to your advantage by making the right half your destination from the tee. The driving line should be to the right of that first pair of bunkers, and perhaps slightly left of

The defences around the green

the monument on the hill above and to the right of the green.

Along that right side is a good 10 yards of light rough, and even at the height of summer growth, it should allow you a decent shot out of it. In fact if the 12th tee were placed up on the plateau above the 11th green, as some have

Watch for subtle borrows on this green

*2nd shot at the 12th*

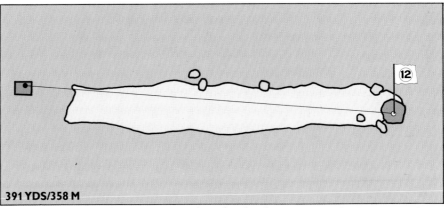

**391 YDS/358 M**

suggested, it would add only some 25 yards to the hole, maintain it as a par 4 and make the drive into a more pronounced dog-leg to the left. If this were done, the present bunkering might have to move, and on the right new bunkers, or better still a stretch of gorse bushes, would have to be considered, at around 220–250 yards. This I think would make it a much more dramatic hole.

The present approach to the green, from that right side, is defended inevitably by a bunker 30 yards short, and a secondary bunker close by the right front of the green. The other bunker you see 30 yards short on the left is so wide as to be of no great consequence. From a point level with the second left-side fairway bunker, you will be exactly 200 yards from the centre of the green, so even with your best drive, you will be looking for a healthy hit with your second.

The green is built up, with a dip then a slope up to the front, and the important thing is to have enough club to get you there. Be quite sure of your yardage and your club selection, and try to be past the pin – behind the green is a slight rise which should stop the long shot. The green slopes slightly left to right, and extra care is needed when putting. This green does have some quite subtle borrows.

## What's in the name?
The Monument on the hill above the green commemorates the airmen of two world wars stationed at Turnberry.

Target area for the drive to the right of the fairway

**TICKLY TAP**

# 13

### 379 YDS/346 M
## PAR 4
### STROKE 14

This hole is rather an odd-man-out on the Ailsa in that it is quite flat, and is a drive and a short pitch, one of the shortest par-4 holes on the course. It is dominated by a grassy hollow and a ridge on the right, which contains a lusty bunker, some 225 yards out, at the angle of the right dog-leg. There is ample fairway space to the left here, as much as 50 yards in places as it swings round to the right, and beyond the angle, about 280 yards out, is another substantial bunker, this

Target area for the drive inside the left-hand bunker

No bunkers around the green but a difficult surface to hold

2nd shot at the 13th

**379 YDS/346 M**

one edging into the left fairway.

You must obviously play to the left of that right-side bunker, and your aiming point might well be the more distant trap, on the left. But what must concern you most on this tee are the ground conditions – wet or dry, slow or fast – and the overhead conditions, particularly the wind. If you play the hole in summer, with hard ground and down a stiff breeze from the north-west, your ball may skip all the way to that left bunker. At any time of the year, you must avoid the rough on the right.

From the right-hand bunker to the centre of the green is 145 yards. From the left-hand bunker to the centre of the green is 100 yards, so some kind of pitch shot is on. The green is free of all bunkering. It is in fact a plateau, raised some three feet above what looks like a plain level fairway. You can see all of the green save the far left-hand corner, and the whole thing is flat, possibly just sloping away from you fractionally. However, the defences are there, even if they are subtle and not obvious. There is a slight dip in front

of the green and a sharp rise up to the putting surface. And the green is set diagonally across the shot, from 4 o'clock to 10 o'clock. All of this, particularly downwind, with nothing much at the back to check the ball, makes this approach shot testing, and perhaps rather difficult to stop. You might even consider under-clubbing slightly.

### What's in the name?

A subtle hole, most of all at the approach to the green where you will be faced with a 'tricky little hit'.

The green has some subtle borrows

Ridge and bunker at 225 yards

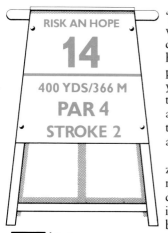

RISK AN HOPE

# 14

### 400 YDS/366 M

## PAR 4

### STROKE 2

This is very probably the most extreme par 4 on the course, and you would do well to 'hope' rather more than you 'risk'. Into any kind of wind at all, it will demand two very fine hits, even from a professional, so before you pull anything out of the bag on this tee, accept that you are about to play a par 5 hole, or, at best, a par 4.5.

In the short driving zone, the fairway is very narrow. In the long driving zone, the fairway is also very narrow. In between there is a reasonable sector of friendly space. Dominating the drive, 150 yards from the tee, is a bunker on the left and a solid mass of gorse on the right. The gap between is little more than 15 yards, and you must get through there, or over it. Beyond that gap the fairway spreads itself nicely, but from about 220 yards on, it shrinks again to about 20 yards across. Through the original gap, especially towards the right half, there is a flat area and that is where you must be. The rough on the right side of this hole can be quite punishing.

The green – it looks miles away – is strongly defended centre-right and centre-left by particularly strong, deep bunkers. An exceptionally big fairway trap covers the centre-left of the green. It is a good 10 yards deep from front to back, and leaves only some 10 yards from its back point to the edge of the putting surface. Into wind, you will be well advised to – and may have to – play short of it with your second, then pitch over it. Even in still air you will want a very fine second shot to carry it. And if you have persuaded yourself that you are really playing a par 5, I suggest you hit your second shot on the

line of the right-hand bunker, to be just short of it. Then you will have an open third into the green, and may make it with one putt for a 'birdie'.

The green is large and wide and slopes towards you, so if your shot to the green is to be your third, then you have plenty of room in which to work and get it fairly close to the pin.

**400 YDS/366 M**

## What's in the name?

This hole is true to its daunting label, for your first two hits must be both bold and very good.

Deep bunkers protect the green on both the left and right sides

*2nd shot at the 14th*

Narrow fairway

Punishing rough on the right

Left:
A view from the tee showing the bunker at 150 yards

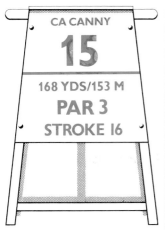

CA CANNY

# 15

168 YDS/153 M

## PAR 3

### STROKE 16

**C**a' Canny is the perfect example of a very demanding, and punishing, short hole. As the professionals say, there is 'nowhere to miss', nowhere but the green to be if you are to avoid serious trouble.

From the medal tee it plays at 168 yards – from the championship tee more than 200 – and into a strong headwind you may well need anything up to and including a driver. Wind and weather conditions again can be decisive here. The green is set into a sand dune which overlooks it slightly at the left side and the back, but in practical terms the green is unsheltered. There is a very sharp and steep slope to the right, plunging down towards the 8th fairway in a good 30-foot drop. There is no usable ground between tee and green, unless you care for an ocean of heather, and the hole demands a shot carried all the way to the putting surface. Finally, there are three very deep bunkers all along the left side, and the last of the 'Ca' Canny' ramparts is another deep trap, positioned front-right at the top of the downslope, and put in specifically for the 1977

*The 15th Green*

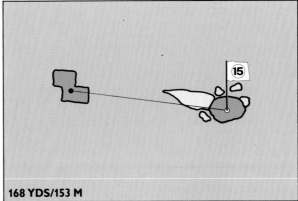

**168 YDS/153 M**

The two deep bunkers
at the front of the green

Open Championship.

It immediately became a controversial bunker. Many contended that in a championship a loose shot could be held by it, whereas if it wasn't there the ball would kick far down the slope into rough ground. They suggested that such is the skill of the modern professional playing from sand that a bunker shot would be that much easier for him than trying to recover from rough 30 feet below the putting surface. They were probably right. The severity of this slope will certainly take the ball all the way to the bottom, and that usually means

The middle of the green is the
only place to go

an instant four.

The green is 35 yards from front to back and reasonably wide. It helps you a little from the left side, taking the ball into the centre, and also slopes up towards the back, which will help hold the shot. But you will get little else in the way of help from this hole, and the main object is simply to hit confidently for the middle of the green – and get there.

**What's in the name?**

'Take care' is the watchword. Any error at the 15th comes in for heavy punishment.

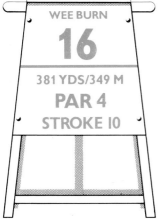

WEE BURN
# 16
381 YDS/349 M
## PAR 4
STROKE 10

**A**pleasant little hole for the professionals, who would consider it no more than a 'drive and a flick' in normal circumstances, but a fearful hole for the average player. In fact fear, the fear that Wilson's Burn puts into the mind of the player, is the real and only defence of this hole.

There is one bunker set into the left side of the fairway, just over 200 yards out. Then there is the burn. No one now seems to know who Wilson was, but his burn

runs along the bottom of a ravine which crosses the front of the green. The burn itself is not particularly deep, but the ravine is, with rather steep sides. It has the same effect as the rather

more famous Swilcan Burn at the first hole of the Old Course – it is there, and it has to be crossed. Anything over-short can dribble down the near bank and into the water. Anything that

carries the burn but is not positively 'up' on the green, will dribble back down the far bank, and into the water. Although it is a substantial physical barrier, the problem for the player is

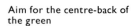

Aim for the centre-back of the green

*The 16th Green and Wilson's Burn*

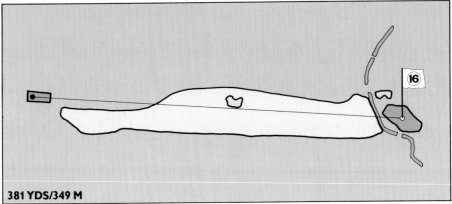

**381 YDS/349 M**

The ravine in front
of the green
is a daunting prospect

psychological – created
by the prospect and the
possibilities in the
terrain rather than by the
terrain itself.

The bunker on the
left is reachable, so keep
right from the tee. The
best driving line would
be on the dome-shaped
shelter you see beyond
the 17th tee. The rough
on the left can be quite
strong. Keep away from
this side. You can miss
by miles on the right,
and still have a shot at
the green, even if you go
all the way wide to the
7th fairway.

There are sand hills to
the left of, and behind,
the green, which is quite
large and a good 35
yards from front to back.
On this hole, you can see
everything before you,
see the green from the
tee. The key is the
second shot. If the
flagstick is cut near the
front, close to the
downslope into the burn,
don't be too clever – hit
a full shot with whatever
club you decide is
needed to get to the
back-centre of the green
and rely on a two-putt
par. If you are
downwind, that is, with
a northerly wind, you
might have a
straightforward short
pitch to this green. If
you are into wind (a
southerly), you might
well need a second wood.
And if you are not
entirely certain, for any
reason, that you can
make the carry, do not
force it. Lay up short of
the burn in two, and
think of a little pitch
over – and why not think
positively then of a
single putt? But if you
do not make par here do
not grieve – it is not all
that easy, and the next
hole should console you.

## What's in the name?

The 'little burn' or
stream is Wilson's Burn –
not so wee when you
have to carry it or suffer
the consequences.

Approach shot must carry this
bank or the ball will run back
into the burn

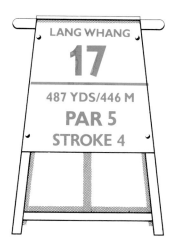

LANG WHANG
**17**
487 YDS/446 M
**PAR 5**
STROKE 4

Lang Whang is yet another Ailsa hole which essentially uses the terrain and its natural contours more than man-made hazards. The second par 5 on the course, the only one on this inward half, it can look a good deal more intimidating than it really is.

A high sand ridge runs along most of the left side. To the right, another broken mass of sand dunes reaches over towards the sixth green. These sand hills almost but not quite join in front of the 17th tee, leaving a gap and a path

along which we reach the fairway proper. The view from the tee, across the bridge from the 16th green, lets us see only a slice of the left half of the fairway. Immediately in front of the tee, falling beneath us, Wilson's Burn in its deep valley winds away across the 7th fairway to the sea. Since the 17th tee seems high above all this, you may feel unprotected and friendless as you stand there and look towards the green. But don't be downcast – the gap ahead of you is a carry of only 100 yards and beyond it is a valley of

fairway as wide as you could wish.

In this great expanse of fairway is one bunker, to the right, at 265 yards. It is so far and so wide that you can forget it. The next fairway bunker you see, ahead of you, is the key point of the entire hole. At 375 yards, a high, strong ridge comes in from the right, narrowing down the fairway to a tight 20 yards or so. The bunker is set in the end face of this ridge, squeezing the fairway into an uphill gap; it then becomes narrow, level or slightly uphill, all the way to the

*The bunker in the end of the ridge and the narrow uphill fairway*

green. If you get off a good drive, say 225 yards, you will then be 150 yards from that bunker, which in turn is 100 yards from the green.

The bunker in question might, incidentally, make a good driving line. There are no hazards behind it, save an uneven, rolling, rather up-and-down stretch of fairway. Before you get into your second shot would be a good moment to stop and think what you are

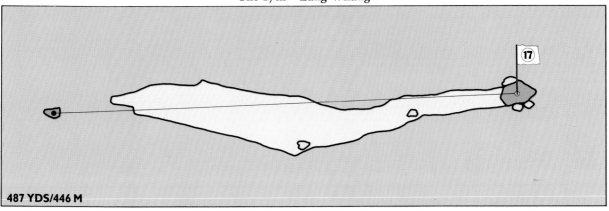

**487 YDS/446 M**

*The 17th Fairway*

Fairway narrows to 20 yards

Bunker set in the face of the high ridge

about. The next critical factor is the green, strongly protected by one big trap on the left, and two on the right, but with a very open front. It is of medium width, but quite long – 35 yards. So you have a fair chance of hitting and holding it with a third shot.

The 17th is, I feel, an attractive hole for the average player who should be confident of making par if he is thinking rationally. But the real examination is on the second shot – how that key bunker and its narrow, uphill gap are played. The prevailing wind will be against you, and into wind you might think it sensible to be just short of it, reaching the bottom of the slope in two, then making a longish pitch to the green from there. Downwind, you may well decide that you can ignore it and fly the ball well past it. Such are the fascinating dilemmas posed here by terrain and weather.

## What's in the name?
A 'good whack' is called for here, to set yourself a reasonable chance of making the green in three.

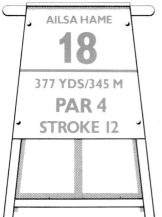

AILSA HAME
## 18
377 YDS/345 M
## PAR 4
STROKE 12

**A**lmost there. Almost finished with the Ailsa – but not quite. The red tops and white walls of the Dormy House and the Turnberry Hotel may give you thoughts of other pleasures, but there is still a furlong or two to go.

Stand on the medal tee of the 18th and you may feel the last pangs of Ailsa terror, such as you felt at the 7th or the 9th, for you are on top of the sweeping ridge which forms an amphitheatre around the 5th green, beneath you to the right. And you are facing a tee shot across a sector of that ridge, presenting in front of you what looks like a wall of heather and rough, with a path to the Dormy House running along the top.

Fortunately, the carry over that lot is no more than 100 yards and you are playing a hole which is honest and open, a perfectly pleasant finishing hole with everything in view before you. For the Open Championship and major professional tournaments, the 18th tee of the Arran course,

Uneven fairway but no other greenside hazards

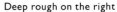
Deep rough on the right

*The 18th Green and the Turnberry Hotel*

# The 18th – Ailsa Hame

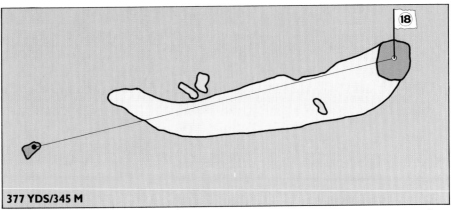

**377 YDS/345 M**

Putting out – a view from the left back of the green

off to the left beyond the 17th green, is used to make the Ailsa home hole a dog-leg, but I must say I think the hole played straight from the medal tee is no less attractive.

A pair of bunkers is set in the left rough covering the range 165–185 yards and I would expect you to pass them to the right. A distant bunker, 300 yards out on the right, should not be in play, but it makes a good driving line from the medal tee. Perhaps the greatest danger on this hole is a very heavy bank of gorse along the right side, quite close to the fairway and running from about 175 yards almost all the way to the

green. Keep clear. Get yourself in there and you are likely to be stone-dead.

The fairway is quite generous. The final 80 yards or so from that distant bunker to the green is uneven, an area of humps and hollows, but there are no greenside sand hazards. There are some swales around most of the green which might make short chip shots slightly tricky if you miss the green, but even from one of your less-than-perfect drives, you might reasonably be thinking of reaching this green, and making the par. It is in truth an inviting green to hit to, and if you were required to

make four to win on this hole, even for something as serious as a monthly medal, I'm sure you would feel that it was not impossible.

The Ailsa's 'big finish' is really holes 14–17, and this gentle last hole is just the kind of thing to send you off thinking that, on one of the world's finest golf courses, perhaps you didn't do too badly after all.

## What's in the name?

The home hole on the Ailsa course – open and straightforward just so long as you don't rush it.

# Turnberry

The Ailsa Course of the Turnberry Hotel must now be considered with Royal Troon as the classic West of Scotland Open Championship venue. Although it had staged professional events, including the Match Play Championship, and an Amateur Championship and Walker Cup matches, it was not until 1977 that it became an 'Open' course. In the event, it produced one of the most dramatic of all Open Championships – Tom Watson and Jack Nicklaus battled each other with brilliant stroke-making until Watson prevailed by only one stroke with a record aggregate score.

### Course Record (Ailsa Course)
63 Mark Hayes (USA)
(Open Championship 1977)

### Open Championship
1977 Tom Watson (USA) 268

### Double Diamond World of Golf Classic
1975 The Americas

### European Open
1979 Sandy Lyle 275

### PGA Club Professionals' Championship
1980 David Jagger 286

### PGA Match Play Championship
1957 Christy O'Connor (Ireland)    1960 Eric Brown
1963 David Thomas

### John Player Classic
1972 Bob Charles (New Zealand) 285    1973 Charles Coody (USA) 289

### Amateur Championship
1961 M F Bonallack

### Walker Cup
1963 GB 8    USA 12
(Four matches halved)

### Home Internationals
1960 England

### Ladies' Amateur Championship
1912 Miss G Ravenscroft    1921 Miss C Leitch    1937 Miss J Anderson

Left: Miss Cecil Leitch, four times winner of the Ladies' Amateur Championship and winner at Turnberry in 1921

Top left: Michael Bonallack, winner of the 1961 Amateur
Championship at Turnberry, with his wife Angela who was the
beaten finalist in the Ladies' Amateur Championship at Royal
Birkdale the following year. Right: Deane Beman (USA) chipping
to the 16th green during the 1963 Walker Cup match.
Above: David Thomas, 1963 PGA Match Play Champion

Above and right: Gale force winds tore up the tented village
at the 1973 John Player Classic but order was restored and
Charles Coody took the trophy

# Turnberry

Top: The 5th green during the 1977 Open. Above: Tom Watson and Jack Nicklaus who played almost stroke for stroke through all four rounds. Left: Tom Watson the 1977 Open Champion. Right: Sandy Lyle, winner of the 1979 European Open, is presented with the trophy by 1978 winner Bobby Wadkins

**Playing the course** Guests of the Turnberry Hotel have preferential rates and exclusive access to the tee at certain times, but otherwise the course, like its partner the Arran, is open to everyone. These courses can be very busy in season, and advance reservations are recommended. These can be booked directly through Golf Course Reservation at Turnberry Hotel, Maidens Road, Turnberry, Girvan, Strathclyde KA26 9LT, tel Turnberry (06553) 202, or through the professional's shop at Turnberry, tel Turnberry (06553) 370. There are no restrictions on ladies' play.

**Adjoining course** The Arran, laid out 'inside' the bigger Ailsa course, is rather less dramatic, without the seascapes and tumbling dunes of the Ailsa, but providing a tight test between avenues of gorse.
Arran 6276 yards   SSS 70.

**Recommended courses in the surrounding area** The local course at Girvan (5 miles) is open and sporty, if short, and the Troon-Prestwick courses are within comfortable reach – Royal Troon, Prestwick, Western Gailes, Glasgow Gailes and the Kilmarnock GC at Barassie are particularly recommended.
Girvan GC, Municipal Golf Course Road, Girvan, Strathclyde;
tel Girvan (0465) 4272.
Royal Troon GC, Troon, Strathclyde; tel Troon (0292) 311555.
Prestwick GC, Links Road, Prestwick, Strathclyde; tel Prestwick (0292) 77404.
Western Gailes GC, Gailes, Strathclyde; tel Irvine (0294) 311357.
Glasgow Gailes GC, Gailes, Strathclyde; tel Irvine (0294) 311347.
Kilmarnock GC (Barassie), Barassie, Troon, Strathclyde; tel Troon (0292) 311077.

**Where to stay** Turnberry Hotel can provide all of man's wants and needs, and there is more inexpensive accommodation at the Dormy House. The Caledonian Hotel in Ayr would be a good central point for all courses in this region.
Turnberry Hotel, Maidens Road, Turnberry, Girvan, Strathclyde KA26 9LT;
tel Turnberry (06553) 202.
King's Arms, Dalrymple Street, Girvan, Strathclyde; tel Girvan (0465) 3322.
Caledonian Hotel, Ayr, Strathclyde; tel Ayr (0292) 69331, telex 76357.
Savoy Park Hotel, Ayr, Strathclyde; tel Ayr (0292) 66112/63469.

# MUIRFIELD

## Muirfield

'The Honourable Company of Edinburgh Golfers' – what a marvellous title, with a grand medieval ring to it. Such grandeur is appropriate, because the Honourable Company, which owns the course at Muirfield, played a critical part in the creation of golf as an organized sport, and is generally accepted as the oldest golf club in the world, dating from 1744.

Perhaps inevitably, the Scots being as they are, this is disputed, principally perhaps by the Royal Burgess club on the other side of Edinburgh, but on the basis of continuously documented records the claim of the Hon Coy is sound. It was in existence ten years before the Royal and Ancient, and the Society of St Andrews Golfers.

A spectacular part of the course considered by many to be the finest championship course in Britain

# Introduction

What the Hon Coy did beyond any dispute was to formulate the first regulations for playing the game, now widely known as 'The 13 Articles'. This 1744 code was adopted almost word for word when St Andrews drew up its rules a decade later, and they still form the basis of the present body of rules.

So when you step into the spacious, comfortable clubhouse at Muirfield, you step into golfing history. The solid red sandstone encloses centuries of golfing memorabilia, including portraits of past captains (and powerful Scottish personalities they all seem to have been), plans of the evolution of the course, and the club's fine old silver.

Like all such aged institutions, the club has seen good times and bad, has been rich and poor. It started when 'several Gentlemen of Honour, skilful in the ancient and healthful exercise of golf' petitioned the City of Edinburgh to provide a silver club for annual competition on the links of Leith (five holes) in the spring of 1744. To their credit the City Fathers obliged, and the 4th 'silver club' was presented to the club in 1980.

By 1836, the links of Leith, which were public land, had become too crowded and the club moved to Musselburgh. In 1891 it moved further away from Edinburgh to a piece of ground near Gullane which Andrew Kirkcaldy, as caustic of tongue as he was skilled at 'the golf', dubbed 'an auld watter meadie' (an old water meadow). With

the spread of the railway system came a branch line to Gullane, leaving a stroll of some three-quarters of a mile to the course, and the members were able to disregard the distance from Edinburgh. Only one year later, they were able to stage an Open Championship, won by Harold Hilton.

'Bench and bar' were strongly represented in the membership in the early years; the notables of Scottish law are much in evidence in the original records, and that trend persists. The club has always favoured matches and wagers, holding that the man-to-man match, or at least foursomes play, is the true essence of the game. The Hon Coy does not much fancy par and bogey, it has no need for a professional or professional's shop, using instead the services of the professional from neighbouring Gullane.

The course itself is something of a marvel. When you stand in front of the clubhouse, the property lies before you in splendour – spacious yet strangely private, with everything open to be seen. It is all very different from the King's

Course at Gleneagles, where every fairway is secluded from its neighbour. Save for a few houses set well back from the first fairway, on the left side, the course is not overlooked at any point. With Portmarnock (1893), it was one of the earliest courses in the world to use the design concept of two loops of nine, running contra to each other. Muirfield is clearly the gem of that wondrous East Lothian golfing coast, and many eminent golfers, not the least of them Jack Nicklaus, hold it to be the best and fairest test of all the championship courses of these islands.

If there is one outstanding feature of this course, it is the bunkering. The three par-five holes are quite magnificent. There is a healthy blending of long and medium par fours and all the short holes are testing. Everywhere the bunkering is subtle, devious, menacing, and often quite penal.

In the driving zones, and in the angles of the dog-leg holes, the bunkers compromise the drives quite specifically. It is a platitude to say that to play well you

THE HONOURABLE COMPANY OF EDINBURGH GOLFERS

**MUIRFIELD CHAMPIONSHIP TEES**

| hole | metres | yards | score |
|---|---|---|---|
| 1 | 411 | 449 | |
| 2 | 319 | 349 | |
| 3 | 346 | 379 | |
| 4 | 165 | 181 | |
| 5 | 510 | 558 | |
| 6 | 431 | 471 | |
| 7 | 169 | 185 | |
| 8 | 406 | 444 | |
| 9 | 452 | 495 | |
| OUT | 3209 | 3511 | |

| hole | metres | yards | score |
|---|---|---|---|
| 10 | 434 | 475 | |
| 11 | 353 | 386 | |
| 12 | 348 | 381 | |
| 13 | 140 | 153 | |
| 14 | 409 | 447 | |
| 15 | 362 | 396 | |
| 16 | 172 | 188 | |
| 17 | 496 | 542 | |
| 18 | 409 | 447 | |
| IN | 3123 | 3415 | |
| OUT | 3209 | 3511 | |
| TOTAL | 6332 | 6926 | |

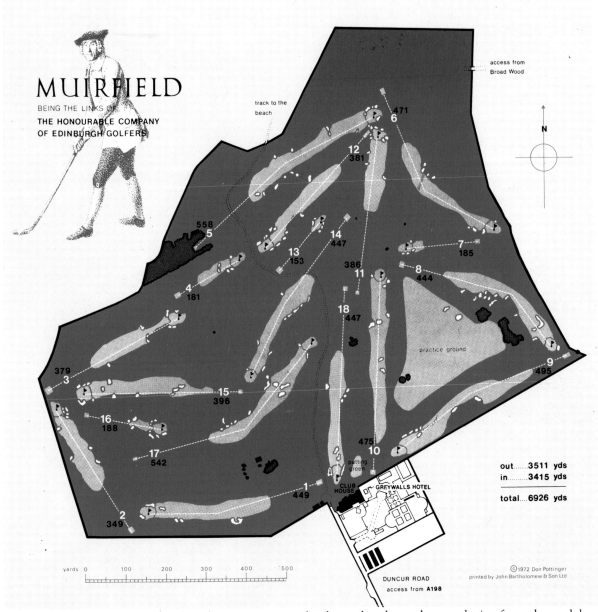

MUIRFIELD

BEING THE LINKS OF

THE HONOURABLE COMPANY
OF EDINBURGH GOLFERS

track to the beach

access from Broad Wood

6 471

12 381

5 558

13 153

14 447

7 185

11 386

8 444

4 181

18 447

practice ground

3 379

9 495

15 396

16 188

17 542

475

10

1 449

putting green

2 349

CLUB HOUSE

GREYWALLS HOTEL

| out | 3511 yds |
| in | 3415 yds |
| total | 6926 yds |

yards 0 100 200 300 400 500

DUNCUR ROAD

access from A198

© 1972 Don Pottinger
printed by John Bartholomew & Son Ltd

must drive well – that should apply to every golf course. But at Muirfield there are none of the margins which you might find at St Andrews or even occasionally at Carnoustie. Muirfield is a driver's course. They say that Henry Cotton, in winning the 1948 Open Championship, missed

Left: A view inland and to the south

only four fairways in 72 holes, and Jack Nicklaus in 1966 seldom used a driver in order to hold his shot in prescribed positions. The greenside bunkering and comple-mentary slopes are major hazards at Muirfield, and one characteristic which should be early apparent is the pair of fairway

bunkers, placed anywhere from 30 to 80 yards short of the green, used on so many holes.

Muirfield is hallowed ground as much as is St Andrews. It has produced such Open Champions as Vardon, Braid, Hagen, Cotton, Player, Nicklaus, Trevino and Watson. Yet for the average player,

playing from the medal tees, there is great pleasure and a good deal of success to be found. No water, no trees, no crippling carries – the course is fair and open to all who play sensibly and well, and who bring to it the respect it merits and demands.

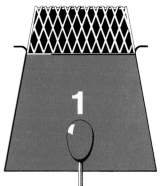

## 444YDS 406M PAR 4

The long bunker at the front right of the green threatens any approach from that side

This is the most difficult opening hole of any of the great Scottish links courses, a very severe test which only underlines the fact that you should be properly warmed up before you tackle Muirfield. The hole is flat, running to the west, and the fairway is narrow. There is a very large C-shaped bunker to the left, on the edge of the fairway, extending from 202 to 230 yards out from the tee. You cannot quite see all of it from the tee, but it is quite driveable for the average player, and into a strong wind would still be in play for the professionals.

Thus the drive is tricky. The hole seems to tend to the left, then angles back slightly to the right. The actual teeing ground gives the impression of being aimed to the right of the line, so make quite sure of your alignment – it is very easy to aim off to the right without quite realizing it, and be in the rough. Check the quality of that rough – there are no bunkers on the right side of this fairway, and if the rough is light, it is better to be there than in that left-hand bunker. If you are in the

Two bunkers in the short rough

Large bunker at 200–230 yards must be avoided at all costs

2nd shot at the 1st

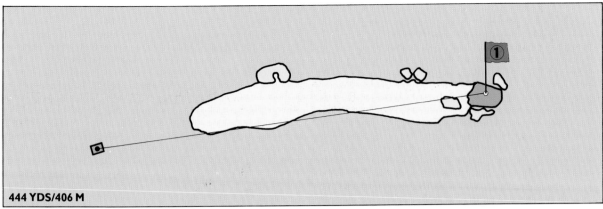

**444 YDS/406 M**

bunker, you are dead in terms of making any kind of score on this hole, so, ideally, be in the fairway to the right of it. Beyond the bunker, the fairway narrows. The further you drive, the narrower the fairway becomes until, at about 300 yards, it broadens again.

No matter how well the average player drives, he will be facing a long and difficult second shot. Against a rather strong wind, I have hit two of my best shots and still not reached the green. The back point of that bunker is 186 yards from the front of the green, so

if you have driven that far, you may well be 210 yards from the flag. The second shot, all things considered, is possibly even more complex. There are two bunkers in tandem up on the left, only just in the rough, about 90 yards from the middle of the green. Again, you may not see them clearly from the position of your drive. There is a long, rather than a cross, bunker short of the green which rather blocks off the right half of it. There are greenside bunkers along the right side, and at the back left. Thus the left-

front quarter of the green is open, and that should be your way in – precisely why these two bunkers are placed where they are at the edge of the rough, short left, to check people from going wide to the left to open up the green even more.

This first hole is a perfect illustration of the point-to-point nature of the game of golf, and quite obviously demands very careful positional play. Ideally your second shot should pass right of the two bunkers in the left rough, but at the same time stay to the left of that long fairway

bunker. If you are not quite sure of making the distance, aim at that fairway bunker and stay short of it.

This may indeed be your best plan. You must accept that this is a difficult hole, and the average player would do well to play it as a par 5. Being short of the fairway bunker will leave you a tidy pitch to the centre of the green, which is reasonably flat, sloping only slightly left to right, and if you score five on the hole, do not fret – you can be well content with that.

Left front of the green is the best target area

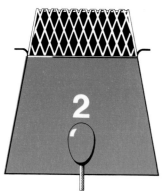

## 345 YDS 315M PAR 4

**A**t first glance, after the rigours of the first hole, this one looks like a catch-your-breath hole, an innocent, perhaps even a birdie hole, but beware. It does not play quite as easily as it looks. The hole runs almost due north-west, and your first task, as ever, is to get the ball on the fairway. It does look inviting. This fairway is broad, but rather undulating and in the driving zone will be inclined to turn the ball from right to left, and much of it slopes downhill, throwing the ball forward.

The drive may bring into play a variety of traps. There is a bunker in the right rough at about 160 yards, innocent enough. A little past the 200-yard mark a pair of bunkers straddles the fairway, one on either side, just in the rough. Plenty of room between them. The backs of these are 100 yards from the front of the green, so if you are in the fairway level with them, or just past them, you should have a pitch-type shot to the green. There is yet another bunker on the

Above:
The broad fairway sloping downhill most of the way

Out-of-bounds wall comes close to the left side of the putting surface

*2nd shot at the 2nd*

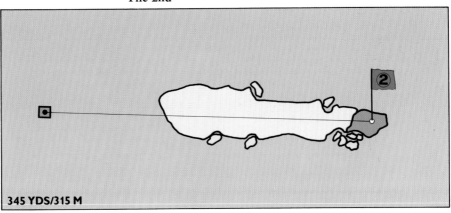

**345 YDS/315 M**

left side, almost 300 yards from the tee; who knows, in very dry conditions, downwind, pitching your absolutely best drive on a down-slope, you could just

reach it. In these circumstances, many professionals would use an iron from the tee for accuracy and the precise length they wanted. The rough, particularly on the right side, is usually quite strong on this hole.

The approach shot is rather less easy than it may seem. You will not get any particular hold on this green, since the landing zone on the front part of the green slopes downhill, away from you. It might make sense to drive a shade short on this hole, taking a line five yards inside the right-hand bunker, giving

yourself a full shot at the green, rather than a half or three-quarter shot. This gives you a better chance of getting more control on the ball.

There is an army of bunkers by the green – five of them, in varying sizes, all to the right. To the left of the green, a stone wall, which marks the out-of-bounds along the whole left side of this hole, angles in quite close to the putting surface, with only a few feet of fringe between. The green, although quite strongly contoured, is very large, and you should not have major

problems in hitting and holding it. There is no reason to think that you cannot make par here – and optimists have little reason not to think of a possible birdie. One factor to consider, however, is that you may not be fully into your stride, may not be warmed up properly, may be still a little stiff. This is reason again to stress the need to prepare well on the practice ground, and to concentrate extra hard over the opening holes of your round, just as you will need to over the closing holes.

Cluster of bunkers guarding the right side of the green

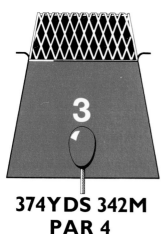

**374 YDS 342M
PAR 4**

For the third hole you turn through 90° and head eastwards. This is the first of three holes running in the same direction and the longest such stretch on the course. It is a medium-length par 4 which in some conditions could play quite long. The green is past a gap in a distant ridge (at 300 yards), and cannot quite be seen from the tee. Your driving line should be exactly on that gap, or a shade to the left of it, which would allow you to see a more generous slice of the green on your second shot. The driving zone is very generous, as much as 90 yards across in places, so I would expect the drive not to be a major problem for you. There is a bunker in the right rough at 160 yards, so hit well to the left of that and dismiss it.

Set into the hillocks or ridges on either side of the gap are quite substantial bunkers which might distract you. I would suggest that you try to eliminate them from your mind and concentrate on your target for the second shot, the green. This may require an extra effort, since you may not be able to see too much of it. The centre of the green is about 100 yards beyond that gap. The green, which is a huge rectangle, has two

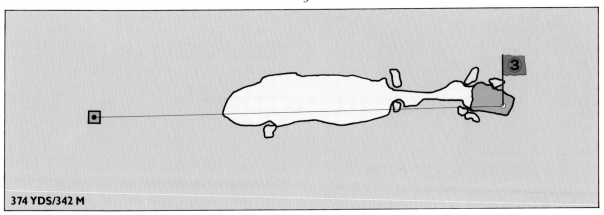

**374 YDS/342 M**

bunkers at the right-front corner, a bigger one at the left front, and another left centre, so it is quite strongly defended. You may not see any of these on your second shot, but there is a healthy, open frontage to the green and even if you are a shade off-line with your second, you have a reasonable chance of catching the putting surface, part-blind shot or no.

There are two important points to be made about this green, and therefore the shot to it. It is 44 yards long, and there is no trouble at the back. Thus there is a difference of four club-lengths from front to back, so you must be sure of your yardage. Walk forward by all means to check the pin position. If you are short, the ground from the gap to the green is flat and friendly, and you may be able to bobble the ball on. But the word here is long, not short. Take more than enough club if you are in any doubt. The green does go slightly uphill, which will help hold your shot. All told, a good par-4 hole which I rather like, but one which can play very differently from day to day depending on the conditions.

Left:
The generous driving zone in front of the ridge

Ridges hide greenside bunkers on the left and right

Gap at 300 yards with a deep bunker on either side

*Approach to the 3rd*

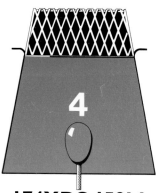

# 174YDS 159M PAR 3

The first of Muirfield's short holes, the 4th, like the other three, is a rigorous test of your striking ability and accuracy with an iron club. All the same, let me tell you that this hole can play almost any length – I have used a driver here!

The green is built high – you will be hitting up to it – and is ferociously bunkered by fearsome traps; it falls off down very steep slopes on all sides. Even at the front there is a pronounced slope up to the putting surface, and this slopes up very positively from front to back, so if you are over the green, you will have to pitch back onto a slithery downslope.

The critical requirement with your tee shot is to pitch the ball on the putting surface. If you do that, or at least onto a reasonable part of it, you have a fair chance of staying on. I do not believe that this is an unfair hole, but I have no doubt that it is a very dangerous one, particularly when the wind blows.

There is one cross-bunker, about 100 yards out from the tee, and two bunkers just past it on the right, and another on the left front of the green. The rest of the green is unprotected, and a little bank rises above the right side towards the back of the green. But the bunkers are lethal. Any ball pitched just short, on the upslope to the green, perhaps even on the first few feet of the putting surface and not on a proper line, will be spun off and will run down wicked slopes into these traps. They are deeper than a tall man, with vertical revetted faces, and if you do get in there it can take you a lot of strokes to get out.

The green is 40 yards long, or three or four clubs' difference from front to back, and makes a severe test. Do not be too proud to take wood. You must consider the wind and weather conditions; you must take the right club; you must find the right line, which is slightly left of the centre front of the green, and you had better make sure you hit

## The 4th

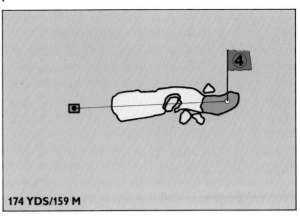

174 YDS/159 M

the shot well. If you score three here, be well pleased with yourself. I rate the hole at the very least as a par 3.5. I also have to tell you that Brian Barnes, in an Open Championship, actually scored one on the hole, so be of good cheer. I will not mention that Brian was so overcome by this that he scored seven on the next hole.

The yellow flags to the right mark the 12th and 13th greens

Green slopes up from front to back

Steep slopes and ferocious bunkers around the front of the green

From the 4th Tee

## 506YDS 462M PAR 5

The 5th is the first of Muirfield's three par 5s, and all of them, I'm bound to say, are really great golf holes. This one keeps turning to the right throughout its length, and for that reason all the right side is firmly protected by strong rough and an outburst of bunkers, strategically placed. Into a hard wind, you might struggle just to reach the fairway – you must carry a good deal of broken ground and reach out a good 150 yards from the members' tee. That would leave you another 350 yards to cover, which sounds rather ridiculous. Yet for the average player, on a fairly still day, there is no reason to fear this hole. It can be a great pleasure, and very thrilling.

From about 150 to 250 yards, the right side of the fairway is closed off by five bunkers. There is one placed on the left, on the edge of the fairway at about 240 yards, with a smaller, supporting bunker 25 yards beyond it. The drive should be aimed exactly at that second bunker on the left, which will keep you out of all that débris on the right. From about 200 to 240 yards out, there is plenty of fairway; getting the ball in there will give you a good look forwards along and up the fairway. You must at all costs keep out of bunkers on this hole.

They are designed and placed at different ranges to catch long and short hitters alike, and there are 16 of them altogether.

Up ahead, you will see a cross-bunker coming in from the left. It is 100 yards from the front of the green, and it does narrow the fairway somewhat. It might therefore be 150 yards or more ahead of you, and you have to decide whether, under the conditions, you can carry it, or get past the right-hand end of it. If you do that, you will have an open shot at the green. But the 5th hole will not have finished with you. You then have to cope with a remarkable green.

It is fairly undulating, sloping down to the left, two-tiered, and with a slight ridge making the right side higher than the left. There are four bunkers all along the left side, from front left to back left, in general below the putting surface. On the right side of the fairway, 40 yards short of the green, is a bunker, backed by two more 30 yards behind it, only just in the right rough. And at the right centre, nudging into the putting surface, is the last of the traps, small, deep and sinister. After all that, please note that the ground just short, immediately in front of the green, will be likely to turn the ball from right to left, so that the open shot I spoke of may still be possible, but will require some extra care.

If you can bring this green within range of three shots, then I suggest that on the third

you concentrate on nothing but getting onto the green. Do not be tempted by the pin position. If it is tight to one side, play to the other side, or at least for the centre of the green. Do not be greedy with the pitch. Those green-side bunkers can undo all your good work.

In general, the hole is uphill all the way. That means your shots will fly a little higher, and cover less distance, with less run. If you are into a hard east wind, the 5th will seem endless. But, wind or no wind, if you go about the challenges of this hole rationally, you have a good chance of making par. And whatever you score, your compensation when you get there will be well worth it. You will have arrived at the highest

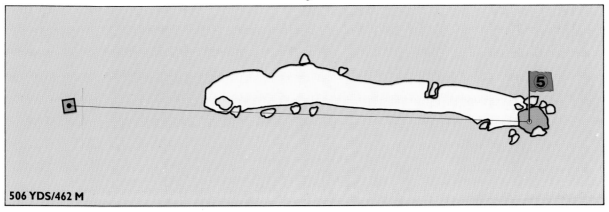

**506 YDS/462 M**

point of the Muirfield property and can rejoice in magnificent views of the Firth of Forth, Bass Rock and Berwick Law through the Lomonds of Fife and Gullane Hill and on up to the noble City of Edinburgh and the dramatic bridges beyond it. And again I must tell you, although you may well find it difficult to believe, that the American player, Johnny Miller, in the 1972 Open Championship, scored two on the hole. He used a driver and a 3-wood, and probably thought how simple it was, and wondered why he didn't do it every time he played the hole!

The fairway is liberally strewn with bunkers to left and right

Cross bunker 100 yards from the green

Go for the centre of the undulating green rather than risking greenside bunkers by attacking the pin

*Approach to the 5th*

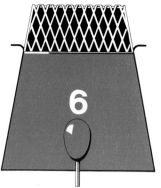

# 436YDS 398M PAR 4

The 6th is not an easy hole by any means, nor am I really sure what to say about it. In turn, I have the feeling that it is the weakest, the poorest, the strongest, the least fair of all the Muirfield holes. First time out, it really is quite difficult to know where to drive. You look up a rising fairway which has two bunkers eating in from the left. They are 212 yards from the back tee, and therefore driveable. These bunkers are clearly visible and virtually form the horizon, so to that extent, since you are driving 'at the sky', this is a blind drive. Officially

Stone wall is 116 yards from the front of the green

2nd shot at the 6th

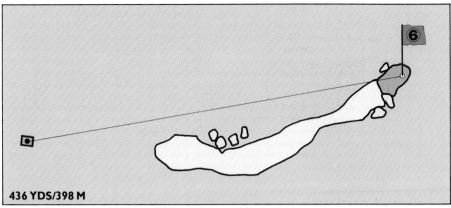

**436 YDS/398 M**

A view of the green showing the more generous entrance to the left

Muirfield is proud of the fact that, unlike many other links courses, it has only one blind shot, the drive at the 11th, but I would be inclined also to rate this one a blind drive.

Immediately behind these two bunkers, completely out of sight but in close support, are two more; all are wicked, insidious traps, and so deep and with such high revetted faces that you may even have to play out backwards or sideways. Your line therefore must take you to the right of them, which will put you into a valley area from which the hole turns to the left. Just to complicate your life, if you drive too far into this valley, the ball will over-run the fairway into tangly rough.

From here you will still be a long shot, perhaps 200 yards, from the green. Level with the last of the four bunkers on the left, a path crosses the fairway, 175 yards from the front of the green. In addition, because of the folding ground, you will probably see very little of the putting surface, so put your faith in your yardage. You will see a stone wall, by the way, coming in from the left. The end of that wall, where it stops just short of the fairway, is 116 yards from the front of the green.

There are two big bunkers, one short right and the other at the right-front corner, with a smallish pot at the left centre. A dip in front of the green is deceptive. A ball pitching short and to the right will probably break into one or other of these bunkers, which are penal. If you are in there, and the pin position is set on the right of the green, you will have a horrible shot in prospect. I should aim slightly left of centre of the green on this second shot – the ball will tend to go right towards the centre. But I still think this is a rather cruel hole; if you make four here you have every right to feel ecstatic.

Dip in front of the green will make the ball break right towards the bunkers

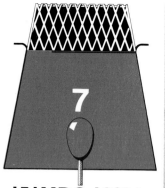

## 7

## 151YDS 138M
## PAR 3

This hole runs to the west and so, if there is any wind prevailing, you will be playing directly into it; on such days the 7th becomes positively hostile. In its design and contouring it is probably not as extreme as the 4th (it is also 20 yards shorter), but with any kind of wind it can be very challenging. Of all Muirfield's four short holes, this is the only one which plays in a westerly direction, the others – 4th, 13th and 16th – running easterly, which you might judge a design fault, but all four are very demanding holes.

*From the 7th Tee*

## The 7th

The 7th, in common with the 13th, may be able to cope with a 'run-on' shot, but in general terms you should not be short at any of these holes.

The green is quite large, on a high plateau, so you will be hitting uphill all the way, as at all the short holes on this course. That in itself means you must think of 'one more club', as we say. The hole is closely trapped, one front right, one front left and two more up the left side, and off the back right and back left of the green there are quite brisk downslopes.

From the front of the front tee to the back of the back measures 68 yards and the green is 37 yards long, so your first exercise here is arithmetical – you must know exactly how far the tee in use measures to the flag. There is nothing beyond the green save a distant view of the Firth of Forth and the famous bridges, ancient rail and modern road, so there will be some lack of definition from the tee.

Finally, there seems to be a theory, put about by the Muirfield caddies, that the slope of this green is an optical illusion, and that there are no borrows on any putt. With the greatest respect to the local caddies, a magnificent body of men, don't believe it. There are borrows. I know. I have experienced them. This green is totally exposed, so the requirement here is nothing less than a fine assessment of the conditions, particularly of wind and weather, and your best strike at the ball, a first-class stroke which will get you the distance.

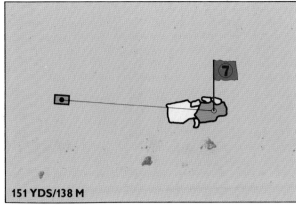

**151 YDS/138 M**

Left:
The line of bunkers waiting for the wayward tee shot

First of three bunkers along the left side of the green

Steep downslope behind the green

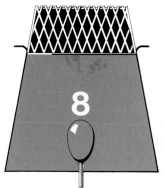

## 439YDS 401M
## PAR 4

Of all the Muirfield holes, the par-4 8th illustrates perfectly the local philosophy of fairway bunkering in the driving zone, intended above all to lengthen the second shot, to funnel you towards the narrowest part of the fairway, and to reinforce the hole's Phase Two defences, ie those around the green or in play from the second shot. All this is as it should be, of course, if golf is to be more than a slugger's game, and points up the greatest single demand that Muirfield will make of you – for straight and accurate driving.

The 8th is a dog-leg turning to the right. In the angle, there are no fewer than nine bunkers, covering the range from 200 to 260 yards. There is no bunker on the left side of this hole, as well there might at around, for example, 250 yards. These nine traps look like an elephant's grave-yard, and they could certainly be your grave-yard if you get in there. Don't. Be well to the left of all of them. Be in the left rough if you have to – it is not too severe. If you are in these bunkers, you could tango from one to the other and use up three or four strokes to advance 50 yards.

Even if you drive nicely into the fairway, you will still not see the green. Two big cross-bunkers, set on a slight

The drive must be aimed left to avoid the mass of bunkers from 200–260 yards

*From the angle of the Dog-leg at the 8th*

# The 8th

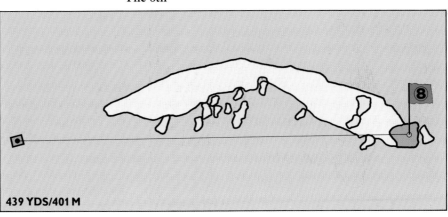

**439 YDS/401 M**

The area behind the cross-
bunkers and the solitary
bunker to the right of the
green

Cross-bunkers 50 yards from
the green

rise, with a third in the rough to the right, screen off everything but the top of the flagstick, and give the impression that the green is set in a bowl or a pronounced hollow. It is not. It is perfectly flat, and the approaches beyond the cross-bunkers are perfectly flat and fair. From the cross-bunkers to the centre of the green is a good 50 yards, so you have plenty of ground to work with beyond them. The thing to do on the second shot is ignore them and fly boldly over them.

You will then find that the green is virtually defenceless and that you have overcome the challenge of the hole. The green is wide, and of good length. There is one smallish bunker at the back left. The fringes and close approaches are all open and reasonably

flat, so if you miss the putting surface you still have an honest chance for par with a chip and one putt. The major ramparts of the 8th are that scattering of heavy, forbidding traps in the dog-leg angle; if you skirt that lot, you have broken the back of the problem. The drive, as so often at Muirfield, is critical.

## 9

## 460YDS 420M PAR 4

The 9th hole has been called an ancient monument, an antique, rubbish, a monster, coupled with a variety of unflattering adjectives, but I choose to think that it is a very fine par 5 from the championship tee, like the two others at Muirfield, and a great golf hole by any standards. It poses intriguing tactical problems, the first being that for medal, as opposed to championship, purposes, it is in fact a par 4, at 460 yards. Championship length is 495 yards and therefore a par 5. Please take my word that if the hole is played into any kind of west wind, no one will reach the green in two shots.

We find ourselves looking towards Greywalls Hotel and the clubhouse of the Honourable Company of Edinburgh Golfers. A long, low greystone wall, an out-of-bounds wall, runs the entire length of the hole along the left. The first striking feature, critical to the playing of the hole, is Bunker A. This is a large cross-bunker coming into the left centre of the fairway some 200 yards from the medal tee. About 60 yards beyond it on the same line is another big bunker. The critical element here is that the rough comes into the fairway in front of Bunker A, continues back to embrace the more distant bunker and eliminates the entire left half of the fairway for a good 80 yards. The right half of the remaining fairway narrows to little more than 15 yards at one point.

In a sense, the decisions about your tee shot are simple. You must not be in Bunker A. You must not be left of it, and you must not be directly over it. You have two choices – either be short of it, and into a strong wind you may not in any case reach it, or you must be to the right of it. Don't be afraid of missing the fairway to the right. The rough, or at least the fringe rough, is not penal – you'll get a shot out of there. The whole thrust of the first part of this exercise really makes you play to the right. The problems set by the second shot mean that you are almost obliged to go left.

Bunker A is 230 yards from the front of the green. As you look forward, you will see a ridge running along the fairway; this leaves the left side, towards the wall, higher than the right. Along the edge of that lower right side is a line of four bunkers, 70 yards long, covering the line of a second shot that might be coming in from the right, or wide from the right.

These bunkers will gather in a shot not played positively towards the left side of the fairway; to complicate that,

The view from the tee

2nd shot at the 9th

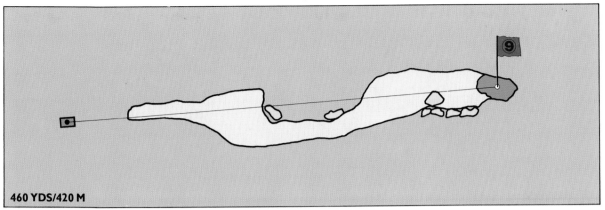

**460 YDS/420 M**

just past the nearest of them, and edging over towards the centre of the fairway, is the big Simpson's Bunker, named after the architect who put it there. So you are being steered left all the way on this shot, and of course that out-of-bounds wall up there is coming more and more into play. Good players have gone over it – Peter Thomson in an Open Championship, for one – but there is more space up there than you might think, or can see. On the second shot, you must get the ball up on that higher left side, towards the wall. I see no reason for you to crick your back going for length on this shot. If you can advance yourself, say, 150 yards from Bunker A, you will be level with or just short of Simpson's Bunker, and will have less than 100 yards to go to the flag-stick, and the best possible look at the green and the flag position.

For most average players, this will be a solid par 5 from the medal tee. Into wind, rate it 5.5. The more you try to be greedy and improve on these ratings, the more certain is the road to disaster on such a hole. There is no greenside bunker, but the green slopes from left to right. If the pin is on the left, or higher, side, you may find it difficult to pitch close. But if you have come this far this well, why not pitch on, take your two putts, score five, and walk off feeling like the Lord of Creation?

Out-of-bounds wall

Bunkers and rough narrow the fairway 220 yards from the tee

Bunkers line up below the ridge on the right side of the fairway

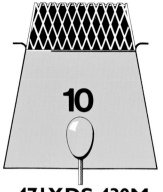

**10**

**471 YDS 430M
PAR 4**

The start of the second half at Muirfield, the counter-clockwise nine, is just as severe as the start of the front nine, and that opening hole. The 10th runs due north and the medal measurement of 471 yards is only five yards short of the par-5 distance. The hole runs due north in a straight line, and you may have difficulty in accepting that it is 11 yards longer than the 9th. The wisest course might be to play this one in five careful strokes. Over all the teeing grounds there is a 69-yard spread, so try to establish accurately which tee is in use and the consequent yardage you are facing.

Again, fairway bunkers compromise the drive. There are two of them on the right side of the fairway. The first is some 240 yards from the back tee, the tee right back towards the stone wall, and the second is perhaps 30 yards further on. These are strong bunkers, so you must aim to the left of them. You will not see the green, only the flagstick, from the tee.

The prospect on the second shot is of a slight ridge across the fairway, still holding most of the green from view, with two cross-bunkers on it. This ridge is about 100 yards from the first fairway bunker, and the

*Approach to the 10th*

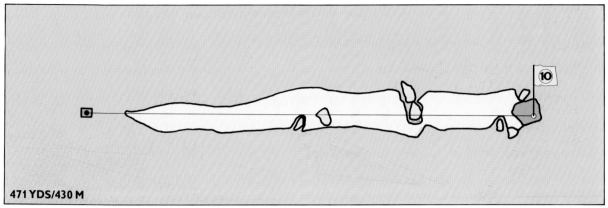

**471 YDS/430 M**

green is another 100 yards on. You may well be facing a lusty second shot of 180 or 200 yards, so you must try to ignore this cross-hazard and fly the ball over it. 'Easy to say,' I can hear you complain, but it has to be done. There is very little space, if any, to sneak past the outside ends of the ridge. Give yourself enough club, and give the shot your fullest and most positive swing. Do not be afraid of being too long – there is a ridge around the back of the green which will at least stop your ball. On the second shot, you will see a right-hand slice of the green, which is not too intimidating. The entrance is quite generous and it is not too tightly trapped. There are two bunkers short and slightly wide to the right, another closer to the green at the left centre. The green also helps by sloping up slightly towards the back.

Left:
A panoramic view of the fairway with the two bunkers on the right threatening the tee shot

Green slopes up at the back and a ridge helps to hold the approach shot

Ridge and cross-bunkers 100 yards from the green

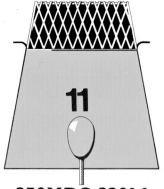

## 350YDS 320M
## PAR 4

**A**gain we have a straight hole, another par 4 running in exactly the same northerly direction as the 10th, but it is a fairly short par 4 and not nearly so forbidding. At first sight you may not be inclined to agree with that, since the 11th is the classic blind-drive links hole, with a high ridge in front of the tee concealing every single scrap of fairway. The ridge looks formidable. You must not allow it to influence your thinking, or your swing, on the tee. From the very back championship tee it demands a carry of 195 yards, but from the very front of the front tee you are talking about 115 yards, an

altogether different matter. So probably what you do, as soon as you have out-stared the ridge, is check exactly which teeing ground is in use, establish the carry required, realize that it is not after all such a terror, and set about it.

Playing the hole for the first time, you would do well to hit directly over the marker-post, or if anything a shade left of it. When you have toiled over the hill, you will find a wide fairway area with good lies and stances. There is a bunker in the rough on the right at around 250–260 yards and another to the left of the fairway, 30 yards on. I don't believe either of these should trouble you, although if you are playing with a strong

Downslope and bunkers on the left

*2nd shot at the 11th*

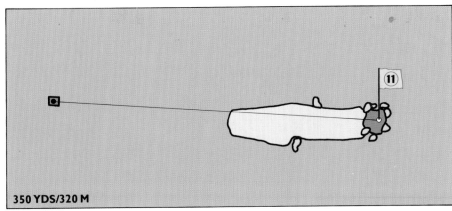

**350 YDS/320 M**

following wind, the one on the right might well be in range of your best shot.

Now that you have negotiated the ridge, you will see where the real defences of this hole lie – all around the green. An interesting green it is, too: clearly elevated, it has a dip in front which might take some of the yardage off your shot if it is a touch short. There is a slight tier effect across the green. The back portion slopes up quite noticeably, which will help hold the ball. The front of the green is fair, the entrance reasonably open and clearly designed to make the second shot a 'target' shot. Apart from the front, the green is ringed around with a garland of bunkers, two on the left, three at the back (pressing in on the putting surface, on a downslope), and two at the right. These last two edge into the right-front corner, and give the impression of a spur of green, spreading away to the right, behind them. There is quite a lot of green in that area, and on high days and holidays you can be sure that the pin will be cut in there!

Given a drive taking you ten or twenty yards over the ridge, the average player should be playing a mid-iron or a pitching club, in still air, perhaps nothing much longer than a 6-iron. This should give you the height you need, and you should aim to pitch the ball on the front centre of the green. It should hold quite nicely at the middle of a green which is 30 yards deep. There is one other point here, and it can be slightly disconcerting. The back of the green in fact forms the horizon, so in a sense you will be pitching up into an 'empty sky', rather like the drive on the 6th hole. But if you have the right club in your hand, do not be afraid of boldness on this second shot. The tendency for amateurs, I suspect, is to be short.

Left:
The ridge is a daunting prospect

Two bunkers cut into the front right of the green

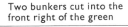

Dip in front of the green

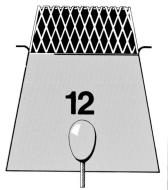

## 12

## 376 YDS 344M PAR 4

For the 12th you turn towards the south-west. It is slightly longer than the 11th, but looks altogether more friendly and sympathetic than most on the course. From a nicely built-up teeing area, we can see everything falling away quite pleasantly before us, all the way to the green. The strongest and most immediate feature from the tee is a ridge edging in towards the fairway to the left, with a big, forceful bunker at the end of it. This bunker is 230 yards out, and could well be your driving line, since the fairway, which up to that point is quite ample, slopes from left to right and will move a ball on that line in towards the centre. If you feel you can reach that bunker, drive to the right of it, but as close to it as you dare. There is a bunker just in the rough, on the right at 150 yards, and I certainly expect you to drive well past that. The rough on the right side of this hole, certainly the fringe rough, should not be all that punishing.

I would assess this as a fairly comfortable driving hole, but the second shot is rather interesting. The big bunker we have noted on the left side of the fairway, by the ridge, is in fact only 100 yards from the front edge of the green, but somehow the shot looks longer, more cramped, more

tricky than it should. I think the bunkering up the fairway and at the green is responsible for this sensation. The green is immediately protected, close up, by five bunkers. Since it is 40 yards long, quite open at both front and back, none of these bunkers really should be relevant to the second shot.

As so often at Muir-field, we have a pair of traps entering the fairway from the right, 40 yards short of the green, goodly-sized and side by side. If you have driven to the right side of the fairway, the line of your second shot may be directly over the inner of these two. There is another, ten yards further out, in the rough on the

Ridge and bunker on the left at 230 yards

2nd shot at the 12

## The 12th

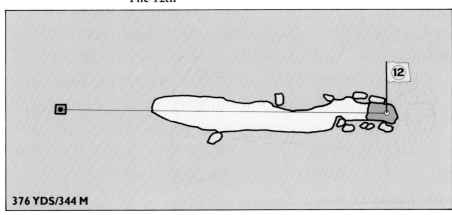

**376 YDS/344 M**

left. These are the traps which give the approach its rather cramped look.

In the area of the green, there is a bunker short and wide of the left-front corner, one halfway along the green on the left, a big one at the right back (these latter two are set in downslopes since this green is built up), and a pair placed tightly together just by the right-front corner. The green

The green and its right-side defences

is roughly rectangular in shape and is about 40 yards from front to back. It does slope off in minor fashion on the left side and at the back, but since it is built up and 'facing into' the shot, the ball should hold quite well. There is a slight dip and upslope at the front, but you could reasonably expect to run a ball on.

The task at the 12th is straightforward, given good 'management'. You

must get off a respectable drive into the fairway, without straining particularly for distance. You must then try to eliminate any illusions the bunkering might suggest; don't attempt to steer the ball but hit an honest pitch at the putting surface. Straightforward golf holes require no more than straightforward golf shots.

Elevated green with downslopes all around

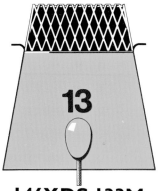

# 146YDS 133M
# PAR 3

The 13th hole at Muirfield is, I believe, one of the world's greatest short holes. It also proves that greatness in a par-3 hole does not mean it has to be more than 200 yards long. It runs in an easterly direction, which offers up one of the few

points of criticism of the Muirfield course, namely that three of the four short holes – the 4th and 16th are the others – run in the same approximate direction, and so most of the time they will be played downwind.

The green here is sited substantially above the teeing ground, and is set into a cleft in a high

ridge. It is almost 50 yards long, but rather narrow, sloping upwards quite definitely at the front, then flattening out rather deceptively at the back, permitting a variety of wicked pin positions. Almost any pin position on this green can be wicked.

It is probably a platitude to say that on

short holes you should ignore the bunkering, since the object of the exercise is to make the ball pitch on the putting surface, and stay there, as close to the flagstick as your shot-making talents allow; but bunkers are bunkers. They often have a hypnotic, magnetizing effect on the golfer. The bunkers on this hole are

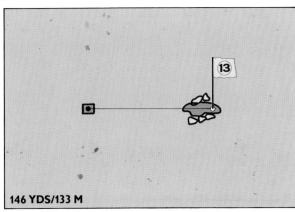

**146 YDS/133 M**

as diabolical as any that Muirfield can offer. There are two on the left side of the green, three on the right, all too close to the putting surface for comfort. These bunkers are set at the bottom of the sandhills which overlook the green on either side, and look more ominous and grasping because of it.

The bigger one on the left, very close to the putting surface, is more than six feet deep, with a vertical face. If you are plugged in there, you can send out for drinks and sandwiches – you may well be in there for the rest of the day. The problems of lie, stance, aim and elevation on the ball will be extreme.

I am not sure if there is a particular way to play this hole. You must know the correct range and have the right club and consider the playing conditions. Ultimately, though, the tee shot is a test of the golfer's courage and faith in his swing – courage at going

boldly for the flag, or at least the fat of the green. The only alternative is to be short and stammer the ball to the front of the green, which also means taking a chance on getting a first putt close. However, you may have 30 yards to go, and uphill!

Front-left bunker is more than 6 feet deep

*The 13th green*

Long narrow green sloping up from the front

The left-hand bunkers are barely visible from the tee

Three ominous bunkers on the right

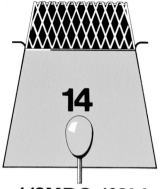

# 14

## 442YDS 403M
## PAR 4

**T**his is an attractive, open and unpretentious hole, with almost everything laid out nicely to be seen from the tee. The hole runs parallel with the 12th and is strikingly similar to it, although a good deal stronger and some 65 yards longer.

The landing area for the drive is really quite friendly in the 220–260 yard range, although it does rather narrow down beyond that. There is an enfilade of three bunkers in the left rough at these distances. On the right, level with the first of these, is a single bunker. The fairway breaks somewhat from

Above:
A wide area of fairway to
the right of the three bunkers

Three bunkers protect the
left side of the fairway at
220–260 yards

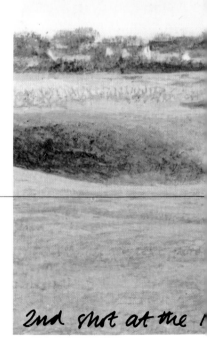

Fairway narrows and breaks
from left to right

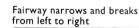

2nd shot at the

## The 14th

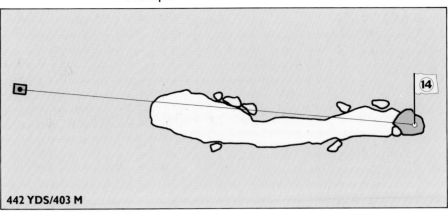

**442 YDS/403 M**

left to right, so a sensible driving line might be on the centre bunker (230 yards) of that left-hand set, with the ball pitching short and breaking to the right. A very good player might well carry past the first bracketing pair, and have the ball finish more or less level with the most distant bunker. For the average player, some care will be needed down-wind – the nearest bunkers would certainly be reachable.

The second shot, depending of course on the drive, can be long, from 150 to 200 yards to the front of the green. Here we see what is becoming another Muirfield characteristic: a pair of bracketing

bunkers, one left, one right, each only just in the rough, about 80 yards from the centre of the green. There is one rather small bunker hard by the right-front corner of the green, another to the left, wide, and perhaps 20 yards from the green. Considering that you may well be playing a fairly long shot – you certainly will if you are into the wind – the green is not too large. The lie of the land suggests that you should come into this green from the left, where the entrance is open, and that is why most of the defences of the hole are along the left side. The back and left sides of the green are fairly clear.

Your second shot has

to be bold and firm, and pointed at the left centre of the green. This is a testing par 4 for the amateur player, and, into wind, a very strong hole for any class of player.

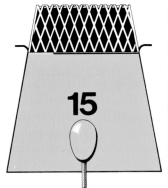

## 15

## 391 YDS 357M PAR 4

**A**nother fine par 4, the 15th is a good deal less intimidating than it looks from the tee. You may even find it almost recreational before you tackle Muirfield's powerful finish, which starts at the next hole.

This one is reasonably straight, and slightly downhill. A diagonal line of cross-bunkers stretching from 140–170 yards out should not cause problems unless there is a strong headwind. We will assume that you can carry them, and a good driving line would

be over the centre one. The fairway beyond is quite wide, slopes from left to right and 'onwards', and should be good for an extra 20 yards on your drive. I would say that this is one of the least demanding drives on the course.

The real test of the hole is concentrated on the second shot and this emerges not so much from the hazards you see as the impression they may make on you. A really good drive might put you about 150 yards from the green. Look up

the fairway and you will see, yet again, the Muirfield twins, bunkers on either side of the fairway about 60 yards short of the green. But this time, 20 yards on and smack in the centre of the fairway, is a third bunker, quite big. This

Green slopes away from the centre into bunkers on both sides

*Approach to the 15th*

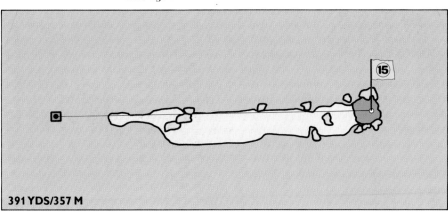

**391 YDS/357 M**

may give you the feeling that the entire area up there is cramping and narrowing. It isn't really. The central bunker is the culprit. It looks very close to the green, but in fact there is a good 30 yards of fair ground between it and the front

A fine view from the tee – the Firth of Forth running inland towards Edinburgh

of the putting surface. You must carry this trap. If you do, and your shot is straight, you have a fair chance of running on.

The green itself is quite heavily trapped. There are three bunkers along the right side, a small one rather wide of the left-front corner, and a very big bunker covering all of the left back. As you will see, the front of the green is quite open. However, it is oddly contoured. The left third falls off to the left, the right third to the right, and the central third is flat but then slopes upwards to the back of the green.

The 15th is a perfectly fair hole, one which needs just a little thought on the second shot. Playing downwind, take extra care that the ball does not run away from you, on both drive and approach shot.

Plenty of ground behind the central bunker

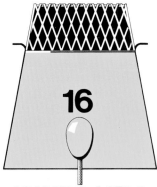

## 16

## 181YDS 165M
## PAR 3

The last of Muirfield's short holes is the start of its ferocious finish. This is probably a good point in the round to realize that you have been playing a very big course, perhaps in strenuous weather which has made some physical demands on you, and that you may be tiring. So resolve to tackle this finish by playing within yourself, by keeping your swing in tight control, and above all by raising your concentration as many notches as you can.

You will certainly need all you can muster on the 16th. All the Muirfield short holes are difficult and challenging, this one – the longest – perhaps most of all. They all have much in common. All the greens are higher than the tees. All the greens are built-up and mounded. All the greens have sharp downslopes around them, and all these slopes feed awesome bunkering. All the greens are quite heavily defended, and finally all have some fierce contouring.

This hole has seven bunkers around the green area, and there used to be two more bunkers about 100 yards out, at the beginning of the 'fairway', if we can call it that. At this point, the ground goes down into a big dip or swale, rising again into the front part of the green. From the

tee, you can see only one greenside bunker towards the right-front corner, but in fact there are two there, with two more covering the right side and three curving around the left corner. The green is reasonably big, but has downslopes almost all the way around it. All these defending bunkers are very deep and penal, with very stiff faces.

You cannot expect to enjoy the luck of Lee Trevino in the 1972 Open Championship, when he exploded from one of these bunkers and saw his ball hit the flag-stick on the fly, and drop into the hole. If he had missed the stick, he might well have scored 5 on the hole. There is no alternative here but to (a) keep out of the

bunkers, (b) make sure you have enough club and (c) add one more club to be quite sure. Then – shoot for the back half of the green.

The danger zone is front right. If you are caught up in any of these slopes, your ball will be fed down into one bunker or the other. If the pin position is on the right, keep left. If it is on the left, keep right. Don't be too clever with this shot. Hit and hold the green. You will not make par easily – you will have to work very hard to score three on this hole – but then you are playing a great championship course, and you should not expect to get anything easily at Muirfield.

*The 16th Green*

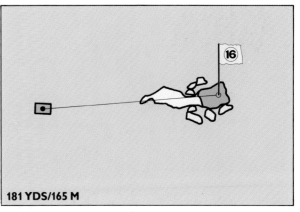

**181 YDS/165 M**

A large green but heavily defended

Back left is the safest landing area

Deep dip in front of fiercely contoured green

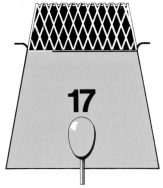

# 17

## 501 YDS 458M PAR 5

This is the last of Muirfield's great par-5 holes, and it may just be the best of them. It is a hole which in almost any conditions of weather poses very serious, but very exciting, problems on every shot. Into wind, for example, it will play very, very long.

Along the right side of the hole, all the way from tee to green, there are no man-made hazards whatsoever. At around 250 yards, the hole dog-legs to the left, and the temptation is to keep to the left, to reduce the distance. It is a temptation you must resist. In the angle of the

dog-leg, stretching along for some 80 yards, is very broken ground and five bunkers. The first of that set of bunkers is 200 yards from the very back, championship tee, and you must at all costs drive to the right of it.

There is plenty of room on that side. Into wind from the medal tee (40 yards in front of the championship tee) you could reach that first bunker. Downwind you might reach the last one, so have a care. Play to

the right – in fact from the tee you can see only the first of these bunkers.

When you get up to your drive, and you are neatly in the fairway and start shaping up to your second shot, you must immediately put on your

A wicked area of humps and hollows 100 yards from the green

*Approach to the 17th*

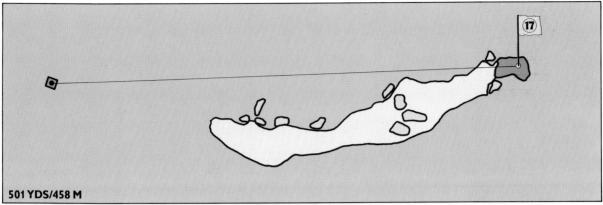

**501 YDS/458 M**

An intimidating view down the 17th fairway

tactical hat. The fact that this is a par 5 does not mean automatically that you will be reaching for a fairway wood, and blasting away. Governing your entire thinking on this second shot is an extraordinary stretch of ground. It covers the entire fairway and measures 30 yards or more from front to back; its centre is about 100 yards from the front of the green. It is an area of humps and hollows and slopes and ridges, and contains three of the biggest, most frightening of all Muirfield's bunkers. If you try to pass this area to the left, there is a hostile bunker hidden just in the rough to snare you. You cannot pass it to the right – there is no fairway, and if you do go right, into the rough, you will have no practical third shot to the green.

You simply *must not* get into this area. It will totally destroy your score on the hole. You must either carry it, or stay short of it, and there is the challenge, and the nuisance, of the shot. Beyond this massive hazard is ample fairway area and a clean shot at the green. Short of it is ample fairway area and again a clean shot at the green, not much more than 140 yards away. If you are into a strong wind, and your drive has been not too good, *think again.* Why not play an iron club that will keep you short of these bunkers, and leave another iron shot to the green? If you are down a strong wind (the hole runs with the prevailing wind at your back), and your drive has been quite good, ask yourself if you can carry that area comfortably. At all events you must take care because, whether you lay up short or carry over this zone, you must be on the left side of the fairway to get the best sight of the green. If the pin is on the right, and you are on the right after two shots, you have no shot on.

The green is long, and has a flat entrance. There are bunkers on either side of the front, and banks along the left, back and right sides. Wind and weather conditions will govern your playing of this hole, but it is a thinker's hole, a planner's hole, a great golf hole. In 1966, Jack Nicklaus virtually won the Open Championship with the birdie he needed on the last round: downwind, he drove with a 3-iron, then hit the green with a 5-iron!

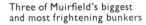

Three of Muirfield's biggest and most frightening bunkers

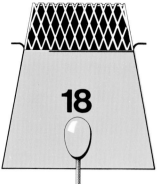

## 18

## 414YDS 378M
## PAR 4

**N**ow you have arrived at the great climax to this exceptional golf course, and possibly the very best finishing hole of all our championship links. By that I mean, of course, the most difficult! I must say I would not feel particularly relaxed if I had to make 4 to win a Championship on this hole. It is straight, running almost due south, and is very sharply, very adroitly,

bunkered. The prevailing wind is right to left. There are problems on drive and second shot alike.

The fairway is narrow. There is a big bunker on the right, 190 yards from the medal tee. There are two bunkers on the other side of the fairway at 210 and 250 yards, and the gap between, equal to the width of the fairway, looks rather inhibiting. In fact, beyond these initial traps the fairway narrows and stays narrow. The drive must

find its way between these bunkers, or at least stay in the fairway, in their general area. A reasonably good player with a reasonably good drive should get past the one on the right, possibly level with or past the first of the two on the left. From there, he will be some 170 yards from the front of the green and about 190 yards from the flag. But to reach this green in two shots needs a very good drive indeed.

You had better not think that it is then simply a matter of

blasting away with your biggest gun – the second shot requires consideration. Up the fairway, a back-to-back pair of bunkers blocks out the left approach to the green. The bunkers are 40 and 20 yards short of the front respectively. The entire left side of the green is covered by one long bunker. The right side is covered by one almost as large, with a distinctive turf-covered 'island' in the middle. Thus if your drive has been good, you have to decide if you can carry

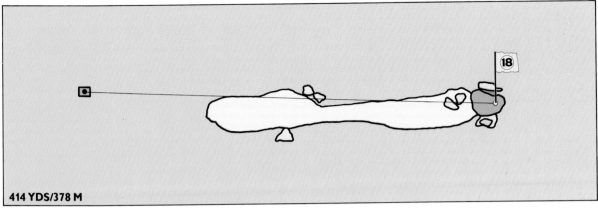

**414 YDS/378 M**

these fairway bunkers, a carry which may be all of 150 yards. There is a good 20 yards of true ground past that second one, which could help you run on. Your line then would be directly over the front of the two bunkers. If you think the carry is doubtful, then aim to the right, perhaps in line with the island bunker – but be short of it! Then you would have a short chip to the flag. The green, by the way, is slightly raised, and slopes up a little from the front.

Henry Cotton, in 1948, had two shots in that island bunker, scored five and still won the Championship. Gary Player in 1959 scored six on the hole, including three putts for a 68, and still won. Jack Nicklaus in 1966 used a 1-iron, then a 3-iron, to secure the par which won him the Open, while in 1972 Lee Trevino hit such a huge drive in the final round that his second shot was an 8-iron. In the last round of the 1980 Open Championship, I had a good drive down the left, and hit a 3-iron three feet from the hole for a birdie. In front of that huge crowd in the 'stadium' around the last green, it was a very pleasing score. It jumped me up quite a few places in the prize-list, and at the same time I was sure that throughout the entire Championship there were more fives than fours scored on the hole. So play it, on your terms, as a par 4.5.

Left:
A view from the tee of one of the finest finishing holes in Championship golf

Bunkers blocking the left approach, but there is room behind them

Two bunkers to the left of the fairway at 210 and 250 yards

*Approach to the 18th*

Prestwick Golf Club virtually 'created' the Open Championship, and staged it for the first 12 years of its existence. By 1873, the Royal and Ancient club at St Andrews, and the Honourable Company of Edinburgh Golfers, then at Musselburgh, joined Prestwick, and the championship rotated around their three courses. By 1892, the Honourable Company had moved to its new course at Muirfield and was able to begin a sequence of marvellous championships played there since.

## Course Record
63 Isao Aoki (Japan)
(Open Championship 1980)

## Open Championship

| | | | | |
|---|---|---|---|---|
| 1892 H H Hilton | 305 | 1935 Alf Perry | 283 |
| 1896 Harry Vardon | 316 | 1948 Henry Cotton | 284 |
| 1901 James Braid | 309 | 1959 Gary Player (S Africa) | 284 |
| 1906 James Braid | 300 | 1966 Jack Nicklaus (USA) | 282 |
| 1912 Ted Ray | 295 | 1972 Lee Trevino (USA) | 278 |
| 1929 Walter Hagen (USA) | 292 | 1980 Tom Watson (USA) | 271 |

## Ryder Cup
1973 USA 16    GB 10
(Six matches halved)

Early winners of the Open Championship at Muirfield:
below, James Braid (1901, 1906); right, Harry Vardon (1896);
below right: Ted Ray (1912)

## Amateur Championship

| | |
|---|---|
| 1897 A J T Allan | 1926 J W Sweetser (USA) |
| 1903 R Maxwell | 1932 J de Forest |
| 1909 R Maxwell | 1954 D W Bachli (Australia) |
| 1920 C J H Tolley | 1974 T Homer |

## Walker Cup

1959 USA 9    GB 3    1979 USA 15    GB 8

(One match halved)

## Home Internationals

1948 England    1956 Scotland    1976 Scotland

## Curtis Cup

1952 GB 5    USA 4

Right: Walter Hagen putting on the 18th green in the final round of the 1929 Open. Below: Henry Cotton drives off the 10th in the 1929 Open watched by Walter Hagen. Nineteen years later, in 1948, Cotton himself was to become an Open Champion at Muirfield. Bottom left and right: Gary Player breaks down by the recorder's hut after taking 6 at the final hole in the last round of the 1959 Open, thinking he has let the title slip from him . . . but in the end he still finishes two strokes clear to take the trophy

# Muirfield

Left: Jack Nicklaus playing out of a bunker at the 12th in the 1966 Open. Centre: Lee Trevino keeps talking and Tony Jacklin is on the receiving end during the 1972 Open. Below: Another long putt goes in for Trevino at the 9th

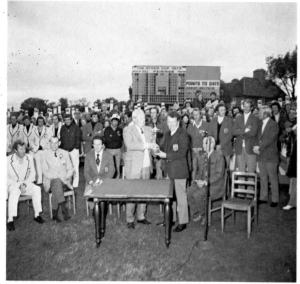

Edward Heath presents the Ryder Cup to US captain Jack Burke in 1973

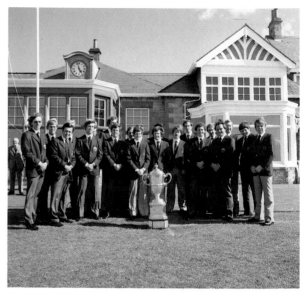

The 1979 Walker Cup teams

**Playing the course** Muirfield, like Royal Troon, is the home of a private club, but the procedure for playing there is rather less intimidating than most people assume. You make arrangements in advance by obtaining an introduction from a member or by writing to the Secretary with an introduction from your own club's secretary. If practicable, a starting time will then be allocated. You will be warmly welcomed, and well instructed. Again contrary to general belief, ladies are permitted to play Muirfield provided they are accompanied in play by a gentleman. The clubhouse telephone number is Gullane (0620) 842123.

**Recommended courses in the surrounding area** There is no course immediately adjoining the Muirfield championship course but less than a mile away in the village of Gullane are the Gullane courses, numbers 1, 2 and 3, all delightful to play, rising and falling over Gullane Hill. Also within comfortable reach by car – a few miles – are Luffness New, Longniddry, Royal Musselburgh, Kilspindie, Dunbar and the famous and quite historic North Berwick.

Gullane GC, Gullane, East Lothian; tel Gullane (0620) 843115.

Luffness New GC, Aberlady, East Lothian; tel Gullane (0620 843114.

Longniddry GC, Longniddry, East Lothian; tel Longniddry (0875) 52141.

Royal Musselburgh GC, Prestongrange House, Prestonpans, East Lothian; tel Prestonpans (0875) 810276.

North Berwick GC, West Links, Beach Road, North Berwick, East Lothian; tel North Berwick (0620) 2135.

Kilspindie GC, Aberlady, East Lothian; tel Aberlady (08757) 216.

Dunbar GC, Dunbar, East Lothian; tel Dunbar (0368) 62317.

**Where to stay** Greywalls Hotel is literally on the course, by the 9th green and 10th tee. There are hotels and guest houses in Gullane itself, and a wider range of accommodation in neighbouring North Berwick.

Greywalls Hotel, Gullane, East Lothian; tel Gullane (0620) 842144.

Queen's Hotel, Main Street, Gullane, East Lothian; tel Gullane (0620) 842275.

Bisset's Hotel, Main Street, Gullane, East Lothian; tel Gullane (0620) 842230.

Dirleton Open Arms, Dirleton, East Lothian; tel Dirleton (062085) 241.

Marine Hotel, Cromwell Road, North Berwick, East Lothian; tel North Berwick (0620) 2406, telex 727363.

Right: Tom Watson on his way to the 1980 Open Championship
Below: Isao Aoki after breaking the course record

# GLENEAGLES

### Gleneagles

Gleneagles Hotel is unique. World-famous as a first-class resort hotel, it is also one of the most beautiful golfing centres you will find anywhere. Its four 18-hole courses – King's, Queen's, Prince's and Glendevon – are laid out on a sheltered moorland plateau which makes delightful, natural golfing country of firm turf, banks of golden gorse and purple heather, tall pines and burns and lochs. There are superb views for as much as 40 miles in all directions. The Ochil Hills are to the east and south, with the striking cleft of Glendevon leading through to Fife; the nearer of the Grampian Mountains lie to the north, and the mountains of western Perthshire and the Trossachs to the west. It is an enchanting place.

Gleneagles Hotel is built along the lines of a French château and stands in splendid near-isolation in its own estate of some 700 acres in lovely Strathallan, on the very threshold of the Scottish Highlands. It has an interesting history. The story is that one Donald Matheson, then general manager of the Caledonian Railway Company, conceived the idea of such a hotel in such a place in 1910, when he was on holiday in the area. He persuaded his company that a first-class hotel there could compete successfully with the European 'Grand Hotels' which increasingly were attracting the wealthy traveller. Another version has it that Matheson was only too well aware that the Glasgow & South-Western Railway Company had already created Turnberry, and he was not to be outdone. So he sent his scouts along the entire length of the Caledonian lines to find an outstanding site on which he could outdo Turnberry Hotel and its golf facilities.

Construction started in 1914, but was interrupted by World War I when the building was partly used as a hospital and rehabilitation centre for coal-miners. Work was fully resumed in 1922, and Matheson involved himself in every aspect of it. He recruited the famous James Braid to design the King's and Queen's Courses. Braid later collaborated with Major C. K. Hutchison, and by 1924 an exceptional concept had become a reality. Since that time, Gleneagles Hotel has proved itself as one of the 'flowers of Scotland', a national and international treasure, and the only 5-star hotel in Scotland.

In its golden era, in the Thirties, the hotel was an altogether grand place. Wealthy and noble clients arrived at the hotel's own railway station with their personal servants, guns and gundogs, and rods, and all of these were accommodated by the house in the most proper manner.

Left: Typical Gleneagles scenery – the approach to the 13th on the Queen's Course

Top: Gleneagles Hotel from the King's Course
Above: The Starter's Hut on the King's Course

Golf at Gleneagles is a rare experience. The courses are resort courses, open, expansive, with nothing cramped as you find on links fairways, yet still difficult enough to be a stern test for the professionals. Without being of massive championship length, both the King's and Queen's Courses will require all the shots in your repertoire. The supporting courses, the Prince's and Glendevon (opened only in 1980), are shorter.

James Braid held the King's Course to be his finest achievement. On the Queen's, much more use is made of dog-legs and water, and there is much discussion among regular visitors about which is the better, which the prettier. Largely the choice is a subjective matter but you can say that because the King's is a shade longer, and a shade larger, it is therefore a shade more difficult. One of its most attractive characteristics is the fact that almost every hole seems an entity in itself, a world of its own, running along its own private valley

with nothing and no one to distract you.

The fairways are wide and smooth, the greens immaculate and invitingly large, the hazards well defined, the bunkers not criminally severe. The turf is crisp, the air is crystal clear. The King's is one of the most magnificent courses

in the world, and playing there will be one of the most memorable experiences of your golfing life. You will play in the main from elevated tees, with each hole spread honestly before you. You will be well advised, first time round, to use one of the best of the local caddies –

clubbing on the second shot in this clear mountain air can be puzzling. Above it all, you may well hear the calls of wild geese, of grouse and pheasant, partridge and duck, woodcock and snipe in a setting of lovely flowering shrubs, beech and alder, fir and pine.

PLEASE RING BELL
ON LEAVING GREEN

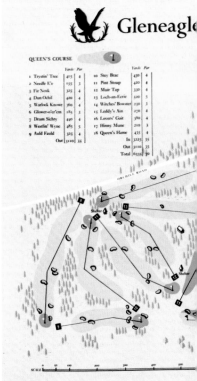

## Gleneagles Hotel Golf Courses

Local Rules

### KING'S COURSE

A ball is out of bounds if it lies beyond the wire fence to the left of the 6th and 10th holes or behind the 2nd green.

### QUEEN'S COURSE

A ball in the ditch at the 1st, 3rd, 4th and 5th holes may be lifted and dropped under penalty of one stroke.

A ball played from the 10th tee to the right of the boundary line between the post on the hill and the tee is out of bounds.

### GENERAL

All water (other than casual water) on the course is to be treated in accordance with the Rules of Golf applying to lateral water hazards.

Far left, above: A view to the south across the Prince's Course
Far left, below: A request to those leaving the 3rd green on the King's Course
Below: An early plan of the courses before the extension of the Prince's, and long before the Glendevon

| HOLE | NAME | S.S.S. 71 LENGTH IN YARDS | LENGTH IN METRES | HANDICAP | PAR | | | | L.G.U. S.S.S. 74 LADIES' LENGTH IN YARDS | LENGTH IN METRES | HANDICAP | PAR | SCORE |
|---|---|---|---|---|---|---|---|---|---|---|---|---|---|
| 1 | Dun Whinny | 362 | 331 | 6 | 4 | | | | 338 | 309 | 6 | 4 | |
| 2 | East Neuk | 406 | 371 | 14 | 4 | | | | 372 | 342 | 14 | 4 | |
| 3 | Silver Tassie | 375 | 343 | 9 | 4 | | | | 336 | 307 | 9 | 4 | |
| 4 | Broomy Law | 465 | 425 | 2 | 4 | | | | 434 | 397 | 2 | 5 | |
| 5 | Het Girdle | 167 | 153 | 16 | 3 | | | | 126 | 115 | 16 | 3 | |
| 6 | Blink Bonnie | 476 | 435 | 8 | 5 | | | | 418 | 382 | 8 | 5 | |
| 7 | Kittle Kink | 429 | 392 | 4 | 4 | | | | 416 | 380 | 4 | 5 | |
| 8 | Whaup's Nest | 170 | 155 | 17 | 3 | | | | 148 | 135 | 17 | 3 | |
| 9 | Heich o'Fash | 354 | 324 | 12 | 4 | | | | 320 | 293 | 12 | 4 | |
| **OUT** | | **3204** | **2929** | | **35** | | | | **2908** | **2660** | | **37** | |
| 10 | Canty Lye | 450 | 412 | 1 | 4 | | | | 408 | 373 | 1 | 5 | |
| 11 | Deil's Creel | 233 | 213 | 10 | 3 | | | | 152 | 139 | 10 | 4 | |
| 12 | Tappit Hen | 399 | 365 | 13 | 4 | | | | 345 | 315 | 13 | 4 | |
| 13 | Braid's Brawest | 451 | 412 | 7 | 4 | | | | 416 | 380 | 7 | 5 | |
| 14 | Denty Den | 266 | 243 | 15 | 4 | | | | 237 | 217 | 15 | 4 | |
| 15 | Howe o'Hope | 460 | 421 | 3 | 4 | | | | 437 | 399 | 3 | 5 | |
| 16 | Wee Bogle | 135 | 124 | 18 | 3 | | | | 121 | 111 | 18 | 3 | |
| 17 | Warslin' Lea | 374 | 342 | 11 | 4 | | | | 350 | 320 | 11 | 4 | |
| 18 | King's Hame | 531 | 486 | 5 | 5 | | | | 440 | 402 | 5 | 5 | |
| **IN** | | **3299** | **3018** | | **35** | | | | **2906** | **2656** | | **38** | |
| **TOTAL** | | **6503** | **5947** | | **70** | | | | **5814** | **5316** | | **75** | |

Marker's signature ......................

Player's signature ......................

| GROSS | HANDICAP | NETT |
|---|---|---|
| | | |

## el Golf Courses

### 'WEE' COURSE

| | | Yards | Par |
|---|---|---|---|
| 1 | Fairy Hillocks | 312 | 4 |
| 2 | Nickie Ben | 183 | 3 |
| 3 | Cheerie Lea | 375 | 4 |
| 4 | Knowe Tap | 395 | 4 |
| 5 | Heckle Birnie | 350 | 4 |
| 6 | Clean Drap | 115 | 3 |
| 7 | Muckle Boukit | 435 | 4 |
| 8 | Hill o' Ferlic | 340 | 4 |
| 9 | 'Wee' Hame | 140 | 3 |
| | Total | 2625 | 33 |

### KING'S COURSE

| | | Yards | Par | | | Yards | Par |
|---|---|---|---|---|---|---|---|
| 1 | Dun Whinny | 370 | 4 | 10 | Canty Lye | 485 | 5 |
| 2 | East Neuk | 405 | 4 | 11 | Deil's Creel | 215 | 3 |
| 3 | Silver Tassie | 395 | 4 | 12 | Tappit Hen | 405 | 4 |
| 4 | Broomy Law | 485 | 4 | 13 | Braid's Brawest | 465 | 4 |
| 5 | Het Girdle | 175 | 3 | 14 | Denty Den | 285 | 4 |
| 6 | Blink Bonnie | 480 | 5 | 15 | Howe o' Hope | 465 | 4 |
| 7 | Kittle Kink | 455 | 4 | 16 | Wee Bogle | 150 | 3 |
| 8 | Whaup's Nest | 175 | 3 | 17 | Warslin' Lea | 390 | 4 |
| 9 | Heich o' Fash | 425 | 4 | 18 | King's Hame | 480 | 5 |
| | Out | 3365 | 36 | | In | 3340 | 36 |
| | | | | | Out | 3365 | 36 |
| | | | | | Total | 6705 | 72 |

GLENEAGLES HOTEL

KING'S COURSE

1

**DUN WHINNY**
**362** YDS

STR 6 PAR 4

**J**ust to stand on the first tee of the King's Course at Gleneagles Hotel is one of the great joys of golf. All the features of the hole are in view, and an inviting, very wide fairway beckons. This is one of the most obvious differences between the Gleneagles courses and the great links of Scotland – here are none of those '14 yards across' fairways. Indeed, anyone making a pilgrimage to play all the great Scottish courses one after the other might well consider Gleneagles a benign hospice in the midst of a forbidding journey.

The first fairway looks almost one hundred yards wide in places. There are three bunkers in line on the left side, from 190 yards to 230 yards, two on the right at 160 yards and 200 yards, but there are acres of space in the driving area in between. You will see the green in the distance, raised high above you and bunkered; its height above the fairway is the one essential fortification of this hole. The green rests on top of the very long ridge which runs through the entire Gleneagles property and is the most constant single factor in the architecture of the King's Course. The closer you drive to the green, the less you will see of it, so your second shot is the key to playing the hole.

From a reasonable drive in the fairway, you will be facing a shot of around 150 yards to the flag – a long 150 yards,

because the ground slopes up very abruptly to the putting surface, which is as much as

30–40 feet above the fairway. You must carry the ball all the way on to the green. There is one

Bunkers on the left at
190–230 yards

Slope above the central
bunker must be carried with
the 2nd shot

*Approach to the second from the bunker on the left*

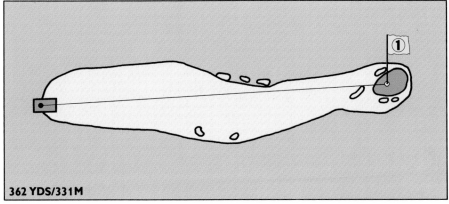

362 YDS/331M

greenside bunker to the left, and two on the right, but since the green is quite large, none of

Above:
The deep bunker and steep slope up to the green

these is particularly menacing. But there is one more bunker, at the foot of the slope beneath the green, and it is dead in the centre, wide, deep and entirely evil. It is critically important to stay out of this bunker. If you do get in, you will have to find a recovery shot which is high enough to top the slope, and long enough to reach the centre of the green – one of the most fearsome shots in golf.

Before you play your second shot, remember that it is not enough just to carry this central bunker. You must carry the slope above it and be somewhere on the putting surface at all costs. If you do not quite carry the slope, the ball will almost certainly first trickle, then rush, back down into the bunker. This will leave you feeling rather humiliated, on the very first hole, and with the prospect of a very difficult third shot.

A 'pyramid' of pine trees behind this green makes a lovely backdrop, and gives good definition, but on the second shot, take a club or two 'more than it looks'. And if the pin is at the back, take another club more – the green has a lot of slope, rising up to the back, with lots of big borrows on it. In the same way, if you have to putt uphill, give it plenty of club; if downhill, seek out the delicate touch. This is a lovely, generous opening hole, but one with a good deal of sting to it.

### What's in the name?

In translation, Dun Whinny means Furze Hill – the name of the furze- or broom-covered slope behind the high, uphill green.

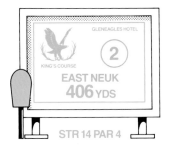

KING'S COURSE GLENEAGLES HOTEL

② 

EAST NEUK
**406** YDS

STR 14 PAR 4

**F**ollowing Dun Whinny is one of the most beautiful and scenic holes you could hope to find anywhere. From the tee, just behind the first green, the hole falls spaciously downhill all the way to a wide fairway. Beyond there are marvellous views across Strathallan to the rising hills, with ripe farmland reaching up to heather-clad tops and the great cleft of Glendevon reaching towards Fife. Turn back and look across the first green and there is a panorama of the professional's shop, the 'twin' 18th greens of the King's and Queen's Courses, the Dormy House, and the great hotel rising above the trees in a pastoral Scottish landscape.

The fairway flows downhill and slopes down from the ridge along the left side of the hole. If you hit one badly off-line to the left, it might well be a 'lost ball' in the heathery slopes of the ridge, which also has some big trees. There is one bunker in the fairway, slightly left of centre, at 175 yards, another wide to the right at 240 yards. A good line, if you can make the carry, is directly over that first bunker, since the ground behind it will break the ball to the right. The right side will give you a clearer sight of the green, which is tucked round the corner to the left, at the end of the ridge. Beware the right-hand bunker. The perfect place to be is just to the left of it, and past it if you can. You are

*2nd shot at the 2nd*

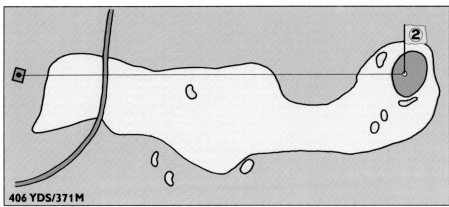

406 YDS/371 M

then in the correct attacking position for the second shot.

Your second is also downhill. In fact, given a good line and distance on your drive, you can make this a gentle hole. With a very good drive you will be playing a pitch second, or at worst a mid-iron, to a green which is quite receptive. It is fairly big with a

The wide entrance to the green and the three right-hand bunkers

bank at the back, so you are not likely to go thundering through. It is not closely bunkered. There are two bunkers short and to the right, another quite short and wide to the left, and a fourth placed rather closer to the right side of the green. But the entrance is wide and generous, and East Neuk is on balance a reasonable

par. It is certainly a hole to encourage you to go for your shots. Swing out freely into a big drive, hit a crisp approach shot, and you are almost there.

## What's in the name?

This is East Corner (neuk is like nook). The green is tucked away in the most easterly part of the course.

Fairway runs steeply downhill and around to the left

Bunker wide on the right at 240 yards

KING'S COURSE
GLENEAGLES HOTEL

**3**

**SILVER TASSIE**
**375** YDS

STR 9 PAR 4

The third hole is a puzzlement. Look in the only direction which could possibly suggest a fairway and you will see a mass of mounds, what looks like a solitary bunker, a high ridge in the distance, but not a sign of anything that remotely looks like a putting green. All very misleading. However, since the ridge in the distance has a marker-post on top of it, we can deduce that there must be a green somewhere beyond.

I would be inclined to take a 3-wood or a 2-iron or something that would get me to the top of the little hill that comes in from the left. However, no matter where you (or I) put the ball, we must still face a blind second shot over the ridge. The important point with the drive is to be in the fairway, avoiding a solitary bunker on the left which is 200 yards from the tee, and hope to find a reasonably flat lie on a fairway with exceptional movement in it. Most of the left side is a succession of mounds which will throw the ball to the right. So accept this hole as a very stiff par 4.

I must say that while I can tolerate the odd blind drive, I do not at all care for blind second shots where the pin – in this case the entire green – is invisible. They might well cut a gap in this ridge and let the player see the green – I don't believe the hole would be any the worse for it. The green is quite tight behind that ridge, not at all far on. If you carry the ridge, over the marker-post, you will certainly be on the putting surface. Having to go over the hill means care with judging distance, so remember that the fairway bunker is 175 yards from the centre of the green, and orientate yourself accordingly.

When you do get over the hill, you will find a very large and very long green, with a firm ridge running right across it, giving two distinct levels. Each of these levels is fairly flat, but if your ball has only just made the front of the green, and the pin is cut on the back, upper level, you are definitely in a three-putt zone and you must work hard on your first putt and get it into a circle not much more than three feet from the hole.

This is not one of my favourite golf holes. On

Looking back down the fairway from the ridge

## The 3rd – Silver Tassie

the other hand, it is there, and it has to be played. It is part of the Gleneagles scene and probably has been like this from the very beginning. So take it by the throat and shake it hard, and don't be too upset if you cannot manage anything better than a five.

### What's in the name?

Once over the mysterious ridge, you will find the green in a tassie- or cup-shaped hollow behind the marker-post.

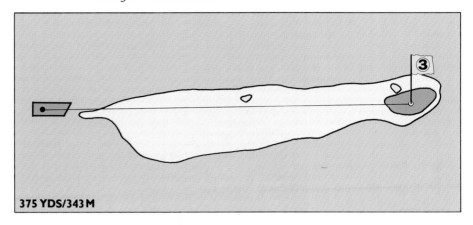

**375 YDS/343 M**

Fairway bunker is 175 yards from the green

Difficult to find a flat lie on the rolling fairway

The 3rd Fairway

KING'S COURSE    GLENEAGLES HOTEL

**4**

**BROOMY LAW**
**465** YDS

STR 2 PAR 4

By contrast with the 3rd, I make the 4th a first-class hole by any standard. It is typical of Gleneagles golf in that it is played up a long, isolated valley, divorced from the world, with the ubiquitous ridge marching along, this time on the right side.

It is also a very demanding hole, worth a good deal of study in advance. You are looking at 465 yards, par four. But it is uphill all the way and only ten yards short of the regulation 475 yards for a par five. If there is a prevailing wind, it will be against. This is a difficult par four for the professionals, so you must certainly play it as a par five.

The first focal point is a fairway bunker in the right centre. It is not much more than 150 yards from the tee, but in a strong headwind it might well come into play. If you feel you can carry it, your driving line should be directly over it. If not, keep left, but as close to it as you dare – there is plenty of fairway past it. The second half of the hole turns slightly to the right, and is uphill all the way to a green cut high into the side of the ridge, with an overshadowing clump of trees. The second shot is critical. You will probably be playing from an uphill lie, and no matter how well and how long you drive the ball, you will be facing a very long second shot.

There are two bunkers on the right of the fairway, at about 240–250 yards from the tee, and a long diagonal bunker on the left, at the 300-yard mark. Across the fairway, not quite opposite, is another bunker on the right side. Over the last 100 yards to the green, the entire left half of the fairway seems to collapse down a

Above:
The green almost hidden by mounds and hillocks

Long bunker on the left at 300 yards

Fairway is uphill all the way

*The 4th Fairway*

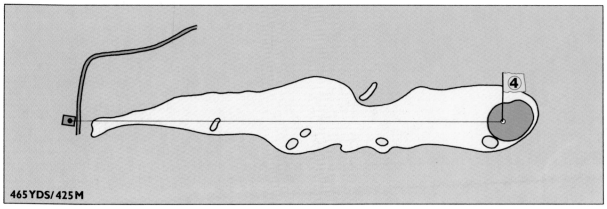

**465 YDS / 425 M**

sharp, rough-covered bank, and there is yet another bunker at the right-front edge of the green, covering that approach.

All this adds up to a daunting prospect, which not only gives the impression of narrowing progressively towards the green, but in fact does narrow. On top of all that, you cannot see much from the fairway – probably just the flagstick, a few mounds and hillocks around the greenside bunker, perhaps a touch of the bunker itself, but no sight of the putting surface. To reach the green, you should ideally fly the ball all the way to the putting surface, and I do not believe that will be possible. So play tactically short.

Aim your second shot well to the right half of the green. Your line could be on the greenside bunker, or even over the corner of the fairway bunker on the right, which is about 140 yards from the centre of the green. That should leave you with a straightforward pitch to the green. Whatever you do on this hole, do not miss on the left. The entire hole plays up the right side.

The green is slightly basin-shaped and looks as though, like many other greens built around the same time, it has been left with some clay in it, with the sides built up slightly so that water and moisture tend to filter into the middle and be held there in dry weather, creating something of a small reservoir.

To sum up, this hole is perfect evidence that golf is a point-to-point game, not a muscle game. If you can knock out two good shots to cover 380 yards – the first just past the first fairway bunker, the second well up on the right side – then you are left with a pitch to the centre of the green, and a stab at one putt: an ideal way to conquer Broomy Law.

## What's in the name?

The 'broom-clad mound' – a reference to that part of the Gleneagles ridge which runs along the right side of the 4th fairway up to the green.

Ridge runs down the right side of the fairway

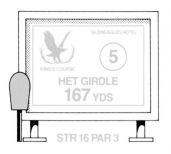

**KING'S COURSE** GLENEAGLES HOTEL

**5**

**HET GIRDLE**
**167** YDS

STR 16 PAR 3

**A**fter that long, uphill slog, a relaxing par 3 might seem just the

ticket, but this is not the one. It is a very fine, demanding short hole. From a high tee nestling in the trees, you play to a high pulpit green. There are several points to be made about Het Girdle.

Since the tee is relatively sheltered, there may be rather more wind above the green than you suspect. Note also that the teeing ground seems

to be set a good 45° to the right of the hole. Make doubly sure of your set-up and alignment. The green is strongly defended. To the front are various obvious defences in the form of differently shaped bunkers, all very big, all very deep. Rather less obvious are the slopes all around the green, which fall away sharply. In fact, even if you miss the

traps, you can scarcely hope to run the ball onto the green, so sharp is the upslope to the putting surface.

In a strong wind, it can be a very difficult hole. The yardage does not seem intimidating, but the tee is quite long, with perhaps two or two and a half clubs' difference from front to back. The green is fairly large, a good 40 yards

## The 5th – Het Girdle

from front to back, meaning three clubs' difference. There are three very large bunkers covering the right side, placed rather wide. They are quite deep and will require recovery shots which get up quickly, then cover a long distance horizontally to the green. Another bunker is close up on the left front. From the depths of that one, you will not see the flag and possibly not even the putting surface above you. In certain conditions this hole will demand a very long tee shot, and the key requirements here are precision in executing the shot, a sharp awareness of yardage, and accurate club selection.

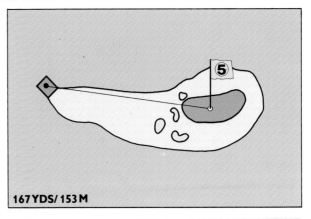

167 YDS/ 153 M

From the 5th Tee

Steep slopes fall away all around the putting surface

Large deep bunkers protect the front of the green

### What's in the name?

The key is in cookery rather than corsetry. It means 'hot griddle' and describes the unusual shape of the elevated plateau green.

Left:
Only the flag is visible from the deep bunkers below the green

Gleneagles

KING'S COURSE • GLENEAGLES HOTEL
**6**
**BLINK BONNIE**
**476** YDS
STR 8 PAR 5

**T**his is the shortest par 5 on the King's Course. Only one yard more than the required minimum for a par 5, it should make an easy birdie for a professional, and a none-too-taxing par for the amateur. Nor is it nearly as difficult as it looks. The fairway bunker on the left, and a tree at the end of a row of trees bearing in from the left, seem to be cramping, but the bunker, on a ridge, is just 160 yards out and there is a friendly downslope and a wide fairway beyond it. A bunker on the right side at about the same distance is set widely enough for you to ignore it. The driving line should be over the right end of the left-hand bunker or a yard or two to the right of it.

The second shot for the amateur player is

Bunker on the left
at 160 yards

Above:
The fairway runs downhill
beyond the bunker

A good drive will be carried
forward on the downhill
slope

*The 6th Fairway*

## The 6th – Blink Bonnie

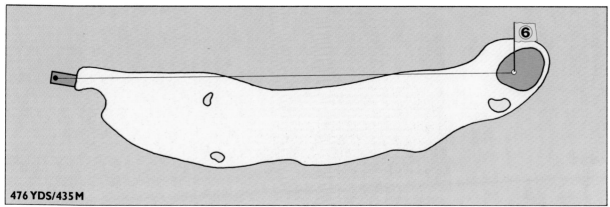

**476 YDS/435 M**

quite long, but everything is open before you and there are no great problems. Along the left side of the fairway, the ground falls off into rough. The fairway itself falls ever so slightly in this area but looks flat enough, and this can make distances difficult to judge. From a good drive, you could be 250 yards from the flagstick. The second shot should be held up to the right somewhat. The green is very big. There is one large bunker, 20 yards short of the green on the right, and wide. That might be a good aiming point for your second shot, since the ground falls right to left and would put you in a good position for a short pitch or chip.

The entrance to the green is wide and uncluttered, though any shot aimed at the left half with a bit of draw on it could be heading for trouble. Most of these greens are rather flat, with only gentle folds and ridges, and are fairly easy to get on and stay on. That leaves the putting problem. Unlike most Scottish links greens, for example, which are inclined to be small, at Gleneagles you can often be facing putts of 35 yards. So, on the King's Course, you need to be sure of your distances between the front of the green and the flagstick.

### What's in the name?

It's a 'charming view' – the backcloth to this hole is a panorama of open countryside leading to the distant Trossachs.

Large bunker 20 yards short of the green on the right

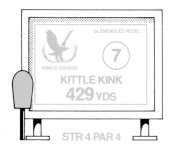

GLENEAGLES HOTEL

KING'S COURSE

**(7)**

**KITTLE KINK**
**429 YDS**

STR 4 PAR 4

**Y**our first adversary here is the view from the tee, or rather the effect it might have on you. It can be frightening. The high tee is cocooned in a clump of trees, and falling off in front of it is a deep ravine. The far side of the ravine rises to a saddle which leads over into the fairway, and the fairway then turns left and runs along a shallow valley. The saddle is framed by two bunkers, but there is a decent gap between them. The hole is very reminiscent in design and terrain of the 7th hole on the Ailsa Course at Turnberry Hotel, if not quite so spectacular or ferocious.

The bunker to the right is only 150 yards out so you can discount that. The one on the left is the key to the drive and to the playing of the hole. The back of this bunker is 190 yards from

The bunker to avoid on the left of the ridge

the tee, and behind it is a critical bank of heather before the fairway can be

reached. To carry bunker and heather would need a shot of some 230 yards' carry – much too dangerous! If you

*Approach to the 7th*

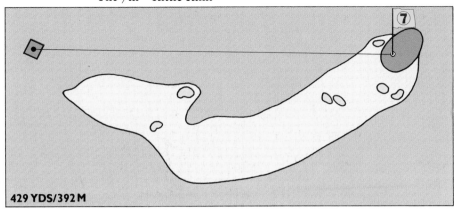

**429 YDS/392 M**

Large bunkers **80** and **60** yards short of the green

Fairway runs along a shallow valley

landed in that heather, you would almost certainly not be able to advance the ball, and it would be a shot dropped before you were anywhere on the fairway. So aim for the marker-post in the middle of the saddle, or even slightly to the right of the marker, to guarantee a place on the fairway.

This will mean a slightly longer second shot, but you must weigh the advantages. A fairly good player might go slightly left of the marker, but, either way, you must find the widest part of the fairway. There is plenty of it. And the further across

the fairway you go, the more open is your second shot to the green. As so often happens in golf, the drive looks much easier in hindsight. When you get to the saddle and look back, you may wonder why you were quite so nervous about it.

The next problem is the succession of traps set for bad and mishit shots. There are two big deep bunkers in echelon in the middle of the fairway, 80 and 60 yards short of the green. Past them are two big bunkers on the right, short and wide of the green. These bunkers are inclined to foreshorten the shot, but I suggest you ignore all four. Try selecting one club more than you think you need – there are no real problems at the back of this green, which

is reasonably large and has a fairly flat entry. Watch out for one more bunker, a rather sneaky one close to the putting surface at the left front, designed no doubt to protect the hole from the shot that comes in off the slope on the left.

Perhaps I have made this hole sound rather easier than it is – it remains a difficult par 4 for amateurs, and one on which I think most professionals would be content to make par. You must hit clean, careful shots every time, and the drive is all-important.

## What's in the name?

Here you have a 'ticklish bend', meaning the left-handed dog-leg which greets you beyond the marker-post.

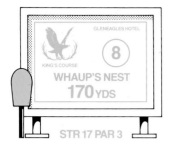

The second of the short holes on the King's Course, this one is as pretty as a picture. From a high tee, you look across a big dip to a lovely, spacious green set, slightly beneath you, into a distant bank and ringed with golden bunkers. All the short holes on this course are very attractive, but they are all a good deal more difficult than they may seem at first glance, and the 8th is no exception.

The first thing to be sure of here is the yardage, since the variety of tees can make a difference of 30 yards. Another point is that the hole is not protected in any way, and so you can reasonably expect the wind to be regular, if not constant, from tee to green. As you view the green from a distance, you will see there are very sharp slopes up to it from the front and the right side, and another going up behind it. You will also see that the bunkers are sited round it at 12 o'clock, 4 o'clock, 6 and 9 o'clock. The second and third of these are substantially beneath the level of the putting surface, and have a good deal of heather around and between them.

The green itself is not quite circular, sitting a shade diagonally across the shot, and must be a good 45 yards from front

Two bunkers in front of the green below the putting surface

From the 8th Tee

258

## The 8th – Whaup's Nest

left to back right. The bunker at the back will not be a friendly place for an over-clubbed shot. You are forced to conclude that, since you are playing over a dip with no fairway whatsoever, your tee shot will have to go all the way to the putting surface. At the same time, it is as well to ask yourself, like the old, rational professional: 'Where do I miss it?' I should favour the left side. The slopes there are much more gentle, and if you can keep out of the left-hand bunker (the one at 9 o'clock), you have very good ground from which to get a neat chip to the flag. Since you cannot run onto this green, whatever you do you must let the tee shot fly high. Be positive.

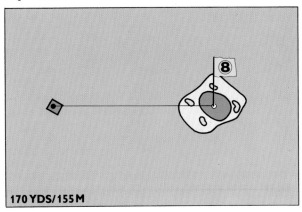

170 YDS/155 M

## What's in the name?

A whaup is a curlew, and, seen across the valley from the tee, the green looks very much like a large bird's nest.

Left:
The green in its spectacular setting

Large bunker to trap the over-clubbed shot

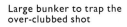

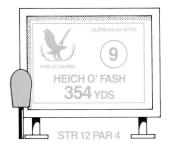

KING'S COURSE
GLENEAGLES HOTEL
**9**
**HEICH O' FASH**
**354** YDS

STR 12 PAR 4

**A**s on so many other tees on the King's Course, your first sight of this hole might be disturbing. But have no fear, it is much less difficult than it may look. The key to success is the second shot. You look at a wide, downhill fairway falling into a big dip or valley in front of the green, which is raised quite sharply above it, rather like the 1st green. At the bottom of the slope in front of the green is a round bunker on the left,

a rather more rectangular bunker on the right. Nearer the green stands a line of trees, rather tight on the right side of the fairway.

If you were to 'skull' a

long iron off the tee, the ball would run on and probably stagger down into the valley. Long hitters, in fact, should beware that they do not overhit and get caught

in one of those bottom bunkers. Downwind, in dry conditions, they would certainly be reachable. Alternatively, you could be very short, not quite get down into

Target area for the drive is the bottom of the deep valley to the left front of the green

All kinds of trouble if you miss the green on the left

Above:
The plateau green beyond the rolling fairway

The 9th Fairway

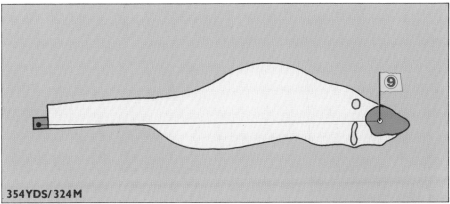

**354 YDS / 324 M**

the dip, and still have a straightforward pitch across the valley to the green. The line of your tee shot should concern you as much as anything. Aim for the left corner of the green, and you should go down nicely and arrive on flat ground in the valley. Getting a good stance for the second shot is important, since the slopes around the valley are quite stiff.

You can see the pin position from the tee, but not from the valley, so check it before you tee off and remember where it is. The green is big, pear-shaped, broad in front, narrowing towards the back to about 12 yards across. It does gather the ball in from both sides a little, which helps, but it is ridged into two levels. Now you can see why it is important to recall the flag position, to give you guidance on the length of your second shot.

If you have moved the ball out well from the tee, and got down into the valley, your second and critical shot will become a routine short pitch. If your judgment of distance is right on this shot, you have a chance for a birdie. Don't forget that if the pin is at the back, the central ridge on the green will slow your ball on its way there. At all events, if you pitch on the green, your ball should go forward at least to the centre, and set up two putts for a healthy par.

Do *not* miss this green on the left. On that side is a sharp downslope, full of unthinkable miseries; real goodbye country.

Whatever happens, when you get up on top and move over towards the 10th tee, you will be rewarded with more of Gleneagles' lovely views.

**What's in the name?**

The Height of Trouble refers to the raised green, and your second shot to it is likely to be the height of your personal ordeal.

GLENEAGLES HOTEL

KING'S COURSE

(10)

CANTY LYE

450 YDS

STR 1 PAR 4

**T**his hole will often play as a par five, so if the conditions suggest it might, do not be over-ambitious. It runs to the west and so is into the wind as often as not. This is another very pretty golf hole, extending to the most westerly point on the King's Course. From an elevated tee, you look across a flood of heather to a generous fairway, 50 yards in width.

The first distraction is a fairway bunker on the left, some 200 yards out. It can play havoc with the average player, who would do well to keep right and give it plenty of room. The very good player might carry over it, but he too would be better advised to carry to the right of it. The direct line to the hole is over the bunker, but it is very tight because beyond the bunker the left side of the fairway falls away into rough. Indeed the entire thrust of this hole is from right to left, with the line of the fairway turning a little to the left, in addition to the slope.

All along the higher right side of the hole is a line of the most magnificent beech trees, marching along towards the green. There is a very big fairway bunker at 340 yards, and therefore about 120 yards from the centre of the green, placed to cover the right half of the highway to the green. Avoid it. From there you would have no hope of reaching the green with your third shot. There are two bunkers close to the right side of the green, again trending all the action towards the left. However, the green is long and large, and offers an open, wide entrance to receive a very long second shot from a first-class player.

So the second shot might be aimed at the right-front corner of the green, the idea being that it will not quite reach the bunker, then break with the ground to the left and towards

The green rising above the right-hand bunkers

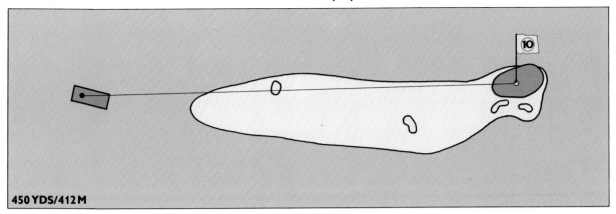

**450 YDS/412 M**

Fairway bunker on the left at 200 yards

Large bunker on the right 120 yards from the green

*The 10th Fairway*

the green after it pitches. From that position, if it is not quite on the green, an uncluttered chip or pitch to the flag is there for the taking. Longer hitters can go for the centre of the entrance, and be on. The green is two-tiered, with a good three-clubs' difference from front to back.

The average player should certainly rate this as a par-4.5 hole, enjoy a moment of delirium if he makes four, and be quite grateful for a five.

### What's in the name?

The 10th fairway has a 'tilted lie', a pronounced slope down from right to left.

GLENEAGLES HOTEL

KING'S COURSE

(11)

DEIL'S CREEL
**233** YDS

STR 10 PAR 3

**T**his I think is the most difficult of the par-3 holes for the average player. Again the tee is fairly high, looking across and down to a big, built-up green set rather across the line of the shot, and heavily defended on the right with three deep and powerful bunkers menacingly placed. There is another bunker, very wide, to the left front. The size of the green can give the impression that it is much nearer than it really is, but I can assure you that this is a very long and testing par 3 which will require a very good shot, almost certainly with a wood, to get on or even close to the green.

The entrance to the green is quite wide, but you will need some luck for the ball to run on to it. The slope up and into the green is rather broken ground, even hump-backed, and anything not quite the right length and a shade to the left can be gathered into the bunker on the left. In the same way, the first big bunker on the right seems to have a magnetic effect. The average player will be playing a long iron or a wood, and these are the clubs with which he is liable to slice. On top of that, any prevailing wind will be left to right, and some pretty pine trees to the left of the hole will not blunt it too much.

Getting properly set up, picking the right club and a good line are therefore very important on this tee. If you pitch the ball too far right, it will spin off into one of the greenside bunkers on the right side. I would recommend aiming at the

## What's in the name?

The 'Devil's basket' awaits you. Not only is this green difficult to hold, it is also surrounded with hazards.

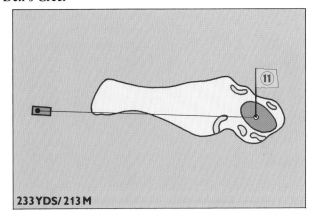

233 YDS / 213 M

fifth bunker on this hole, which is back left at about 10 o'clock, and hope, if you cannot make the carry, to pitch the ball within a few feet of the putting surface. That way you will have passed any evil bounces that the hole might be saving for you, and your ball should run on up the green.

The entrance to the green sloping away on both sides

Slope up and into the green

Wide bunker to catch any shot falling short of the green

The 11th from the tee

KING'S COURSE · GLENEAGLES HOTEL · (12)
TAPPIT HEN
**399** YDS
STR 13 PAR 4

**T**he first time you go round the King's Course, your problem at the 12th hole will be in knowing quite *where* to go. A ridge, garlanded with three bunkers, crosses the fairway and hides the rest of the hole. The left of these three diagonal bunkers is about 180 yards from the back tee, the one on the right 200 yards. If you drive over the marker-post, you will not be far from the middle of the fairway, and you should get a welcome bounce forward from the downslope beyond the ridge, which might put you possibly within a

7-iron shot of the green. Long hitters might go a fraction to the right of the marker, but our old friend the Gleneagles ridge runs along the right side of this hole and its slope has very heavy heather and rough.

If you must miss this fairway, better miss on the left. The rough there is much lighter and you will find a more level stance on that side. By Gleneagles standards the fairway is rather narrow, but the second shot is not over-difficult. The first important requirement is to carry the ridge successfully from the tee.

The green is large, and the more open approach is from the left side. A large bunker, short right and 40 yards from the centre of the green, and another 20 yards behind it, in reserve, close out the approach from the right. A third bunker, short and quite wide on the

The marker-post points the way between the three bunkers in the ridge

Bunker short on the left to catch the hooked approach shot

2nd shot at the 12th

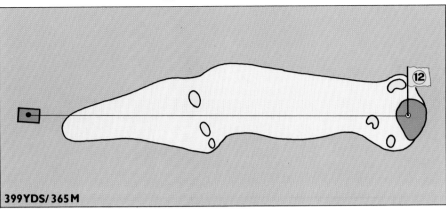

**399YDS/365M**

left, should not concern you unless you are planning to hit a big hook.

This is a pleasant, honest hole – once you have the drive out of the way. You will then be pitching to a big, receptive but interesting green. You cannot see it all that well from the prime position on the left, wide of the fairway, so be sure of your yardage. The first part of the green – ten yards or so – is quite flat, the rest of it, oddly, slopes down and away from

you. So the challenge in the approach shot is knowing and deciding, yet again, exactly where to land the ball. If you are a touch too bold, the ball can run away from you to the back of the green, and you may be tackling a 20-yard putt. Nevertheless, I see no reason why you should not think of this as a potential birdie hole.

Incidentally, if you do land your approach shot past those bunkers on the right, the slopes should kick you into the green. One general point

to think of when playing at Gleneagles is to get the distances right, and trust them, on all approach shots. Many of the holes have rather deceptive ground immediately in front of the greens.

## What's in the name?

The 'Scots tankard' invoked is not so much a description of this hole, more a call to build up strength for the rigours of the final six holes.

Large bunker 40 yards short of the green

GLENEAGLES HOTEL
13
KING'S COURSE
**BRAID'S BRAWEST**
**451** YDS
STR 7 PAR 4

The two bunkers threatening the long second shot

This is probably the most famous hole on the course. Some might consider it one of the most difficult, although on the card it is rated only seventh in order of difficulty. It has some similarities with the previous hole. Again a ridge crosses the fairway, here with one large bunker. The ridge is 200 yards from the back of the tee. Further on up the right side of the fairway, just in the rough, is a small bunker, 300 yards out and therefore out of range for most people.

From the elevated tee, you can see almost everything, including the green, and the driving line should be on the green, or just left of it, which should take you nicely past that first bunker. The long ridge runs the length of the hole on the right, with a path along the top used by spectators. The downslope from it to the fairway is heather-strewn and dangerous, but the sloping right side of the fairway will carry the ball off to the centre or centre-left of the fairway, which is where you want to be. The entire hole undulates pleasantly, and has a lot of character to

Bunker on the left of the fairway 60 yards from the green

Fairway narrows

The 13th Fairway

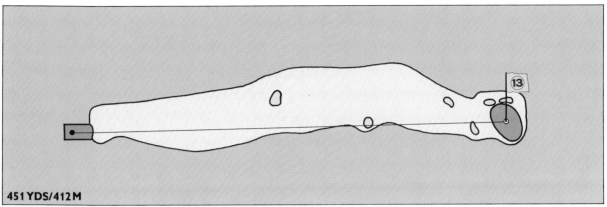

**451 YDS/412M**

it. The green will be slightly above you on a plateau. It slopes down from right to left, and also dips down from the front into a bowl-like area, then goes up again quite noticeably to the back. Its defences are interesting. From about 100 yards in, the fairway narrows. Sixty yards from the centre of the green there is a fairway bunker on the left. You must certainly be past this with your second shot. To the right is another, a cross-bunker,

20 yards from the putting surface. To the left of the green, where there is a sharp downslope, are two pot bunkers; from down there you would probably see only the top of the flagstick.

You will be facing a healthy second shot, and it is quite difficult to decide where to place it. You must certainly get past the left-hand fairway bunker, and avoid the cross-bunker. If you can carry the cross-bunker, the fall of the ground should put you on the

green. If you catch the left-hand bunker, it will take an exceptional shot to reach the green. And pitching the ball at the left front or left-front quarter of the green might see you spin into those traps on the left. Probably the correct line, and your best option, is to shoot for the centre, or right centre of the green. This may well demand one of your best shots, and if you are not completely sure of making it, try aiming for the cross-bunker, staying

a few yards short of it, and going for a short pitch at the flag from there.

### What's in the name?

'Braid's best' is a tribute to the architect of the course, James Braid. The 13th is certainly the most famous hole, if not the most difficult.

Bunker 20 yards short of the green on the right

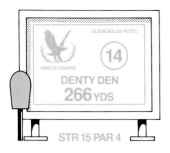

KING'S COURSE     GLENEAGLES HOTEL

**14**

**DENTY DEN**
**266**YDS

STR 15 PAR 4

This is a dainty little hole that should encourage you to think of birdies and, at most, an easy par 4. The challenge of the hole is entirely in the tee shot, which will govern your score in a way that does not happen at many other golf holes. More accurately, the challenge may be in your frame of mind as you look at the hole from the tee. I hope you will believe me when I say that the hole is not nearly as difficult as your first sight of it may suggest.

Once more, a ridge crosses the fairway and the tee shot is blind to the extent that you

cannot see the green. The ridge is not all that high, and a stand of tall pines beyond it, and a tall white marker-post, form a backdrop to the green. The ridge is embedded with five bunkers, four strung straight across it with the fifth some 20 yards behind the one on the far right. You must not allow yourself to be intimidated by these bunkers – they are almost cosmetic. Of course, people get into them, but only because of mishits and rank bad shots. This ridge is 175 yards from the very back of the tee, so the distance is not frightening. Carry the ridge, and the downslope beyond will send your ball smoothly on its way.

The most important consideration is to get the line of the drive right. The marker-post is your line, or a shade to the right of it, and this would take you over the second bunker from the

left. Do *not* drive to the left of that line, otherwise you bring into play the hole's more effective

defences. These are three big, deep traps at the left side of the front of the green, placed beneath

Three big deep bunkers at the left front of the green

*Approach to the 14th*

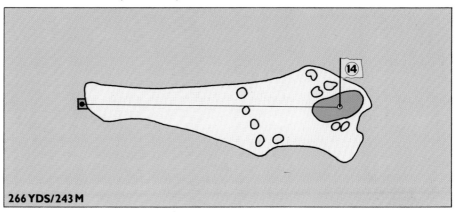

**266 YDS/243 M**

high mounds which overlook the entire scene. The dead ground behind the ridge, that is, the ground you cannot see from the tee, is fair. If you drive on the correct line, it will run you down truly to the putting surface. Go too far left and you will be caught in sand. Go wildly, extremely, to the right, and you will vanish down a very steep, hostile bank.

The left-hand bunkers, although quite deep with high faces, are not hopelessly penal. If you can make a reasonable stab at bunker play, you can still splash out onto the putting surface. Incidentally, there are two other bunkers, at centre right and back right, close to the putting surface, but they seldom seem to come into play.

The green is big, and very long. It has just a suggestion of a basin in the middle, making for some very tricky borrows, and it is 45 yards from front to back. You might well be faced with a long approach putt. The thing here is initial confidence – confidence on the tee to crack the ball over that ridge, on the right line.

### What's in the name?

The 'pleasant dell' is the shady glade where the green is sited – but a poor tee shot could spoil your enjoyment of the scenery.

Left:
The marker-post directs the drive over the ridge

Green is very long from front to back

KING'S COURSE   GLENEAGLES HOTEL
(15)
HOWE O' HOPE
**460** YDS

STR 3 PAR 4

The 14th and 15th holes on the King's Course are, I am inclined to think, respite holes, where you can catch your breath before facing the course's intriguing and testing finish. The 15th in its fashion is a lovely hole, downhill all the way, straightaway, rather like the 2nd but without a

kink in it, and with striking views beyond the hole. Played in the opposite direction, it would be a very strong par 5, but since it is downhill, it is comfortably within range of two shots. One minor problem, in fact, will be to decide just how far you have driven the ball.

The Gleneagles ridge persists along the left side of the hole, wooded in places, and a belt of rough down the right separates this hole from the 4th, which runs in a reverse parallel. Out from the tee there is a band of rough, lumpy ground with splotches of heather, but you will

carry that comfortably. If anything, the fairway slopes from left to right. A long way down – 370 yards – is a pair of fairway bunkers, twinned in the centre of the fairway. The driving line is not quite so critical on this hole. You have plenty of margin. Just the same I should knock it directly over the marker, perhaps on a line with the fairway bunkers or left of them, and stride out optimistically.

There are five bunkers around the green, but none of them is aggressively close to the putting surface save the one at the back. Two are

short on the right side, two quite wide on the left, and the entire centre and left front of the green is open to a clear approach from the left side, which explains why you should favour that side from the tee. The green and the 16th tee behind it are screened by pretty firs and, all told, the 15th green is an attractive target for your second shot. The ground immediately in front is true, and you can surely hope to run the ball on successfully if you have to. It's a quite exhilarating, and none too demanding, hole to play.

The broken ground between tee and fairway

**What's in the name?**
Optimism should spread through your system as you look downhill to the attractive green in its 'hopeful hollow'.

Approach to the 15th

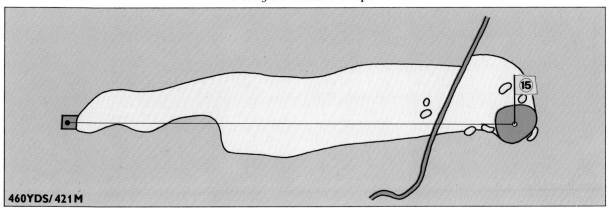

460YDS/421M

Two bunkers wide to the left of the green

Two fairway bunkers at 370 yards

Fairway runs downhill all the way

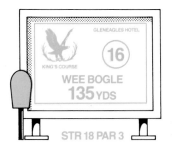

GLENEAGLES HOTEL

**KING'S COURSE** (16)

MINIATURE

**WEE BOGLE**
**135** YDS

STR 18 PAR 3

Architecturally, this is a gem, a perfect golfing miniature, as pretty a golf hole as can be found anywhere. The tee is set in a grove of trees behind the 15th green, and the 16th green is a good deal higher than the tee. It is a long green, running more or less along the line of the shot, decently broad at front and back but nipped in at the waist, where the pin position always seems to be. This green is ferociously protected by no fewer than nine bunkers.

A high bank dominates the left side of the green, falling down quickly to two large, quite deep bunkers close to the putting surface. Three bunkers are strung along the right side, where there is a downslope into heather and rough. All of these bunkers are very severe and, apart from the absence of a sandhill on the right, the hole reminds me very much of the 13th at Muirfield in the power of its greenside bunkering.

As if all this was not enough, the entire front is screened by four very healthy bunkers, with quite narrow gaps between. They run along the line of the shot rather than across it, and they might just as well have been one long continuous trap, 50 yards across. Finally, at the back of the green, is a quick, hairy downslope, going nowhere. It's a devilish little hole, true to its name.

What to do about it? On balance, I would say that line is more important than length. You must carry the bunkers at the front, which are no more than 100 yards from the tee. You must *not* get into the side bunkers. They are so deep, with such tall faces, and so close

*The 16th Green*

to the putting surface that if you get in there, particularly with a plugged ball, you are easily facing a score of five on the hole. If you carry the bunkers across the front of the green, you will almost certainly be on the putting surface. So the trick of the tee shot, apart from getting a good line, is to be confident in hitting the ball right at the flagstick. The green will certainly hold well a properly hit shot.

# The 16th – Wee Bogle

High bank on the left falling into two deep bunkers

Long narrow green with a steep downslope at the back

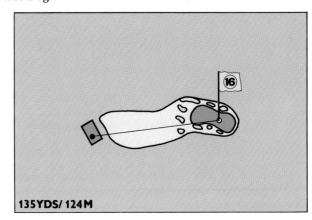

**135YDS/ 124M**

## What's in the name?

Bogles are no-good imps and this hole, while wee, has nine bunkers round its green to snare anything off-line.

Some of the nine bunkers that protect the narrow green

**T**his is the tightest driving hole on the course. The problem is to hold the ball on the fairway, which is no more than 20 yards across at its narrowest point. The fairway slopes very strongly from left to right, and the hole dog-legs to the left, so that the entire camber is against the ball holding on the left side. All along that side is a mass of gorse and bracken and heather, in which the ball will certainly stick, so the decision on the drive – the gamble on the drive, I should say – is to take a line as close to the left edge of the fairway as you dare.

There is one bunker, on the edge of the fairway on the right, forming the narrowest neck. Beyond it the fairway increases in width. This bunker can have a strong, almost hypnotic effect on the player. The ground will certainly gather a short shot towards it or into it, but it is only 160 yards from the tee, much closer than you may think, and you certainly must be well past it with your tee shot. You need a shot as long as you can hit – the back of that bunker is 200 yards from a raised green, so you must try to get well past it.

The fairway turns left at this point and rises up to the green. There is a pot bunker to the left, about 140 yards along and some 80 yards from the green, which should not trouble you. But the slope up to the green, on the right front, is laced with three very dangerous and big traps which will gather anything short, cut, or perhaps off-line to the right. Your second shot is uphill all the way, all carry to the putting surface. In addition, you must consider the size of this green. It is at least three clubs' difference from front to back, so making the right club selection is really important. I should always take at least one more than your vision or instinct might tell you. It is much better to be too long here! If you want to be conservative, and are not sure of carrying these traps to the right, shoot for the left half of the front of the green. The left side, and around the back, is all quite open, and if you miss the putting surface, this is good ground from which to chip, or even try a putt from off the green.

This 17th is a strong hole. You will break

The narrow fairway sloping down towards the right-hand bunker at 160 yards

even with it only if you get the line of the drive right, and if you make sure you have enough club on the second shot.

## What's in the name?

Welcome to Troublesome Valley, renowned for its narrow sloping fairway and tenacious rough. The secret is to proceed circumspectly.

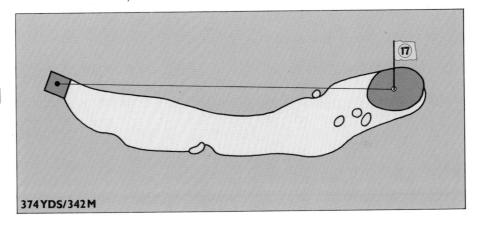

374 YDS/342 M

Three dangerous bunkers on the right in the slope up to the green

Bunker on the right at the narrow neck of the fairway

The 17th from the Fairway Bunker

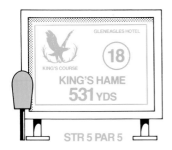

KING'S COURSE
GLENEAGLES HOTEL
(18)
KING'S HAME
**531** YDS
STR 5 PAR 5

**J**ust as the prospect from the first tee was a delight to the eye at the start of the round, so here is a beautiful finish, a fine par 5. There is a high and spacious teeing area. It is so spacious that the first thing to check is which tee is in use. The distance between front and medal tees is a good 80 yards, and the professionals are pushed even further back.

The 18th is an excellent driving hole. The fairway is wide all the way. First obstacle is a high ridge in front of you (what would Gleneagles be without its ridges!), with a necklace

of four bunkers in its face. From the forward tee, this is the best part of 200 yards. From the medal tee, it is 280! About 100 yards on from this first ridge is a secondary ridge, with a

slight basin between them. You have to decide if you can get over that first ridge. There is a good gap between the left bunker and the bunker second from left, and you might

well run the ball up and over. If you succeed, the downslope will carry you forward in dandy fashion. If you think you cannot handle the ridge, play short, to the bottom of it. You are never likely

Above:
A good drive should
bisect the two bunkers

Fairway runs downhill to an
enormous green

*Approach to the 18th*

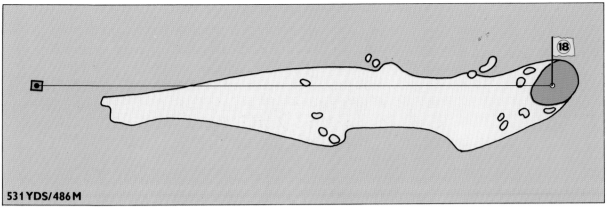

**531 YDS/486 M**

to hit this green in two shots, so be rational about it. The length of your drive is thus a major decision.

If you are short of the ridge, make sure your second shot carries beyond the secondary ridge, a shot of about 160 yards. Again you will get a handy run forward from the downslope and be within comfortable reach of the green. As you come over these ridges, the first thing that may strike you, apart from the

staggering vision of Gleneagles Hotel and the views to the north, is the size of the green ahead of you. It looks enormous, and it is – probably 50 yards from front to back and 50 yards across. It seems acres in extent, and it surely must be one of the biggest single greens in the country.

There are lots of bunkers – three to the right and short, two to the left and short, with only one really tight against the putting

surface, a small one at the right centre. The entrance is quite wide enough, considering that the green should be receiving a pitched shot of some kind. Try to get the ball well up into the centre of the green with this shot. As you can imagine, it is easy to find yourself in the three-putt zone on such a big green.

This is a lovely, spacious par-5 hole. Play it sensibly as such, and it will be a marvellous finish to

crown your experience of a superb golf course in a gorgeous corner of the kingdom.

**What's in the name?**

The home hole on the King's Course, with the Gleneagles Hotel to greet you as you cross the last ridge.

Small bunker to the right centre of the putting surface

The courses at Gleneagles Hotel were designed for resort golf, but the King's Course has staged many professional championships, the Ladies' Championship, and a Curtis Cup match. The King's, and indeed the Queen's, have become even more internationally famous as the venues for various televised matches, and the BBC Pro-Celebrity series. The King's has recently been lengthened for championship play but, not being a links course, it is unlikely that the Open Championship will be staged there.

## Course Record (King's Course)
63 Brian Barnes
(Double Diamond World of Golf Classic – Skol Individual Championship 1977)

## Professional International
1921 GB 9      USA 3
(Three matches halved)

## Double Diamond World of Golf Classic
1974 England      1976 England      1977 USA

## Penfold Tournament
1935 Percy Alliss 273      1948 Fred Daly 273

## PGA Senior Professional Tournament
1980 Paddy Skerritt 286

## Ladies' Amateur Championship
1933 Miss E Wilson      1957 Miss P Garvey

## Curtis Cup
1936 GB 4      USA 4
(One match halved)

Left: Play during the first official match between the professionals of Great Britain and the United States which was played at Gleneagles in 1921. A second match was played at Wentworth in 1926 before the Ryder Cup was formally constituted in 1927. Below: Abe Mitchell and Walter Hagen in play during their singles match which was halved

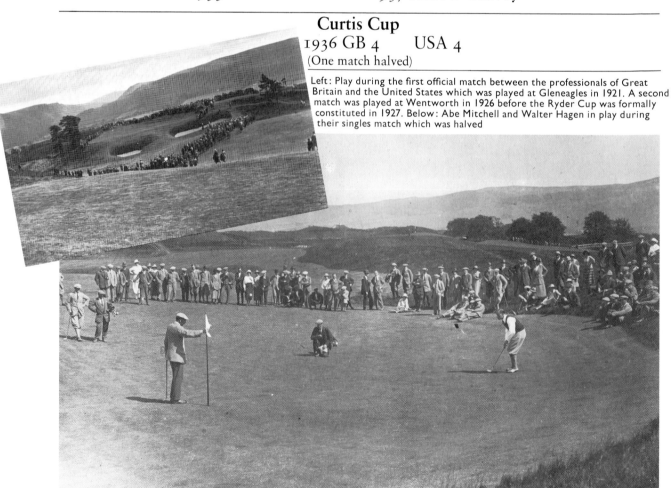

Above: Play during the Gleneagles Silver Tassie Competition in 1930. Below: Mrs E H Vare, the US captain, drives off the 4th tee during the Curtis Cup match of 1936

# Gleneagles

Left: Philomena Garvey during the final of the Ladies' Amateur Championship in 1957 in which she beat Mrs G Valentine by 4 and 3
Below left: England, winners of the Double Diamond World of Golf Classic 1974: (l to r) Maurice Bembridge, Tony Jacklin, Lord Derby (President, PGA), Peter Oosterhuis, Tommy Horton, Peter Townsend
Below: Winners again in 1976. Tony Jacklin receives the trophy from Lord Derby

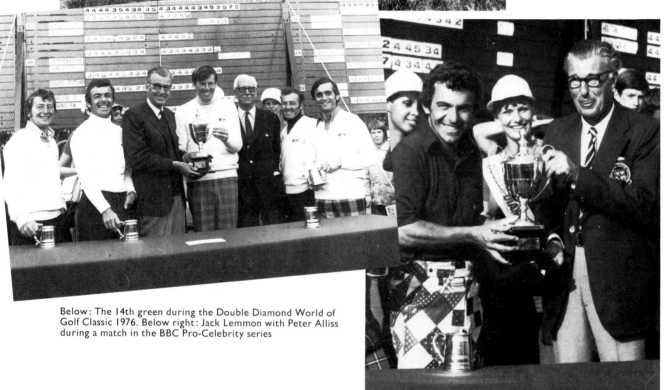

Below: The 14th green during the Double Diamond World of Golf Classic 1976. Below right: Jack Lemmon with Peter Alliss during a match in the BBC Pro-Celebrity series

**Playing the course** Hotel residents have preferential terms, and some priority on the various tees, but the courses can be played by all. There are no restrictions on ladies' play. For tee reservations call the Golf Manager, Gleneagles Hotel Golf Courses, Auchterarder, Tayside PH3 1NF; tel Auchterarder (07646) 3543.

**Adjoining courses** The Queen's is the major supporting course, equally attractive and with the advantage of water in play on several holes. The Prince's is similar in character to the other two, but shorter and more of a fun course, while the Glendevon is complementary in the sense that it is a more open, parkland course.

Queen's 6278 yards   SSS 70

Prince's 4678 yards   SSS 64

Glendevon 5762 yards   SSS 68

**Recommended courses in the surrounding area** Auchterarder, Dunblane, Crieff and the Perth courses are all within easy reach of Gleneagles which is also a marvellous base for visiting Rosemount, Carnoustie, St Andrews and the Fife courses, all within a one-hour drive of the hotel.

Auchterarder GC, Orchil Road, Auchterarder, Tayside;
tel Auchterarder (07646) 2804.

Dunblane New GC, Dunblane, Central; tel Dunblane (0786) 822343.

Crieff GC, Perth Road, Crieff, Tayside PH7 3LR; tel Crieff (0764) 2397.

Craigie Hill GC, Cherrybank, Perth, Tayside; tel Perth (0738) 24377.

King James VI GC, Moncrieffe Island, Perth, Tayside; tel Perth (0738) 25170.

Murrayshall GC, Murrayshall, New Scone, Perth, Tayside;
tel Scone (0738) 52784.

Royal Perth Golfing Society, 1/2 Atholl Crescent, Perth, Tayside;
tel Perth (0738) 22265.

Blairgowrie GC (Rosemount), Blairgowrie, Tayside; tel Blairgowrie (0250) 2383.

Carnoustie Golf Courses, Links Parade, Carnoustie, Tayside;
tel Carnoustie (0241) 53249.

St Andrews Golf Courses, St Andrews, Fife; tel St Andrews (0334) 75757.

**Where to stay** Gleneagles Hotel, 5-star, is the ideal place to stay. There is also a Dormy House with limited overnight accommodation. Auchterarder has some accommodation, and there is a wider range in Perth, 12 miles away.

Gleneagles Hotel, Auchterarder, Tayside PH3 1NF;
tel Auchterarder (07646) 2231, telex 76105.

Queen's Hotel, 20 High Street, Auchterarder, Tayside PH3 1AA;
tel Auchterarder (07646) 2493.

Station Hotel, Leonard Street, Perth, Tayside PH2 8HE;
tel Perth (0738) 24141, telex 76481.

Salutation Hotel, 34 South Street, Perth, Tayside PH2 8PH;
tel Perth (0738) 22166, telex 76357.

Royal George Hotel, Tay Street, Perth, Tayside PH1 5LD;
tel Perth (0738) 24455.

Gleneagles

Sandy Lyle, more fully Alexander Walter Barr Lyle,
born in Shropshire of a famous Glasgow golfing
family, is perhaps the outstanding British golfer of
his generation. He has represented England at Boy,
Youth and Full International level, and has played in
both Walker Cup and Ryder Cup matches. On
turning professional in 1977, he took the Scottish
'nationality' of his father Alex, professional at
Hawkstone Park Golf Club, and led the European
Order of Merit in 1979 and 1980. He has been Open
Champion of Nigeria, Scandinavia, France and
Europe, and he won the Individual Award at the
World Cup of 1980.

# Appendix

Caddies are expected to take an interest in the game. A golfer engaging a caddie is entitled to expect a service in excess of merely having his golf clubs carried or pulled around the course. He should be able to leave the sighting and finding of his ball entirely to his caddie and, where the caddie is a man of experience with an intimate knowledge of the course and its greens, be able to assume that any advice sought and given on the borrow of greens or line of play will be well founded.

Under all normal circumstances in foursomes the caddie of a player driving should go with him to the tee. The caddie of the player due to take the second shot should go well forward to a position where he can see the ball being driven coming towards him. It is not good enough to be standing at right angles to the intended line of flight of the ball some 50 or 60 yards from the tee whence sighting the ball in flight is at its most difficult. In singles where a player is driving into the sun his caddie should position himself well forward so as to be standing with his back to the sun to facilitate sighting the line of flight of the ball.

Caddies should clean the ball regularly and club heads should be wiped down after each shot.

A good caddie by his knowledge of the course and his positioning throughout the game can be of great assistance to a player, can save him losing balls, and is fully worthy of the fee he receives. It is unfair to good caddies that a caddie who is little more than a carrier of a bag of golf clubs should receive a similar fee for a much lesser service.

The above notice is reproduced by kind permission of PWT Hanmer, Secretary, The Honourable Company of Edinburgh Golfers.

# Acknowledgments

## Paintings

Ken Turner is a landscape and wildlife artist
with a growing reputation. Although he had no
previous interest in golf, he soon became absorbed
with his new subject and his paintings reflect the
immediate impact of the spectacular scenery of
these famous Scottish courses.

## Photographs

The photographs used throughout this book
were taken by David Pocknell over a period of a few
days in the late summer. They reflect the rapid
changes in weather conditions which are a
feature of the Scottish coastal regions – the shadows
of the early morning and evening sunshine and the
spectacular cloud formations, sometimes dark and
threatening but often quickly broken and dispersed
by the strong prevailing winds.

## Other Picture Acknowledgments

Pages 50–53, 96–99, 142–145, 188–192, 234–237,
280–283: Action Photos, BBC Hulton Picture Library
and William Paton.

Royal Troon

Turnberry